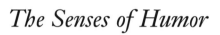

The Senses of Humor

DANIEL WICKBERG

THE
SENSES
OF
Self and Laughter
in Modern America
HUMOR

Cornell University Press   ITHACA AND LONDON

First published 1998 by Cornell University Press.

Printed in the United States of America.

Library of Congress Cataloging-in-Publication Data
Wickberg, Daniel, 1960–   .
   The senses of humor : self and laughter in modern America /
Daniel Wickberg.
      p.   cm.
   Includes index.
   ISBN 0-8014-3078-X (cloth : alk. paper)
   1. American wit and humor—20th century—History and criticism.
2. United States—Social life and customs—20th century.
3. Laughter—Social aspects—United States.   4. Self in literature.
I. Title.
PS438.W47   1997
817'.509—dc21   97-30301

Cornell University Press strives to utilize environmentally responsible
suppliers and materials to the fullest extent possible in the publishing of
its books. Such materials include vegetable-based, low-VOC inks and
acid-free papers that are also either recycled, totally chlorine-free, or
partly composed of nonwood fibers.

Cloth printing   10   9   8   7   6   5   4   3   2   1

To my parents, Ellen and Edgar Wickberg

Contents

Acknowledgments

Anyone who has ever written a book knows that, despite the generic displays of camaraderie and obligation that preface the text, most of the work is done alone. All that lonely work is, however, made possible by the efforts, accomplishments, and support of many. Although we may write alone, we do not think alone; our minds are populated with the ideas of those who have gone before and the presence of those with whom we live. Many of those to whom I am obligated for their ideas and research are acknowledged in the citations of this book. A brief word here about the others.

This book began life while I was in the American Studies Program at Yale University. There I was able to do the kind of truly interdisciplinary work that would not have been possible within a traditional discipline; I am grateful for the support and encouragement given by various people connected to American Studies at Yale of what must have initially seemed a rather strange project. In particular, I owe a debt to David Brion Davis, Alan Trachtenberg, and especially Jean-Christophe Agnew, who both set an example in his own work and provided support, criticism and encouragement in the darker hours of my own research and writing.

I had the privilege of critical readings and advice from two good friends: Chris Shannon and Glenn Wallach. Chris has set a high standard in the rigor and insight of his own thinking; his assessment was invaluable. Glenn's thorough and careful reading provided the breakthrough that made it possible for me to revise the manuscript. An earlier detailed criticism of drafts by Michael Schaffer proved helpful, as did the anonymous readers' reports for Cornell University Press. I am stubborn, of course, and so failed to take many of the suggestions made by my readers, but I am thankful for them nonetheless.

In the early stages of research and writing, this project was supported by a John F. Enders Research Grant and a Paul C. Gignilliat Dissertation Fellowship, both administered by the Yale University Graduate School. The members of the history department at Colgate University made it possible for me to be gainfully employed while I worked on revisions, no small accomplishment in the present academic job market. Jill Harsin and Andy Rotter served as my advocates during my extended visiting appointment at Colgate; I owe them a great deal of thanks. My appreciation also goes to Dennis Kratz, Dean of the School of Arts and Humanities at the University of Texas at Dallas, who came through with a generous subvention as the book was in press. The research for this book was conducted using the libraries at Yale, the University of Washington, and Colgate. The efficient interlibrary loan service at Colgate was particularly helpful.

Peter Agree at Cornell University Press has been a patient and accommodating editor. He made sure that I could write the book I wanted to write, while at the same time letting me know what the consequences of such action might be. I appreciate his frankness and advice. The manuscript was edited by Charles Purrenhage, who did a fine job of clearing the debris from my writing without intruding upon the substance or style of the book. Every author should have such good fortune in the editing process.

The support of my parents, Edgar and Ellen Wickberg, has been a constant. My father read the manuscript in an earlier form and provided an astute analysis that reflected both his own scholarly perspective and the experience of having grown up in the world I describe. My mother awaits the book for her reading; at long last, here it is. My debt to my parents is enormous; I have tried to begin to acknowledge it in the dedication of this book.

My wife, Susan Evans-Wickberg, has lived with (and without, sometimes three thousand miles away) me and this book from before it was a book. It has now been a decade since the initial idea for this project struck me; in those ten years, Susan has made our life together possible. The road has not been an easy one. I am grateful. More than that, I cannot say—she knows.

D. W.

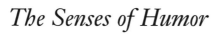

The Senses of Humor

Introduction

Everyday language and ordinary speech in twentieth-century America
find a place for something called the "sense of humor." We routinely
describe individuals as possessing this trait; we use it as a shorthand for
recommending the personal quality of people; we look for it in our
associates and friends as a sign of their good nature and compatibility.
Anyone who has read letters of recommendation or glanced at the personal ads that fill the back pages of urban weekly newspapers knows that
the term "sense of humor" recurs with amazing frequency. It is a simple
description of a universally recognized personality trait. And yet its use
and appearance in everyday speech, as with so many of the routine
phrases we use, is rarely accompanied by critical inquiry into its meaning.
This is as it should be; if we are to stop to analyze the meaning of
every commonplace, we will soon find ourselves unable to speak. But the
question remains: What *do* we mean when we describe someone as having a sense of humor?

This book is an extended answer to that question. The answer takes
the form of a history of the term, but the question itself seems of a
different order. It is at once anthropological and philosophical: anthropological in the sense of posing an exploration or unpacking of the
meaning of a term and value within a particular culture, namely our own;
philosophical in the sense of requiring an analysis of a human faculty in
terms of its relevance to the constitution and identity of persons in the
abstract. Indeed, I hope the present work will be accessible to those who

come to it from backgrounds in related humanistic and social scientific fields. We live, after all, in a time of "blurred genres," as Clifford Geertz reminds us, and those of us loosely connected to something called "cultural studies" can scarcely forget it.[1] Nevertheless, this book is written primarily as a work of history, albeit history of an interdisciplinary nature. More than half a century ago, the philosopher and historian R. G. Collingwood argued that history had supplanted philosophy as the foundation of knowledge of the human mind;[2] I concur that the best answer to a philosophical question is the writing of a history, that to know the meaning of an idea is to understand its history.

This, then, is a history of the idea and meaning of the sense of humor within Anglo-American, especially American, culture. Even having said this, however, I must point out what it is *not*. At the risk of seeming to define this project in largely negative terms, I have come to the conclusion that the best way to avoid misunderstanding is to address the initial expectations many readers may have. Cultural history today takes many forms, and frequently seems to have as many meanings as it has readers. The legacy of structuralist thought has left us with the notion that what *is* is defined by what *is not*. My purpose in describing what this book *is not* is simply to make my aims and intentions clear, to define exactly what kind of cultural history the reader might expect to find here.

Those who come to this work with the expectation that it represents a cultural history of American humor as a literary or popular form—that is to say, as a "tradition" or a body of texts—will be disappointed. There is a voluminous literature on American humor understood in this sense, and although I touch on some of the issues with which that scholarship is concerned, I approach them very differently.[3] The reader will not find, for instance, an interpretation of southwestern humor here. I do not focus on the meaning of particular humorous texts or the literary and cultural traditions in which they reside; I *am* interested, at least in part, in what makes possible the identification of these texts as "humor," and in this sense the tradition of scholarship on American humor is framed within my analysis. One way to put this is to say that I am interested less in the language of humor and more in its metalanguage. Thus, Mark Twain's discussion of the technique and structure of humor, "How to Tell a Story," is a primary source for this work, but his humorous stories themselves are not.

It would be a mistake, however, to say that I am concerned with the history of attitudes toward humor, or ideas about humor, rather than with the history of humor itself. The notion of a history of attitudes assumes that there is an independently existing body of things toward which people have changing "attitudes," that there are "ideas" on the one hand and "reality" on the other. The old dualism of mind and matter, superstructure and base in Marxian language, that in various forms continues to undergird most intellectual and cultural history, is embedded in the idea of a history of attitudes. Rather than a history of attitudes toward humor, or ideas about it, this is a study of the *meanings of* "humor," "sense of humor," and related terms, not as reflections, refractions, or indices of some other "real" thing, but as themselves elements of a cultural reality. Insofar as other realities slip into the narrative— under the names, for instance, of "individualism," "corporate capitalism," "bureaucracy," "market society"—they do so not to play the role of deus ex machina or philosophers' stone, nor to provide a solid ground upon which ideas can rest, but to add breadth and dimension to the cultural changes explicated in my analysis of the sense of humor, to make those meanings yet more meaningful.

Nor should this book be seen as a history of intellectuals and their ideas of humor. Although there are some prominent or "canonical" names appearing throughout the text—Ben Jonson, Francis Hutcheson, Mark Twain, Reinhold Niebuhr, John Dewey, Gordon Allport—there are also more obscure figures—Thomas Masson, E. P. Whipple, William A. Jones, Agnes Repplier, William Moulton Marston—and others who by traditional criteria might not be classified as intellectuals at all—Art Henley, Bob Hope, Eli Perkins, Walt Disney, Eliza Leslie. I intend nothing derogatory toward these latter authors by not classing them as intellectuals, nor do I make any special claims for intellectuals as a class. The status of any of these authors as intellectuals is irrelevant to my project. This is not an "intellectual" history in the sense of having intellectuals as its subject matter. The reader will find little of the analysis of psychological and social experience of these figures; they have not been selected because they struggled more mightily with the cultural problems they inherited than the "average" persons of their time, or because they embody certain traditions of schools of thought "important in themselves." In other words, the ideas analyzed in the text are not seen as explicable primarily in terms of the agency of the actors who produced them; this is no social or psychological history of intellectuals, thinkers, or writers. Rather, it is a history of ideas as a form of cultural history. The dramatis personae have been subordinated to the current of ideas, the thinkers subordinated to the things thought.

The texts that form the body of sources for my history are diverse—they range from philosophical treatises to literary ephemera to vaudeville guides and joke books; from novels to etiquette manuals to college psychology textbooks; from guides to rhetoric and oratory to genteel cultural criticism to empirical psychology of personality attributes. What unifies this wide range of source materials is that all of it speaks to ideas of humor, sense, laughter, and personhood. If any text could help me understand the meaning of the sense of humor as a cultural term and value, I have drawn on it; if not, I have discarded it. The authority of my sources rests on their status as cultural signposts, as moments of instantiation of ideas and values within a larger cultural stream. What I have attempted to reconstruct from these sources is not an intellectual tradition or a social agency lying behind them, but that larger cultural stream of which they are a part. It is in this sense that the present book is a cultural history in the guise of a history of ideas.

And yet a history of ideas it is. I would be remiss not to acknowledge the degree to which this work is indebted to the history of ideas tradition associated with Arthur Lovejoy. In fact, that tradition provides the foundations for a critical cultural history. Instead of seeing Foucauldian notions of discursive formation and *episteme* as marking a fundamental break from an older intellectual history, as many today assume, I have found a fundamental similarity and compatibility between the two conceptions of history. Lovejoy's focus on the relationship *between ideas* frees intellectual history from its fixation on individual thinkers and texts, and points it toward cultural systems of thought.[4]

When I began this project, it was to be the history of a relatively discrete idea—the sense of humor. Not only was I curious about why contemporary Americans attached a value to such a personality attribute, but I wanted to know why they actually believed in its existence. It gradually occurred to me that the history I was writing, while about the sense of humor in an immediate way, was also in fact about something much larger—bourgeois consciousness and, in particular, the cultural arrangement of what philosophers call object–subject relations, within bourgeois thought. I found that it was not possible to analyze a single personality attribute without becoming enmeshed in the language of persons as objects and subjects, bodies and minds, extensions and intentions. In our own day, "objectivity"—as the basis for a scientific episte-mology, an impartial journalism, or a professional ethics—is widely perceived as being in crisis, while "subjectivity" is both denounced as inimical to moral and social order and simultaneously elevated as the foundation of experiential truth by, for instance, those in the widespread recovery groups that dot our social landscape. Some scholars have begun to study objectivity as an ideology, a value, or a "construct."[5] Others have looked to the history and cultural status of the self, interiority, and personhood, as ways of getting at what Foucault has called the constitu-tion of the subject.[6] But the cultural histories of objectivity and subjectiv-ity continue to exist at a great distance from each other. My history of the idea of the sense of humor brings them together—in fact, demands that objectivity and subjectivity be seen as paired terms in modern Amer-ican culture, terms that revolve around the status of the self and per-sonhood. Subjectivity and objectivity, in my formulation, are personal qualities, dependent upon each other for their status and existence. That is to say, we speak of people as *being* objective or subjective, and we think of people as having internal capacities that allow them access to the view from nowhere that is objectivity. Objectivity and subjectivity are not simply ideals to strive for or to overcome, but are fundamental to the construction of modern notions of the self.

In fact, it is the theme of shifting object–subject relations, more than any other element, that unifies the present work. I have not tacked the history of the sense of humor onto this theme, simply allowing the former to act as a register or expression of the latter; rather, it has been the terms of the humoral inheritance and the ways in which those terms have been transformed in modern Anglo-American culture that have pushed the issues of objectivity, subjectivity, and personhood to the fore-ground. The potency of the sense of humor as both a descriptive term and a personal value in modern American culture stems from the fact that it has helped to define a model of personhood that holds the paradoxical valuation of both objectivity and subjectivity in place. From the very start, the term "humor" defined a conception of personhood. It has been my task to take that original definition from the world of medieval medicine and bring it into the twentieth century through its many twists and turns and permutations, and then to explore the implications of those new constructions for the modern era. Humor has always been about the ontological status of persons, about persons both as things and as more than things; accordingly, that has been my theme.

Beyond simply an analysis of the sense of humor in terms of object–subject relations, my ultimate concern in this book is with the character and quality of "bourgeois consciousness." The term is notoriously vague, but I have found no better one for that mode of thinking, that tacit way of knowing, that understanding of the self and the world, that is both dominant and pervasive in modern America. It would be foolish to try to define the meaning of such a term in a sentence or a paragraph—the reader will find it present on every page. The term "bourgeois" functions here not simply as a designation for a social class and its characteristic "attitudes," but for a kind of universalist mode of thought that constitutes the world we live and think in today, the world of "everyday life."

In fact, this book has much to say to those who have sought to study everyday life, popular culture, and the previously invisible history of the so-called inarticulate, but it speaks to them from an unexpected angle. "Humor" and the "sense of humor" initially appear to be ideas that refer to the comic forms of popular culture—unlike the ideas traditionally dignified by intellectual histories. The division between "high" and "low" culture does inform this work, but not because I treat the two as opposed objects of analysis, nor because I believe the aesthetic criteria derived from "high" can be fruitfully applied to "low," but because I treat everyday language and common expression ("low") as having not simply a meaning but an intellectual ("high") history. The argument I am making here is that if we are to understand something we call "popular culture," we must understand the history of the idea of "the popular."

One of the central ironies of the writing of this text, and what contributes to its form, is that I set out to write a history of a term and its meaning in everyday life, only to discover that I had to write it as a history of ideas; everyday life receded from my grasp, became ever more inaccessible, the more I tried to approach it. The entire text thus represents an attempt to approach "everyday life" through the thicket of ideas by making each chapter more comprehensive and inclusive than the last in the reality it seeks to capture. I believe, now more than ever, that everyday life is an intellectual sphere, that ideas are the environment in which people live. I have tried to write not one seamless coherent history, exploring a unitary phenomenon with a consistency of tone and method, but a history of shifting levels of reality. Every chapter is thus pitched at a slightly different level from all the others and represents a slightly different approach to history; the book is both one history and many.

The first two chapters address the medieval and early modern background for the initial appearance of the term "sense of humor" in the mid-nineteenth century. The more important context for the appearance of the sense of humor is not the immediate social, political, or economic context of the nineteenth century, but the cultural meanings embedded in the English language from the fifteenth century forward. The first two chapters are not so much a part of the central subject matter as they are a laying out of the context of ideas and meanings for the explication of that subject matter; they present ideas as contexts for both the genesis and the understanding of new ideas. I study sixteenth-and seventeenth-century Britain in order to understand modern America.

I begin with the idea of humor itself. Rooted in medieval medical characterology, humor signified the constitution of persons in terms of fluids having specific properties; it referred to the composition of persons as objective entities. Beginning in the late fifteenth and early sixteenth centuries, the meaning of humor was metaphorically unmoored from its base in physiology. Chapter 1 explores the historical implications of that unmooring in terms of changing notions of personhood and the elements of an emerging individualism. Implicit in the early modern movement of humor away from objective physiology was an emphasis on the subjective consciousness of objective being and its potential for manipulation; the particular eccentricities of persons as individuals rather than types; and the appearance of humor as a mode of seeing rather than a mode of being. The equation of eccentricity of character with the laughable in stage comedy linked humor and laughter for the first time, in a relationship that would persist to the present. The metaphorical abstraction of humor from its physical referent created an instability in the meaning of the word. The task of the first chapter is to capture the larger pattern of change in meaning that has undergirded that instability, to see that shift in meaning as a context for the development of the idea of the sense of humor as a personality attribute.

One of the central points that I make in this book is that the history of the idea of the sense of humor, like the history of any idea, cannot be written independently from its own ideational context. As Lovejoy said nearly sixty years ago, arguing for the breakdown of a narrow disciplinary view of the history of ideas, "Ideas are commodities which enter into interstate commerce."[7] Ideas are neither bounded autonomous entities nor reducible to their immediate social contexts. Even though the changes in the meaning of humor throughout the early modern period seem to follow a logic of their own, they are not fully explicable without reference to the larger world of meanings in which they occurred. Chapter 2 expands the context for understanding the preconditions for development of the idea of the sense of humor in nineteenth-century Britain and America by analyzing humor in relation to changing meanings of laughter, the emergence of a middle-class culture of sensibility, and the construction of the sympathetic imagination as a key faculty defining the relationship between persons. The historical movement of the meaning of laughter away from an antipathetic response to deformed objects and toward a sympathetic perception of incongruity in the eighteenth and nineteenth centuries was an important context for the cultural redefinition of humor. By making humor a term of both sympathy *and* laughter, modern culture reinvented the long-standing eccentricity of characterological humor as "incongruity," collapsed the distance between object and subject by allowing for the possibility of nonderisive laughter *with* rather than *at* another person, and placed a value on the altogether novel capacity of the individual to laugh at himself. The increasing emphasis on the ontological and epistemological importance of the interiority of persons—the proliferation of "senses," the valuation of intuitive and emotional judgment over "objective" criteria or reason, the capacity for feeling associated with sentimentalism or sensibility—was paradoxically accompanied by an expansion of the self outward via the sympathetic imagination. The idea of humor, as a term of both sympathy and laughter, captured the paradox of this new relationship between interiority and exteriority, the self as both subject and object, by incorporating the humoral tradition within the newer understandings of personhood emerging in bourgeois culture.

These early modern contexts help explain why the sense of humor, when it first appeared as a descriptive term in the 1840s, and as a valued personality attribute in the 1870s, could encapsulate a whole set of assumptions about personhood and its relationship to the social world. Those assumptions were to be articulated and transformed in the later nineteenth and twentieth centuries in terms of a culture characterized by what I call "bureaucratic individualism." Chapter 3 explores the idea of the sense of humor as an element of an everyday commonsensical ideology that constructs and values the individual as a unique being, prior to society, on the one hand, and bureaucratic organization as the norm to which that individual must adapt, on the other. It is the sense of humor as a capacity for what comes to be called "self-objectification," a willingness for the self to be the object of its own amusement, that makes it such a valued and ubiquitous trait in the twentieth century. The sense of humor suggests both a deep interiority capable of perceiving incongruities and a capacity for infinite adaptation to the circumstances of social life. It is one of the fundamental traits of a personhood characterized by accommodation between psychological and social modes of seeing and being. The analysis of the continuity of meaning of the sense of humor from the 1870s to the present casts doubt on the supposed distinction between "character" and "personality" as modes of the self that cultural historians have held as central to the shift from a nineteenth-century "producer ethic" to a twentieth-century "consumer culture."[8] The history of the sense of humor suggests, rather, that both "character" and "personality" are comprehended as a relationship between expansive and contractive modes of being by the ideology of bureaucratic individualism. Chapter 3 provides, I hope, not only an analysis of the sense of humor as a valued personality trait in twentieth-century America, but also a new and more comprehensive approach to the ideologies of selfhood and individualism in modern American culture.

Just as the sense of humor became an interiorized faculty of the person, it was also figured primarily as a consumer attribute, a capacity for perception rather than creation. The internalization of humor as a mode of seeing allowed for the reobjectification of laughable "material," in the form of jokes. Chapter 4 explores the development of the joke as a commodity form in terms of the emergence of a commercial market for humor, the changing cultural status of humor and laughter, and the transformation of the terms of humoral thought. The quasi-literary or popular status of the joke form has tended to render it invisible to history; it has long been wrapped in the belief that jokes are universal things, that they have no history properly speaking. Even those who have granted that the specific content of jokes might be culturally variable have not allowed for the fact that the form of the joke itself is not a cultural universal. What I have sought, alternatively, is the historical meaning of a distinctively modern cultural form. I have tried to do for the joke what literary historians such as M. M. Bakhtin and Ian Watt have done for the novel—to see its particular strategies, organizations, and structures as constituting a peculiarly modern ontology and set of values.[9] The joke, as analyzed here, is the B-side of bourgeois consciousness, the obverse image of the modernity that is constituted in the form of the novel. If the novel is expansive, concerned with the detailing of unique character, situation, and everyday life in terms of an empiricist's understanding of mimesis, the joke is contractive, concerned with abstraction, detachment, formal condensation of meaning, and the mechanistic interchangeability of parts. The development of the joke as an object of exchange, a circumstance-neutral commodity, was undergirded by the changes described in the previous chapters, particularly the constitution of humor and laughter in terms of incongruity and the placement of the sense of humor as a capacity for perception. The joke, like the sense of humor, is ubiquitous in modern American culture. I have tried to make it strange.

Despite the generally high regard in which the sense of humor has been held since the later nineteenth century, there have been those who have perceived it as a danger. What is interesting about their concerns is how mild they have been, by comparison with the antilaughter views of previous centuries. The fundamental novelty of the antipathy toward humor and laughter of the late nineteenth and early twentieth centuries was that it did not reject humor itself as a problem, but rather praised it as necessary and appropriate to its sphere. Chapter 5 explores the ways in which the Victorian separation of the humorous and the serious as two distinct spheres sought an accommodation between those values associated with humor—freedom, play, creativity, relief—and those values more often associated, both by scholars and in the public imagination, with Victorianism itself—work, rigid self-control, seriousness, moral duty. One of the purposes of this analysis, like my challenge to the historiographical commonplace of a shift from "character" to "personality," is to revise the notion of Victorianism itself, to see that "the humorous" and "the serious" were paired terms and values within Victorian culture, rather than representatives of historically opposed value systems. But a further purpose is to show the way in which the stability of that opposition, in its reference to objective spheres of behavior and social space, was undermined by the subjective location of the sense of humor. In the twentieth century, the distinction between the serious and the humorous came to refer less to arenas of social life or objects of perception than to modes of behavior and perception. Seriousness and humor became "attitudes" adopted by the individual vis-à-vis an evaluation of situations. The shell of the distinction between the serious and the humorous remains, but it has taken on different meanings and referents in terms of a rearrangement of object-subject relations.

My historical unpacking of the sense of humor has been guided by a desire to make the familiar strange, to thrust common sense and everyday language into the realm of cultural otherness. The distancing strategy, I am not unaware, shares much with the very meanings I have sought to unravel: the disengagement from the narrowness of present concerns in order to have "perspective"; the imagination of the self as other through the attainment of an "objective" point of view; the objectification of "culture" as a body to be analyzed, rather than an environment in which to live. That the strategies and methods I have followed should reproduce, at some level, the very cultural constructions I have historicized should come as no surprise. I have been interested in those cultural constructions precisely to the extent that they are part of the environment in which I think, precisely to the extent they undergird my own consciousness and the culture of which I am a part. To some, this may seem a case of excessive self-referentiality, of a self-consuming text, of an argument that seeks, finally, only to explain its own existence. Those critics may well be right, but if so, it is my claim that the very existence of a stance outside of "culture" looking in, the estrangement that it requires, is a central condition of modern culture and modern ways of knowing. The pervasive irony of so-called postmodernism with its refusal to be caught taking anything seriously, the elevation of the "camp" sensibility as a feature of contemporary life from the 1960s forward, the constant presence of what Jacob Brackman identified in a classic *New Yorker* article as "the put-on": all point to the sense of humor as a primary representative idea in a culture in which estrangement, standing outside of oneself, is the preferred stance.[10]

Finally, I am aware that outside the boundaries of the cultural studies set, the very idea of a history of the idea of the sense of humor is likely to strike many as an amusing exercise, but of little real importance. The "reality" of history, for the dominant sociocultural history of the present moment, lies in social movements, political institutions, the everyday struggle of people with the material circumstances of their lives. When we admit "ideas" and "culture" into our historical visions, as we increasingly have been doing, it should be to illuminate those underlying realities. The ideas historians have deemed important tend to be ideas of social reform or social stasis, political culture, intellectual and cultural traditions that can easily be codified in bodies of texts and tied to some more fundamental social experience. The history of an idea of a personality attribute can only appear, from this perspective, as a kind of ephemera, an inconsequentiality that might be interesting to specialists in a very narrow academic arena, but that has no larger relevance. I can appreciate the nature of such objections. Nevertheless, in the past thirty years, when we have discovered first the history of childhood and of family, and now the histories of sexuality, of emotions, of gestures, of odors, of everyday life, we have redrawn the boundaries of what lies within history and what lies without; history, its practitioners now say, comprehends all those things we have taken for granted as lying in the realm of the everyday. The sense of humor is one of those things. If this book does indeed take its subject too seriously, perhaps an explanation for such a stance can be found in the following pages. Failing that, I appeal to the reader's own sense of humor; I assume the reader has one.

ONE   # The Idea of Humor

The idea of the sense of humor as an attribute of persons, something individual people could be said to have or not have, was first formulated in the Anglo-American world of the mid-nineteenth century. The invention of this new concept was closely related to a specific idealized version of the bourgeois individual commensurate with the new bureaucratic and corporate imperatives of the period. But the story of the sense of humor does not begin in the nineteenth century. The component concepts of "sense" and "humor," in their shifting meanings and growing importance from the sixteenth to the nineteenth century, are both essential to the cultural metaphysics of personhood that have characterized the long-range history of Western individualism.

Individualism

Individualism seems to refer to so many disparate and often contradictory ways of perceiving, formulating, and living the relationship between personhood and social order that it often obscures rather than illuminates the phenomena it describes. Is it, for instance, an explicit political and economic ideology, or a tacit set of assumptions about political and economic man? Does individualism simply involve freeing people from external social bonds and barriers so that they can follow their internal inclinations, or is it a positive construction of those internal guides and motives? Is it a set of normative principles about how societies should be organized, or a neutral description of the way in which some societies are organized? While the distinctions seem stark, varying uses of the term "individualism," both popular and scholarly, have included all of these positions and many of those in between as well. Compounding the problem, these matters of definition generally arise prior to a host of interpretive issues: the causes and origins of individualism, the relationship of capitalism and private property to individualism, the periodization of individualism, and its relationship to specific national or class cultures or to other modern forms of thought.[1]

Recent studies of individualism have focused on the individual as a specific type of person central to modern Western cultures rather than on individualism as an explicit creed claiming political status for persons. The concern has been less with individualism as the basis for political liberalism, for instance, than with the conception of the self as a private interiorized being. The critical intellectual project of reconstructing individualism as a historical process of representations of concepts of the person has taken a multidisciplinary and cross-cultural approach. While varying in terms of methodology and disciplinary convention, scholars seem to agree that concepts of the person are culturally constituted and that the individual is a particular kind of cultural construction, unlike the ideas of personhood in most societies.[2]

The anthropologist Louis Dumont argues that individualism has its antithesis in what he calls "holism," and that a holistic method is itself necessary to see what kind of construction individualism is. For Dumont, writing under the influence of Durkheimian sociology and anthropological structuralism, the individual emerges in Western ideology as a configuration at the most abstract structural level of thought. As an assumed value, the individual figures not as an element of ideology to be questioned in a discourse, but as the unquestioned foundation of that discourse itself. The characteristics of individualism that make it antithetical to the structural holism Dumont sees in caste societies such as India are its construction of the person as a moral being prior to and independent of society, its notion of essence rather than relation as the basis of self-definition, and its positing of the individual as sui generis and of society as a collection of atomized individuals. Holism, on the other hand, assumes that social structure both exists prior to its parts and defines them.[3]

In this light, the growth of individualism can be seen as a gradual process by which ideology obscures relations within the social whole in favor of an increased subjectification and internalization of those relations. Values and codes of behavior come to appear as intrinsic to the self, the sphere of economy emerges as a realm defined by a construction known as "self-interest," and the internal process of thought and feeling is integrated, unified, and given new dimension by the construction of a range of new motives. Market relations penetrate all realms of cultural space; what had once been ordained social relationships and beliefs are now seen as matters of choice. All qualities of objects either become qualities of subjects—individuals—or lose their social character altogether and take on the features of commodities.[4]

This historical process of internalization represents a transformation in the relationship between person and social order; the self is abstracted from society and becomes the object of its own contemplation or exploration. The self, in fact, virtually becomes a piece of property. As Charles Taylor says in reference to the dual process of internalization and self-disengagement, "So we come to think that we 'have' selves as we have heads. But the very idea that we have or are 'a self,' that human agency is essentially defined as 'the self,' is a linguistic reflection of our modern understanding and the radical reflexivity it involves."[5] The growth and development of individualism, or the idea of the self, then, is not only a process of internalization and subjectification, but is also a transformation of object-subject relations; the person is conceived of not just as a subjective entity or an objective entity, but as a relationship between the two. The highest virtue of selfhood is to stand outside the self, to explore it, to manipulate it, to control it.

Finally, individualism is based on the notion that all people are essentially the same in their particularity and difference. Individualism allows one man to stand for and represent, according to Dumont, all humanity, because people are not represented as fundamentally different by dint of caste status or social location.[6] Even the calls we hear today for "diversity" and "difference" are based on a multiculturalism that is, in the last analysis, reducible to the universal autonomous individual.[7] This paradox of generality in particularity is premised on the elevation of everyday life to the status of exemplum, what Taylor calls "the affirmation of ordinary life," the world of production and reproduction, over and above the life of civic duty or public honor.[8] The exemplary or heroic figure whose moral worth is based precisely on his standing outside the mundane reality of ordinary existence is replaced by the figure who represents the common everyday struggles of all people. The new hero is the man who represents all humanity; he is the individual as a type. One way to read this affirmation of ordinary life, of course, is as a triumph of the universalist ideology of the new middle class, or classes, over the particularism of an aristocratic ethos.[9] Individualism posits a new relationship between the particularity of personhood—each person being unique and distinct—and the generality of the moral value of the person—each person representing all of humanity.

What appears here as a rather abstract set of transformations seems far from the mundane world in which we speak of people having or not having a sense of humor. Yet these transformations have everything to do with the history of the terms "sense" and "humor." The idea of sense, in the way it is used in the term "sense of humor," has much to do with the process of internalization, and indeed it can be linked to the eighteenth-century "affirmation of ordinary life" through the idea of the moral sense and its offshoots,[10] and to the universalist democratization characteristic of Enlightenment thought through the modern transformation of the Aristotelian notion of the common sense.[11] In fact, the whole issue of sentiment and sensibility in eighteenth-century culture speaks directly to the issue of internalization, self-exploration, and self-control.[12]

The changing meaning of the word "humor" is also closely tied to the history of individualism, as historians and critics of humor have frequently noted. Charles Read Baskervill, writing in 1911, explained the sixteenth-century conception of humor related to character as a consequence of a new individualism, and Edward Hooker, writing in the 1940s, saw the eighteenth-century meaning of humor as evidence of an era of "rugged individualism."[13] The meaning of humor, as much as it has changed, has for centuries been linked to the conception of personhood. The same can be said for the word "sense." The term "sense of humor" has buried deep within it, then, meanings that refer both to older forms of socially defined personhood and newer forms of individualism; perhaps no better indices of the shifting meaning of personhood could be found.

Humor and Character

Before the sense of humor, there was humor. The word "humor" originally derives from the Latin for moisture or liquid, and that sense of the word is retained in some of its modern usages, even as it is shifted away from the main designation. In the medical profession, for instance, humors are still considered bodily fluids (as, for instance, the fluids in the eye). This medical usage is a direct derivation from the central meaning of the word humor in the Middle Ages. Humoral theory, as adapted from Galen, defined physiology in terms of a temperament (from the Latin for "mixture") created by the relative proportions of the four humors—blood, phlegm, choler or bile, and melancholy or black bile—in the body. Each humor was said to possess special qualities, so that a dominance of any one humor in the constitution created a specific kind of temperament. Too much blood made the temperament sanguine, while the phlegmatic, choleric or bilious, and melancholy types all arose from excesses of the other humors in the constitution.[14]

It is not quite correct to say that temperament was conceived of as an effect of which humoral dominance or mixture was the cause, although in modern terms a kind of causal relationship seems to be the only way to talk about physio-psychical relationships. In medieval medicine, however, temperament was conceived of as the literal mixture of humors. Black bile, for instance, didn't cause melancholy by its excessive presence in the physical system; rather, melancholy was literally in black bile so that its physical and characterological presence were one and the same. Humoral physiology, then, posited a radically different conception of the ontological status of personhood than does modern characterology. According to Charles Taylor, humoral theory is characterized by a conception of personhood that is not localized in a way that separates levels of reality into subjective and objective states. The conceptual leap is a difficult one for moderns to make. It requires a rejection of typical ways of thinking about causality, and a willingness to see a continuum, rather than a sharp distinction, between the objective physical and the subjective mental qualities of persons.[15]

Early meanings of humor were tied to the person conceived of as a physiological entity, and to a set of symptoms by which to know that physiology. Temperament signified an abnormality, or humoral imbalance in the body, but not a substratum of personality in the modern sense. The melancholy person, for instance, was a diseased or deviant social type that was susceptible to medical treatment and cure. Humoral balance was the norm to be obtained, and it was to be achieved through physiological and not psychological treatment. The four humors had much to do with a social and characterological constitution of the person, but nothing at all to do with the psychological entity we designate as the self.

The point to be made here is a fairly simple one, but it needs to be made none the less. If we are to understand the historical roots of the sense of humor, and its relationship to individualism, we must do so by resisting the temptation to make easy reductions of the language and thought of the past to that of the present. The danger in such reductions lies in the tendency to conflate ways of thinking so as to make the past reducible to the terms of the present. By conceiving of humoral thought as a form of "psychology," for instance, the modern imagination converts it into the language of motives, cause and effect, and "mind," in effect collapsing the major differences between modern psychology and its classical predecessors. The alternative is not to call for a reading of the past in its own terms—hardly realistic in these days of epistemological self-consciousness—but rather to attempt a strategy of distancing by historical contrast. The point of such a strategy is to deliberately render the past as "a foreign country." The question, in this context, then, becomes one of how we have moved from the alien world of humoral medicine to the altogether familiar notion of the sense of humor as a personality characteristic. How has the word "humor" changed its meaning so as to serve as an index of two fundamentally different notions of personhood?

Although humoral medicine persisted as a dominant mode of understanding the temperament and its characteristics well into the eighteenth century, new meanings of the word "humor" began to arise as derivations from the original sense as early as the fifteenth century. Slowly, humor shifted from being a designation for the fluids that made up the temperament to being a designation for the temperament itself, particularly the odd or quirky temperament suggested by an imbalance of the humors. This early modern change in meaning marks the beginning of the diminution of the physiological, and the elevation of the characterological, elements in humoral thought. The new definitions are characterized less by the notion of imbalance, although that notion remains important, and more by the idea of a state of being. Persons are said to possess humors or to be "in" humors, rather than to be constituted by humors. These new meanings do not indicate the discovery or invention of humor as a subjective faculty or as a way of perceiving; they remain tied to notions of persons as objects, but they do indicate a new direct link between the idea of humor, metaphorically abstracted from its physiological referents, and a notion of personhood defined by states of being.

The *Oxford English Dictionary* gives the first citation for humor as "Mental disposition; constitutional or habitual tendency; temperament," as occurring circa 1475, but it is difficult to know how common this usage was, even well into the sixteenth century. This particular notion of humor as a persistent and normal condition of the person, as opposed to a temporary mood, is not cited again until Shakespeare's use of it in *The Taming of the Shrew* (1596).[16] The notion of humor as a "temporary state of mind or feeling," on the other hand, begins to appear fairly frequently from the mid-sixteenth century on. Both the *OED* and Baskervill give 1525 as the date of the earliest use of humor to mean a temporary state.[17] We retain this usage today when we speak of a person being in a good or ill humor, although "mood" is the more common synonym. From 1565 on, the use of the term becomes increasingly pejorative as it is associated with whim, caprice, fancy, or spurious inclination. According to Baskervill, whose thorough search of sixteenth-century writing still sets the standard in the field,

> the first work in which I have found humour used freely in its derived sense dates from 1567; by 1580 the use of the word has become fairly widespread; and by 1592 humour seems to be the term most often chosen by the writers who deal with the follies of the time to indicate the inclination or moral weakness that leads to evil. The use of the word, indeed, increases in proportion to the attention that is paid to the study of manners.[18]

There are two points worth making here. Despite numerous individual appearances of the term in its derived sense, and the plurality of emergent meanings throughout the sixteenth century, it is only in the last third of the century that humor takes on something of a shared meaning, and that only because of its relationship to a specific discourse. The second point is that it is the didactic and moralistic literature of the sixteenth century that creates the pejorative notion of humor. The move from the medical conception of humors as regulated by physiological balance to the moral notion of humors as manners and characteristics to be reformed through criticism represents the beginning of a process by which humor was tied to the idea of persons as self-conscious subjects.

The idea that humors could be objects of criticism, rather than simply transparent characteristics of persons, was an entirely new one.

By the end of the sixteenth century, then, the derived meanings of humor, still partly rooted in the dominant humoral physiology, had proliferated along two major divides. The first division was between those definitions of humor that stressed its status as a temporary state and those that stressed its persistent and constitutional character. That distinction was roughly one between mood and underlying temperament. The other division arose out of the transition from medical physiology to didactic literature, and is evident in the new meanings of humor as whim, fancy, and inclination. It is the division between humor as artifice and humor as natural. One of the assumptions of the didactic literature of the later sixteenth century was that humors were affectations and, as such, were fit objects for criticism.[19] But the older notions of humors as rooted in a natural temperament coexisted with this idea of humors as affectations. The eccentric or odd person was inclined to be such by the natural constitution of his humors, rather than by his deliberate affectations, according to this view. The view of humors as artifice, as objects of self-conscious manipulation, represents the more modern perspective;[20] the view of eccentricities as natural elements of a physiologically constituted temperament represents, on the other hand, not so much a premodern or traditional construction of personhood as it does one in transition, one that has already been deeply impinged upon by an emerging individualism. Whether natural or affected, it is the notion of eccentricity or oddity that suggests the beginning of a historical diversion from the understanding of persons in terms of static typologies; the odd character stands at the margins of typicality, pushing outside of its boundaries.

This shift in the meaning of humor in the latter decades of the sixteenth century was not an isolated development. The Renaissance conception of the individual tended to move literary representation away from allegory, and the social and moral typologies associated with it, and toward the particularities of individuals, a movement that would ultimately result in the development of the novel in eighteenth-century Britain.[21] The movement from character as type to character as individual involved a new way of looking at the peculiarities of persons as their distinguishing features. What was important in defining the person was less the feature that identified him with the type he represented, and more the feature that distinguished him from the type. When people came to be regarded more as complex objects of dissection than as balanced (or unbalanced) wholes, the notion of a *dominant* quality or characteristic became identified with specific persons. The humor came to represent that element of the person by which he could be distinguished from all other persons, rather than his place in an abstract set of typologies defined by temperament.[22] The notion of humor as it came to be defined at the end of the sixteenth century, then, even as it retained much of humoral theory, significantly contributed to a notion of particularity and individuality based on eccentric characteristics. Such a shift in meaning was part and parcel of the emergence of individualism in early modern Britain.

The Comedy of Humors

The metaphorical unmooring of humor from its physiological foundation in medieval medicine set loose a whole range of potential meanings that would percolate through Anglo-American culture for the next three centuries. It was in the dramatic writings of Ben Jonson, above all, that the modern notion of humor was first developed in a systematic way. Jonson's definition of humor was important not because it was the only definition in Renaissance England, which it was not, nor because it was the dominant definition, but because by responding to the wide range of sixteenth-century meanings it was the first attempt to fix a stable meaning by metaphorical reasoning. As a consequence, Jonson's definition would set the terms for future understandings of humor as related to character.

There has long been disagreement over what Jonson meant by his doctrine of humors as the foundation of the comedy form.[23] Given the seeming multiplicity of meanings surrounding him, it is not surprising that Jonson aimed to establish a "true" definition of humor. His intent, as he has the character Asper speak for him in *Every Man Out of His Humor*, is "To give these ignorant wel-spoken daies / Some tast of their abuse of this word *Humor*."[24] This rhetorical strategy of insisting on defining "true" humor, or correcting the so-called abuses of the term, would be a mainstay of criticism well into the nineteenth century, when Thomas Carlyle, most notably, would seize upon it. The perceived need to define the word, over and over again, suggests a relative instability of meaning within English literary circles and within the culture at large.[25]

Jonson's most explicit statement on the meaning of humor is in Asper's definition in *Every Man Out of His Humor*:

> That what soe're hath fluxure and humiditie,
> As wanting power to containe it selfe,
> Is *Humor*: so in every humane bodie
> The choller, melancholy, flegme, and bloud,
> By reason that they flow continually
> In some one part, and are not continent,
> Receive the name of Humors. Now thus farre
> It may, by Metaphore, apply it selfe
> Unto the general disposition,
> As when some one peculiar quality
> Doth so possesse a man, that it doth draw
> All his affects, his spirits, and his powers,
> In their confluctions all to runne one way,
> This may be truly said to be a Humor.
> But that a Rooke in wearing a pide feather,
> The cable hatband, or the three-pild ruffe,
> A yard of shoe-tie, or the Switzers knot
> On his French garters, should affect a Humor,
> O, tis more than most ridiculous.[26]

This passage is the standard one on which all readings of Jonson's notion of humor rely, for it is very explicit about what "may be truly said to be a Humor."

The two key phrases for understanding the idea of true humors propounded by Jonson are that a humor lacks power "to containe it selfe," and that humor can be metaphorically applied "Unto the general disposition." The use of a liquid metaphor is a way to describe character as uncontained or not subject to manipulation by a controlling self; the humor controls the direction of character, rather than the self controlling its own eccentricities. Jonson thus argues for a "natural" definition of humor over the ridiculous artifice of those who would "affect a Humor." By applying the term to the general disposition rather than simply to particular characteristics, humor ceases to be simply one attribute in a complex of attributes and becomes the defining characteristic of a person as a whole. The quirky, odd, and eccentric person, for Jonson, is both in a humor and is himself a humor. When he says "This may be truly said to be a Humor," the "this" refers both to the "peculiar quality" and to the man who is possessed by that quality. A man does not possess a humor, as we might think of a person possessing qualities; rather, he is possessed by it and, by generalization of that possession, *is* a humor. In effect, this definition implies a retention of the conception of being associated with humoral medicine. The humor does not cause eccentricity, in a physio-psychological relationship; rather, the humor simply *is* eccentric, and it is this relationship that allows the quality and the person to be called by the same name.

Despite Jonson's metaphorical link of humor to personhood as a way of describing the conditions of being that distinguish particular persons from the abstract model of personhood as type, he did not foresee a modern internalized self. There is nothing subjective in Jonson's notion of humor. As Louis Cazamian says, "One may apply the epithets 'objective' or 'passive' to the Jonsonian use of 'humor' as the word denotes a mode of being which is unconscious of itself, and is perceived as a fact by persons other than the one who harbors it."[27] Jonson was not alone in the Elizabethan period in clinging to a view of humor as characteristic of objective states. Humoral medicine, after all, maintained a continuing prominence and viability through the following centuries. However, he was the first to take the approach to the humors of the didactic critics of character defects, with its implied focus on affectation and eccentricity, and to root that approach in a natural, objective, and unified view of character. The notion of humors as susceptible to criticism allowed Jonson to create the humor as an objective character type: a source of amusement for others in a social relation between performer and audience. In the sixteenth and seventeenth centuries, then, humor both referred to objective character and was potentially associated with laughter for the first time. Whether comedy should raise laughter was an open question, as it had been since Aristotle, but the opening for a link between humor and laughter was initially created through the comic form and its characters.

However, if Jonson's aim was satiric, as has been suggested, it would seem that the characters whose behavior caused laughter would be capable of responding to that laughter by correcting their behavior. But to correct that behavior, to respond to criticism by self-criticism, would be to have a degree of self-consciousness and self-control denied to the "true" humor. There can be little doubt that Jonson's purpose was, at least in part, didactic and satiric. As Asper says:

If any here chance to behold himselfe,
Let him not dare to challenge me of wrong;
For, if he shame to have his follies knowne,
First he should shame to act 'hem: my strict hand
Was made to ceaze on vice, and with a gripe
Crush out the Humor of such spongie soules,
As licke up every idle vanity.[28]

Asper's message is directed not at the humor characters, but at the audience. What the Jonsonian form does is to demand that the audience see themselves in the comic humors; but unlike the humors, the members of the audience are imagined as fully capable of self-reform and self-manipulation. The comic humors within the dramatic structure are true, natural, and objective characters; the audience members are the persons who potentially possess affectations that can be corrected.

Thus, Jonson draws a line between persons as represented in the drama and those outside of the drama, and at the same time draws his audience members into a relationship with his fictional characters by demanding that they see themselves in those characters. The comedy of humors represents a strange fusion of medieval allegory with its didactic moralism and typologies, and a protomodern realism with its insistence on particularity of character and sympathetic recognition of "the real."

Jonson's contributions to the future meaning of humor can be characterized in the following way. By generalizing the eccentricities of humoral imbalance to the eccentricities of objective character types, Jonson linked humor to the emerging individualism of concrete particularity of persons. By making the humor the foundation of the comic form, he inaugurated a new potential relationship between humor and laughter. Finally, by rooting humor in the theatrical relationship of audience to character, with the audience's implied capacity for what in the twentieth century would come to be called "self-objectification," Jonson determined the future direction of the term. Humor would come to be strongly associated with sympathy and benevolence in eighteenth- and nineteenth-century thought. While this association would seem to be antithetical to Jonson's satiric goal of "scourging" the vices represented by the humors, it prepared the way for the eventual emergence of humor as sympathetic—characterized by laughing "with" rather than "at"—by opening the door to audience identification with the particularity of comic character.

Much of Jonson's contribution to the history of the idea of humor was diffuse and indirect; the present meaning of humor does not appear as the end product of a direct line of descent. By the eighteenth century, many of those in literary, dramatic, and critical circles who argued over or attempted to define humor would not look to Jonson as the authority or source from which understandings of humor might arise. This tendency to look elsewhere was not so much a rejection of Jonson's definition of humor as it was an engagement with the diverse and contradictory meanings of humor in eighteenth-century Britain, and it signals the extent to which humor had emerged from both its medieval medical milieu and its locus in sixteenth-century didactic literature. By the eighteenth century, humor had become a ubiquitous term, used to signify peculiarities of character, distinctive qualities of persons, literary forms, and thoughts of peculiarity abstracted from persons. The Jonsonian meaning was antiquated, too narrow and specific, still rooted in the ontology of medieval humoral thought; and yet, the eighteenth-century meanings of humor owed their being to the problematics of object-subject relations created in Jonson's definition.

From Object to Subject

Following the metaphorical unmooring of humor from its roots in physiology and medicine, the term underwent a long-term shift in meaning from the sixteenth through the nineteenth centuries. Humor had designated the elements of an objective, phsyiological constitution; it would come to refer to a subjective quality of mind and perception. This process of subjectification was not unique to humor. A host of other terms, some newly coined, others radically transformed in meaning, not only provide evidence of an increasing valorization of subjectivity but help to constitute the very internalization they are used to describe. George McKnight provides a lengthy list of new coinages since the sixteenth century that express precisely this new constitution of subjectivity and selfhood in terms of interior states and emotions.[29]

The interiorization taking place over the past four centuries is, however, best revealed in the changes surrounding the terms of humoral medicine. As Owen Barfield has said:

> When we reflect on the history of such notions as *humour, influence, melancholy, temper,* and the rest, it seems for the moment as though some invisible sorcerer has been conjuring them all inside ourselves—sucking them away from the outside world, away from our own warm flesh and blood, down into the shadowy realm of thoughts and feelings.[30]

In the span of a lifetime, perhaps, the meaning of words seems scarcely to change at all. It is in the perspective of centuries that this change in meaning—from physical to psychical, from exterior to interior, from objective to subjective—can be seen for what it is, a fundamental revolution in the understanding of what it is to be a person.

The seventeenth century, particularly the final third of that century, was the critical period in the transition from the objective notion of humor, rooted in character and qualities of personhood, to a modern subjective notion of humor rooted in consciousness of peculiarity.[31] The growing subjectification of humor as a quality of thought of persons rather than simply an objective characteristic of theatrical personae, can be seen most prominently in Thomas Shadwell's appropriation of Jonsonian humor theory in the context of Restoration drama. The seventeenth-century linkage of humor to Jonson was direct, unlike the indirect proliferation of meanings that would follow it. In fact, Shadwell saw himself reproducing exactly the terms of his self-proclaimed master, Jonson. But, in looking back over half a century, Shadwell read Jonson in terms of the 1670s rather than the early 1600s in which Jonson wrote. It is precisely because Shadwell aimed to reproduce so precisely Jonson's notion of humor as the foundation of the comic form that his rereading of Jonson provides an entrée into the cultural meanings of humor and personhood as they had changed in the course of the seventeenth century.

Shadwell's notion of Jonsonian humor is spelled out in several of his writings.[32] Nowhere is his definition clearer than in his preface to *The Humorists* (1671):

> A Humor is the Biasse of the Mind
> By which, with violence, 'tis one way inclin'd

It makkes our actions lean on one side still,
And, in all Changes, that way bends the Will.[33]

The changes from Jonson's notion of humor are both subtle and momentous. The continuities, on the other hand, are fairly obvious and tend to overshadow the conceptual shift that has occurred. A humor is still imagined as a force prior to and beyond the control of the will, determining the objective actions of the person, and it still refers to the dominant inclination or quality, rather than to any particular eccentricity. These continuities conceal the basic differences between Shadwell's and Jonson's concepts of humor.

In Shadwell's understanding, humor has been freed, even metaphorically, from the humoral physiology Jonson relied on to establish the "true" meaning of humor; there is no mention of a physiological, rather than psychological, temperament that would set the basis for an "objective" notion of character. Instead, humor has been internalized as a quality of "mind." As such, it is the *cause* of peculiarity of character—it "makes our action"—rather than being the peculiarity itself, as it was in Jonson's understanding. Shadwell thus disengages mind from action in his definition of humor, making one the expression of the other. Even as he insists on humor as the controlling force of individual character, he subordinates it to the mind, of which it is imagined as a "Biasse"; ultimately it is mind, of which humor is a part, that controls the will and its actions. Shadwell thus represents a turn toward the subjective in the meaning of humor, even as he remains far from the modern notion of humor as a mode of seeing, rather than a mode of being.

Shadwell also marks the extension of the meaning of humor outside the parameters of theatrical character to characters in "real life." Although his goal is explicit and limited to providing the foundations of a theatrical form, his notion of humor requires not only a conception of theatrical characters, but a conception of character outside the theater. Whereas Jonson distinguished between the affectations of people in society and the naturalness of the fictively constituted humor, Shadwell reconstructed the natural humor as existing both in the drama and outside it. When he defines humor he speaks of it as something belonging to all of "us." Besides the fact that humor is now seen as a possession of persons, rather than that which possesses them, Shadwell's definition breaks down the separation between audience and theatrical character, subjective intelligence and objective behavior. As a result of this dissolution, Shadwell demands a kind of realism of character:

> For if a man bring such a humor upon the Stage (if there be such a humor in the world) as onely belongs to one or two persons, it would not be understood by the Audience, but would be thought, for the singularity of it, wholly unnatural, and would be no jest to them neither. . . . [F]or a humor, being the representation of some extravagances of Mankind, cannot but in some thing resemble some man or other, or it is monstrous and unnatural.[34]

Shadwell is able to speak of humor as being a "representation" at the same moment as he demands not only that it be *thought* to be natural by the audience, but that it actually *be* natural. It is the fact of resembling socially recognized types of persons that sets the criteria by which the humor is deemed natural. Men are able to bring humors upon the stage because they exist off the stage, and can be recognized by the audience as drawn from society. Nowhere does he mention affectation or distinguish between true and false humors in terms of affectation.

Shadwell sought to restrain the anarchic and individualistic implications of the concept of humor as eccentricity by ruling in favor of humors as recognizable social types rather than independent and sui generis individuals. While rejecting an extreme individualism of particular differences, however, he contributed to the subjectification of the idea of humor. Although Shadwell's humors were hardly the possessions of self-conscious subjects, the location of humor in mind contributed to the centuries-long shift responsible for the modern notion of humor. Subjectification was the ground upon which an individualism of internalized selfhood, rather than one of particular difference, would be developed.

The movement of humor into the subject, as its primary locus, did not gather force until the eighteenth century, and it would not be until the early nineteenth century that it emerged in its modern meaning of a quality of subjective appreciation. According to one 1882 essay, humor "has only within the last two or three generations been stereotyped in its present meaning."[35] The "double-mindedness" that was "the germ of a new soul," according to Cazamian, was based upon the process by which the Jonsonian humor made "a growing discovery of the significance of his own oddity."[36] Yet this growing subjectification of humor, its being placed as an irreducible mental quality, remained incomplete into the late nineteenth century, as older meanings coexisted with it. "A humor is not always the quality of mind we call humor," said U.S. Senator Samuel S. Cox in 1876. "A humor may be a particular mannerism; a humor may not be funny, but humor is."[37] With Cox, we are a long way from Shadwell's notion of humor as a quality of objective character types, and yet notions of a "particular mannerism" still seem close to humor's seventeenth-century meanings. It was in the later seventeenth century that the turn toward the subjective meaning of humor began in earnest, and it is in the writing of Shadwell in particular that this turn can be documented. That the revolution in humor's meaning remained incomplete two centuries later speaks to the persistence and tenacity of older meanings in the face of a fundamental reorientation from object to subject.

The Humorist and the Man of Humor

This retention of older meanings points to the central fact that the process by which subjective meanings replaced objective ones was never sweeping and unidirectional. For instance, the history of the idea of the humorist, a term first used in the seventeenth century, reveals the persistence of an objective notion of character as laughable at the same time as it shows the increasing concrete particularity and uniqueness associated with individualism. Not until the mid- to late nineteenth century did the term "humorist" come to refer to the self-conscious creator of a product called "humor." Mark Twain, in fact, was probably one of the first humorists in this modern sense, and the American humorists of his era, with their deadpan ironic delivery which only hinted at the intelligence that lay behind it, probably did much to change the meaning of "humorist" to its modern sense. From the seventeenth through the nineteenth centuries, a humorist was more closely related to what Jonson had called a humor—that is, the objective character controlled by his unbalanced temperament.

Shadwell's seventeenth-century use of the term "humorist" retains the meaning of objective character, although by the mid-eighteenth century that usage had apparently diminished. Corbyn Morris, writing in 1744, assumed that most of his readers would be unfamiliar with the term:

The Character of an HUMOURIST, I expect, will be strange to most of my Readers; and if no Gentleman is acquainted with a *Person* of this *Cast*, it must pass for a *Monster* of my own Creation.[38]

Whether the term had simply disappeared in the seventy years between Shadwell and Morris, or whether Morris was simply trying to pass it off as his own invention, it assumed a new visibility in the following century. Morris was likely responding to the change in the meaning of humor, for once humor was unmoored from its physiological base in character, it became increasingly capable of being understood as simply a quality of character, either natural or assumed. Humor had become an object of manipulation, a subjective quality of mind, perhaps even a mode of treatment.

Because of the new meanings of humor, Morris was compelled to distinguish between what he called a "man of humour" and a "humourist," in a distinction that would be taken up by others in the eighteenth century:

> A Man of HUMOUR is *one, who can happily exhibit a weak and ridiculous* Character *in real Life, either by assuming it himself, or representing another in it, so naturally, that the* whimsical Oddities *and* Foibles, *of that* Character, *shall be palpably expos'd.*
>
> Whereas an HUMOURIST *is a* Person *in real Life, obstinately attached to a sensible peculiar* Oddities *of his own genuine Growth, which appear in his Temper and Conduct.*[39]

While Morris's repeated assertions that humor must appear "in real Life," as opposed to the fictive life of literature or drama, suggest the extent to which humor has been naturalized and drawn away from the dramatic relations in which Jonson and Shadwell had embedded it, Morris's distinction seems to parallel that between false and true humors, affectation and natural eccentricity. Our contemporary notion of a humorist, however, seems much closer to Morris's man of humor than to his humorist. The man of humor does not so much affect a particular behavior; rather, he assumes a role, and in doing so reveals a manipulating intelligence behind the mask of the unknowing humorist he pretends to be. The man of humor is conscious of the amusement caused by the eccentric character of the humorist, and plays his role so as to amuse. Here is the Jonsonian humor becoming conscious of himself; but here also, in concert with this new self-consciousness, is a reaction against it. The humorist is resurrected as the objective character type, as if a necessary counterpart to the increasingly subjective meaning of humor. The man of humor *possesses* knowledge of oddity; he is active. The humorist is *possessed by* oddity; he is passive.

The influential Scottish Enlightenment thinkers Lords Kames and Monboddo were both comfortable with this notion of the humorist as a type of character, whether they received it directly from Morris or not; it was an idea in the process of cultural formation in the mid-eighteenth century. Kames clearly views the humorist as an object of laughter rather than a self-conscious creator of laughter. "When we attend to the character of a humourist," he wrote, "we find that it . . . makes him in some measure ridiculous."[40] Monboddo reproduces Morris's distinction between the man of humor and the humorist in almost precisely the same terms. A humorist "is a man of character singular and odd," while a man of humor is one who "has the faculty of imitating, in speaking or writing, such a character."[41] The difference between Monboddo and Morris is that the former doesn't insist on real life as the locus of humor characters; he assumes that the sphere of humor is real life, while the sphere of the man of humor, at least in his representations, is theatrical or fictive. The whole issue of the status and location of the humorist has become one that can be assumed, rather than a subject for argumentation as it is in Morris's account. Unlike Morris, Monboddo casually suggests that the definition of a humorist is "agreed by all." In the thirty years between the publications of Morris and Monboddo, the concept of the humorist had become widely recognized as a term describing the odd and singular objective character.

While the concept of humor itself became increasingly subjectified and internalized as it was abstracted from character, the concept of the humorist also contributed to an increasingly prominent individualism by moving character away from the typologies clung to by Jonson and Shadwell and toward the unique and particular. Stuart Tave has argued that the literary cult of the humorist that arose around specific literary characters in the eighteenth century represents just such a change in values:

> The humorists have an individuality as detailed and strikingly vivid as their creators can fashion. Their claim to universal significance rests less and less, in the later eighteenth century, on their being representa-

tives of a species, manner types, and more and more on their unique-ness. The smallest details of their existence are recorded because it is in these that reality resides.[42]

Corbyn Morris had insisted that humorists exist in "real life." The eigh-teenth-century literary characters represented as humorists maintained their identity as humorists to the extent that their "reality" was the reality of particularity and concrete detail, that of everyday life. The irony of the eighteenth-century humorist lay in a universal significance premised on uniqueness and particularity. The more the humorist was odd, eccen-tric and different from all other individuals, the more he came to embody all mankind. The humorist thus represents a central feature of an indi-vidualism where the individual, as a distinct moral being, is made to stand for all mankind; this is an individualism where the hyper-concreteness of quotidian detail and the universal abstraction of humankind are not op-posed models of personhood, but are held together as one.

The notion of the humorist as a unique, singular, concretely detailed character was a literary mainstay from the late eighteenth century to at least the middle of the nineteenth century, both in Britain and in the United States. The American essayist William A. Jones, for instance, maintained the distinction well into the 1850s. "A humorist is not, neces-sarily, *a man of humor*, but of *humors*," said Jones. "He cannot describe, or point out humorous peculiarities in others; but affords, in himself, a subject for the comic painter."[43] Similarily, Melville describes Stubb in *Moby Dick* as "one of those odd sort of humorists, whose jollity is some-times so curiously ambiguous."[44] Melville and Jones both drew on the literary meaning of humorists as comic characters that came out of eigh-teenth-century Britain. They clearly did not understand a humorist to be a conscious creator of humor.

The use of the term "humorist," however, was not limited to literary depictions of character. As Morris had spoken of humorists existing in "real life," so they did, in effect providing a justification for their repre-sentation in a literature of increasing realism. The general understanding of the concept of the humorist can be seen in a short anecdotal item that appeared in a Philadelphia journal near the end of the eighteenth century under the title "The Humourists." The story concerns two men of "an odd turn of humour" who encounter each other in a narrow lane; both are so obstinate that neither will step aside to let the other pass. At an apparent standoff, the first humorist produces a newspaper and settles into reading it; the second, not to be topped, asks the first for the paper when he has finished with it. Struck by their similarity, the two men become fast friends. This item was a rather trivial and inconsequential insert in the paper, but its triviality reveals to some extent how common was the use of the term "humorist" in this way. The item was clearly produced for the amusement of its readers, who, it must be assumed, would laugh at the peculiar and illogical behavior of the two humorists. There is no detailed drawing of literary character in its concrete particulars; rather, there is an assumption that the reader knows what humorists are as a general kind of person marked by a peculiar and obstinate bent. These humorists are representations of persons in "real life," not in drama or literature. They certainly are not humorists in our twentieth-century understanding of the term: conscious creators of amusement.[45]

The notion that humorists were generally regarded as persons in "real life," rather than simply literary characters, is given further support by the nineteenth-century understanding of black Americans as humorists. The "Sambo" characterization of blacks as childlike eccentrics who were continually saying amusing things, albeit unconsciously, adapted itself well to the language of the humorist. John Bernard, the English comedian and American theater manager, spoke of blacks as "the great humorists of the Union," full of the "confusion of ideas and difficulty of clear expression, pouring words out of their mouths on the high tide of natural drollery, as broad as it is rapid." Bernard's notion of "Samboisms" as unconsciously amusing behaviors and sayings fit perfectly with the idea of the humorist as an oddly amusing objective character. Just as whites imagined themselves as capable of manipulating amusing behavior in accordance with an underlying deliberative intelligence, so they also imagined blacks as incapable of such manipulation and, as a consequence, "natural" and "simple" in their behavior. This distinction is caught perfectly in the institution of blackface minstrelsy, so prominent throughout the middle of the nineteenth century; whites imitated blacks, and in doing so revealed both their conscious awareness and intent to amuse as well as the stereotyped conception of blacks as objects of amusement rather than subjective creators of amusement. The distinction between whites in blackface and the blacks they sought to imitate reproduces Morris's distinction between the man of humor and the humorist—but in new, racial terms.[46]

But as Melville's understanding of Stubb as a humorist, and the general white conception of blacks as humorists, suggest, humorists were not imagined simply as objects of amusement. The appeal of the humorist lay not only in his oddity and eccentricity, but in his own amusement and good nature. These latter qualities allowed him both to be treated as an object and to be imagined as happy in his objecthood. The result was a mitigating of any potential guilt that observers may have felt in laughing at the humorist by a claim that such laughter expressed an endearment to the naturally happy and jolly figure.[47] Herein lay the ambiguity of the humorist in the nineteenth century, the point at which objectivity faded into a potential subjectivity, where the distinction between "laughing at" and "laughing with" began to appear fuzzy and indistinct. Humorists were amusing because they were amused. What observers found funny about the behavior of humorists was not the same thing that humorists themselves found funny, but it was the fact that the humorists were amused that allowed those observers to laugh at them. The observer's laughter was tinged with the benevolence and amiability that had begun to surround the concept of humor in the eighteenth century.[48] Every act of laughter at the peculiarity of humorists was thus made ambiguous; it was a laughter shared with the humorist, but also at his expense.

The distinction between laughing *at* and laughing *with* is a universally recognized one in our culture, and we take it that all occurences of laughter, save abnormal cases of insanity and hysteria, can be divided into those two categories. This distinction, however, is an entirely modern one; prior to the eighteenth century, no such understanding of laughter was possible. All laughter at the behavior of persons was conceived of as distancing the laugher from his object of amusement, or made possible by a previously existing distance. Traditionally, as one historian of comedy has said, comic figures "were objectified and removed from us in a way that made them distinctively other people." In the modern period, however, "the comic figure tended to be a person whose behavior was more like that of the average man. His excesses were no longer so aberrant, and he himself became less of an abstraction."[49] This narrowing of the distance between object and subject—a narrowing that began with Ben Jonson—resulted in a recognition of self in the other, and consequently a new notion of laughing "with" rather than "at." This development will be explored more thoroughly in the next chapter. I mention it here to point to the way in which the emergence of the distinction between sympathetic and antipathetic laughter was clouded by the ambiguities of object and subject suggested by the use of the term "humorist" well into the middle of the nineteenth century. The sympathetic/antipathetic distinction was, and is, recognized as a real and valid one, but every instance of laughter also seems to express a potential ambiguity in its emotional meaning and content. Why else has the defensive statement "I'm not laughing at you, I'm laughing with you" entered the stock of cliché expressions? The continued insistence on the distinction suggests the continuing ambiguity of the meaning of laughter.

From Character to Discourse

The notion of the humorist became ambiguous in this particular way partly because the meaning of humor in the eighteenth and nineteenth centuries shifted from eccentric character to writing about eccentric character. As humor became identified less with an objective state of being, and more with a subjective way of seeing, it was abstracted from character and moved to the discourse by which character was represented. At first glance this process of abstraction appears as the antithesis of the increasing attention to subjectivity and interiority so central to the growth of individualism. Instead of being more personalized and character-specific, humor, in the eighteenth century, became more and more depersonalized as it was abstracted from the peculiar qualities of the concrete individual (the humorist); it finally came to rest in a set of texts, practices, and discourses, objectively accessible to all persons. The term "humor" could now designate a piece of writing or a literary genre, rather than a quality of character. If humor remained largely concerned with character, as it did throughout the eighteenth and nineteenth centuries, it was not because humor was seen as a quality of persons; rather, it was seen as a means of representing persons, a way of writing *about* the qualities of persons.

On the surface, humor was depersonalized. Instead of being rooted in the constitution of particular people, it had an external existence. Ironically, however, this depersonalization of the meaning of humor *did* represent the growing importance of subjectivity in modern culture. The movement away from character located humor as a self-conscious creation in the mind, rather than in the unknowing character as object of amusement. Humor came to represent a way of perceiving and representing the world that was under the control of its self-conscious creator. Instead of simply referring to the world as it was, objectively, the new meanings of humor increased the power of the subjective self through its ability to represent that world in terms of oddity and eccentricity. By objectifying humor in writing, the eighteenth century diminished the objective quality of character and elevated the subjective quality of consciousness.

The move from character to discourse, from object to subject, can be seen in the definitions of humor given by writers in the eighteenth and nineteenth centuries. Jonathan Swift, for instance, in "To Mr. Delany," seems to counter a new definition of humor that would link it to wit, and thereby to the process of self-conscious creation of the amusing:

> Humor is odd, grotesque, and wild
> Onely by Affectation spoild,
> 'Tis never by Invention got,
> Men have it when they know it not.

The issue of affectation vs. naturalness had provided one of the central ambiguities of the meaning of humor since the time of Jonson. Swift turned that ambiguity into an argument against the encroaching notion of humor as a process of subjective creation. If humor was the process of self-conscious creation, or even its product, then, for Swift, it was to be denounced as an affectation: not "true" humor. Humor is not a mode of treatment of characters, but naturally occurring objective character itself (although it should be noted that it is a *possession* of character, not its controlling force). For, as Swift says,

> What Humor is, not all the Tribe
> Of Logick-mongers can describe;
> Here, onely Nature acts her Part
> Unhelpt by Practice, Books, or Art.[50]

The key phrases, for Swift, in his battle against those who would abstract humor from character, are that "Men have it when they know it not," and that humor is not subject to learned analysis as a technique or process of representation, that it is "Unhelpt by Practice, Books, or Art."

This position would be repeated by others throughout the eighteenth century, even as it became the less accepted view, because it accorded with the important distinction between wit and humor. But important changes made their way into this understanding of humor as a natural and unself-conscious character attribute. For instance, John Witherspoon, one of the most influential figures in eighteenth-century American education and often credited with being the main source of the establishment of Scottish Common Sense philosophy in America,[51] could observe that "the talent of humor is often possessed in a very high degree by persons of the meanest rank, who are themselves ignorant of it; in them it appears chiefly in conversation, and in a manner that cannot be easily put upon paper."[52] While Witherspoon's understanding of humor points clearly to the dimension of social class or "rank" that came to characterize the distinction between wit and humor, it should be noted that his main goal in this passing comment is not so much to make a social distinction as to preserve the Swiftian idea of humor as rooted in the objective and unself-conscious character. Humor could be a mark of class distinction precisely because it was not dependent on education, cultivation, or conscious creativity; it was natural and unlearned. Despite his disparaging tone, his understanding of the concept of humor is similar to Swift's; it is something to be found in character, not in writing, and it is a natural and naive attribute.

But given the essential continuity between a definition of humor such as Swift's and that offered by Witherspoon later in the century, the difference between the two, not so much in attitude or evaluation of the relative merits of humor, but rather in understanding what sort of thing humor is, reveals the extent to which the concept of humor was being subjectified. For Swift, humor is an attribute possessed by persons unconscious of it. For Witherspoon, on the other hand, humor has been raised to the level of a *talent*—specifically, a talent in the modern sense. While the premodern idea of talent was, much like the premodern meaning of humor, understood to be a disposition or inclination characteristic of a person, the modern meaning, clearly by the eighteenth century, had become associated with the idea of a specific creative ability with which a person was endowed.[53] The notion of humor not simply as an attribute, but as a talent or creative ability, points away from the idea of objective character and toward the aptitudes of the conscious individual. The distance between Swift and Witherspoon, between the early and later eighteenth century, marks a further stage in the movement from humor considered as a possessing quality of persons to humor considered as a possession of persons.

While Swift and Witherspoon both sought to preserve humor as a feature of character, for many others the concept was easily abstracted from character to a mode by which character came to be represented in literature, that is, in writing. George Campbell, in his *Philosophy of Rhetoric* (1776), which, along with Hugh Blair's *Lectures*, would come to be one of the two standard texts on rhetoric in nineteenth-century America, could confidently state that "the subject of humor is always character," assuming that humor was a mode of representation rather than a feature of objective character itself. For Campbell, humor was still intimately linked to character, and inconceivable without it, but humor no longer referred to a characterological substance or quality. Rather, it was a way of treating or viewing character. The elements of character treated by humor were, for Campbell, what had previously been conceptualized as humors: "not every thing in character; its foibles, generally, such as caprices, little extravagances, weak anxieties, jealousies, childish fondness, pertness, vanity, and self-conceit."[54] What Campbell meant by humor was different from what was meant by Swift or Witherspoon, for the latter two still located humor *in* character rather than in the *representation* of character.

Other eighteenth-century writers were aware of the ambiguity of the term, and they attempted to draw a clear distinction between the two loci of humor. Kames, for instance, was explicit in stating that "humour in writing is very different from humour in character." The humorist was a natural character possessed by humors, while humor in writing was created by "an author, who, affecting to be grave and serious, paints his objects in such colours as to provoke mirth and laughter."[55] The tension between "natural" and "affected" states that had characterized the term "humor" since the sixteenth century was reproduced by Kames and others in the distinction between humor in character and humor in writing. Humor in writing was self-conscious and affected in the same way that the man of humor was; it involved the donning of a mask, a wink to the reader, an acknowledgment of the difference between the author's comic intent and his apparently serious form of expression. In this way, the objective meaning of humor slowly bled into the subjective meaning as it was abstracted from character, as "natural" eccentricity produced "affectation" in its representation.

Kames was not alone in making the distinction between humor in character and humor in writing. Monboddo could casually speak of humor as something "in speaking or writing" apart from the elements of character.[56] An anonymous "Essay on Humour" in an American periodical in 1790 reproduced the distinction made by Kames, but in far more muted terms:

> Thus far have I spoken of humour, as belonging to character: I shall now consider that which is found in composition. Singularity and a certain air of seriousness, indicate humour in character, and they are also the marks of humour in writing. . . . An author possesses real humour, when, with an air of gravity, he paints objects in such colours as promote mirth and excite laughter.[57]

The terms used by the author are nearly identical to those used by Kames, suggesting either a loose borrowing, as was common in critical essays of this period, or a meaning that had become thoroughly conventionalized by the end of the eighteenth century.

It remained something of a truism throughout the eighteenth and nineteenth centuries that humor was intimately related to character, but the nature of that relationship was vague enough to allow for the increasing abstraction by which humor came to refer not only to the representation of character in writing, but the process of mind by which that representation was accomplished. The ultimate abstraction was to detach humor from character altogether, as Sydney Smith did in his lectures delivered at the Royal Institution in 1804, 1805, and 1806:

> Most men, I observe, are of the opinion that humour is entirely confined to character;—and if you choose to confine the word humour to those instances of the ridiculous which are excited by character, you may do so. . . . All that I wish to show is, that this species of feeling is produced by something besides character.[58]

That "something," for Smith, was the principle of incongruity, by which all particulars of character were reduced to an abstract relationship in the mind. The issue of incongruity as the basis for humor is an important one that I will discuss at some length in the next chapter. What is important to note here is that the notion of incongruity allowed Smith to abstract humor entirely from both character and its representation, thus effecting a final break from its roots in humoral medicine and medieval notions of personhood.

Smith was able to do this, in part, because the common assumptions of his audience had moved well beyond the original derivations of humor from medieval characterology. When Smith indicates that most people limit the use of the word "humor" to character, he does not mean that they view humor as an element of objective character. Rather, by the early nineteenth century it is clear that humor has become primarily a mode of representation. Smith's limiters would be those who choose "to confine the word humour to those instances of the ridiculous which are excited by character," not those who would confine the word "humor" to the attributes and qualities of character itself.

One can ask of any mode of representation "what" is represented and "how" it is represented. The first question leads to the object, the thing being represented. The second leads to the subject, the mind of the creator and its fashioning of the terms in which that object is viewed. Once humor was established as a mode of representation, rather than a natural substance or quality, it could point in two directions: to the object it represents, which is to say, character; and to the subject who represents it, and consequently the subjective logic by which the representation is accomplished. The measure of the triumph of the subjective meaning of humor in Smith's analysis is the extent to which the object of representation becomes obliterated. The object appears only as an arbitrary instance or occasion for the true common principle of humor, which is a principle of mind and subjective assessment. Character, for Smith, appears incidental to humor; it is the principle of representation in the mind, the principle of incongruity, that is essential.

The location of humor in the mind of its creator and its appreciators, rather than in the objects of its representation, would create the dominant meaning of humor in the nineteenth century. Even those who harkened back to seventeenth-century definitions of humor as a way to maintain its characterological foundation found that newer developments overwhelmed them, circumscribing the possibilities of meaning. Leigh Hunt, for instance, writing in 1846, attempted to maintain the distinction between objective and subjective meanings of humor, only to find the objective meaning untenable:

> *Humour,* considered as the object treated of by the humorous writer, and not the power of treating it . . . is a *tendency of the mind to run in particular directions of thought or feeling more amusing than accountable;* at least in the opinion of society . . . [humour] deals in incongruities of character and circumstance, as Wit does in those of arbitrary ideas.[59]

Humor is that mode of treatment which deals in incongruities of character; it is not a quality of character itself. At the very moment that Hunt insists on the distinction, he finds himself forced to speak of humor as a way of representing objects, rather than as a category of objects represented. The notion of incongruity has entered the very definition of the object treated, not simply "the power of treating it." The object of amusement has become contingent on the terms in which it is represented. Humor is no longer "in" character; at best, it is "about" character, and character is increasingly incidental to it.

English Liberty

The transition from the sixteenth- to the nineteenth-century meaning of humor, from the objective and characterological to the subjective and discursive, represents one relatively minor aspect of the increased internalization that is characteristic of modern individualism. The shift in the location of humor in relation to concepts of personhood may seem relatively rarified and abstract, having little to do with the larger implications of individualism for modern economic and political systems. In another sense, however, contemporaries from the seventeenth century through to the nineteenth century have given explicit recognition to the relationship between humor, individualism, and the organization of particular societies. The distinctiveness of "humor" as a term in the English language gave rise to a doctrine of Anglo-American exceptionalism, founded on a link between political liberty and humor. The relatively abstract transition from object to subject outlined above was accompanied by a more explicit recognition of humor as a product of distinctively English institutions and character structure.

The recognition of humor, in a nonmedical sense, as a specifically English term is usually credited to Sir William Temple, who in 1690 spoke of humor as "a word peculiar to our language too, and hard to be expressed in any other." For Temple, humor was dependent upon English liberty. Unlike other countries, where conformity was enforced by politics and climate, in England, "every man follows his own, and takes a pleasure, perhaps a pride, to shew it."[60] The result was a diversity of characters, with all the odd and eccentric attributes associated with the word "humor." Temple was echoed, even more explicitly, by William Congreve five years later:

> I look upon *Humour* to be almost of *English* Growth; at least it does not seem to have found such Increase on any other Soil. And what appears to me to be the Reason of it, is the great Freedom, Privilege, and Liberty which the Common People of *England* enjoy. Any Man that has a *Humour* is under no Restraint, or Fear of giving it Vent.[61]

The explicitly political meaning of humor as a peculiarity of English people based on liberty, would become a widely recognized one in the eighteenth century.

The question of whether or not humor, in its protomodern derivations, was exclusively or primarily an English term has been raised by a number of scholars.[62] To some extent, it makes no difference whether humor was or was not distinctively or uniquely English; what is important is that so many Englishmen clearly thought it was. And they thought so because they were able to link it to specifically English notions of political liberty, character, "race," and nationality. Thus began a tradition of nationalism associated with humor that continues to our own day. Who has not heard the claim, most passionately advocated in the nineteenth century, that citizens of some nation other than one's own lack humor? The English have said it of all the continental Europeans at one time or another, the French have been quick to accuse the Germans, the Germans have denied it to the Dutch and, most fittingly, the Americans have repeatedly declared that the British themselves have no humor. This notion of not simply national differences in humor, but absolute possession or nonpossession of humor as an attribute of national character, is rooted in the British claim of national exceptionalism.[63]

There were generally two related but separate reasons given for the British preponderance of humor in the eighteenth century. The singularity of English people, their oddity and unaccountability, was seen either as a consequence of the institutional structures of government or alternatively as based in the national, racial characteristics of the English population. The first position, articulated by writers like Corbyn Morris or Hugh Blair, characteristically located English individualism not in a conception of natural selfhood unimpinged upon by external forces, but rather in a concept of liberty as a positive outgrowth of political traditions, institutions, and manners. For Morris, the humorist, understood in the eighteenth-century sense, was "the last and noblest *Weed* of the Soil of *Liberty*." He was dependent on freedom for the very conditions of his existence.[64] Blair extended the basis of liberty to English manners as well as "free Government." The two together allowed every man to live "entirely after his own taste" and afforded "full scope to the display of singularity of character, and to the indulgence of humour in all its forms."[65] Both Morris and Blair echoed Temple and Congreve in repeating what had become an accepted observation on the distinctiveness of English liberty and its relationship to humor.

One of the alternatives to seeing the distinctive presence of humor among the English as a consequence of external arrangements—manners, customs, political traditions—was to see it as rooted in the physiological or "racial" characteristics of the English people. As the playwright George Farquhar wrote at the turn of the eighteenth century, England was "different also from other Nations as well in the Complexion and Temperament of the Natural Body, as in the Constitution of our Body Politick." As a consequence of the "Mixture of many Nations," in England "we have the most unaccountable Medly of Humours among us of any People upon Earth."[66] Farquhar developed a theory of English comedy as rooted in the diverse humors of the English audience; looking back, on the one hand, to the physiological roots of humoral characterology, and forward, on the other, to a view of character attributes as nationally and "racially" specific, Farquhar also drew humor away from the representation of characters on the stage, and located it in the diversity of the audience. Once the humors represented on the English stage were viewed as a response to the humors of the English public, humor as a distinctive quality of the English people had to be explained. For some the explanation was politics and customs; for Farquhar, it was the "racial mixture" of the population.

If liberty and racial diversity seemed likely explanations for the prevalence of odd and eccentric characters of many types in English society, such arguments would seem even more appropriate in a later American context. In an article on American humor, for instance, William A. Jones would announce that buffoonery "can only exist in an enslaved country," but "Humor is a manly quality, and requires the pure air of freedom to expand it."[67] Samuel Cox, in the last quarter of the nineteenth century, would extrapolate from Blair and others in seeing the United States as particularly amenable to the individualism of both political liberty and racial admixture—characteristic of humor. For Cox, "the American man ought to be more potent in his individuality than any other," because "his life is intertwined more with his fellows of every caste, degree, and nation," thus contributing to the most diverse "compend of all time, with all its tastes, affectations, whims, and humors." This individualism, based on the American mixture of peoples, combined with "the greater unrestraint in our 'land of liberty' and in our independent and social life ought to give us a freer and bolder strain" of humor.[68]

Cox made the relationship between political liberty and humor more explicit by claiming its corollary: "The indulgence of humor is incompatible with despotism," he said. "If you would deaden humor, put your government to work with the Procrustean bed, and make men all of a length, and you have machines, not men, and no humor."[69] This argument, as I show in Chapter 5, would reappear throughout the twentieth century, in particular when Americans faced enemies that were decidedly nondemocratic and nonliberal: during World Wars I and II, for example, and especially during the Cold War. It is only much more recently that the reverse argument—that humor flourishes in totalitarian countries because it is one of the few available means of combatting helplessness and despair without directly challenging the political order—has become common.[70] Throughout most of the twentieth century, humor, in its many meanings, has been explicitly linked to political liberty and opposed to totalitarian, despotic, and dictatorial regimes. By pointing to the absence of humor in countries controlled by these types of regimes, its proponents could reaffirm its value and its relationship to political liberalism and individualism.

Beyond the arguments for the distinctive possession of humor by the English, and later by the Americans as well, as rooted in political liberty, custom, or national and racial character, lay another argument which linked humor to *economic* individualism. This argument was less frequently made and repeated than those noted above, but by the early nineteenth century it had become increasingly tenable. According to the Scottish political economist John Millar, humor was most prevalent in "commercial countries, owing to the separation and multiplication of trades and professions," because such a division of labor creates "the greatest diversity of character." Arguing against the notion that political liberty produces humor ("Men do not acquire an odd or whimsical character because they are at liberty to do so, but because they have propensities which lead them to it"), Millar saw English economic development as responsible for England's distinctive possession of humor: "There is, perhaps, no country in which manufactures and commerce have been so far extended as in England, or consequently in which the inhabitants have displayed such a multiplicity and diversity of characters."[71] Commercial development, in this view, explodes the stock typologies of characters prevalent in noncommercial countries, and produces the singularities and oddities of individuals generic to humor. It was not economic individualism in the classic sense of the rational actor as self-directed goal achiever, but rather the individualism of particular difference based on the proliferation of economic functions in modern England, that was held to account for the English possession of humor.

Whether the focus of such arguments was on the political, social, "racial," or economic foundations of humor, what seems clear is that the modern history of humor reveals not only a largely abstract transition from object to subject, from character to discourse, from character typology to individuality, but also a more explicit, concrete, and conventional linkage between humor and individualism at the level of argumentation itself. The reformulation of ontological assumptions about the particularity of personhood and the emergence of an internalized notion of selfhood had their manifestations in arguments about the relation of humor to political, economic, and national identity.

By the end of the eighteenth century, the idea of humor had undergone a fundamental revolution, as had the entire worldview with which humoral medicine had been associated. But humor had not yet acquired its fully modern meaning, and would not do so until the later nineteenth century. So far, I have been able to treat changes in the idea of humor in a discrete manner; these changes appear to present an internal logic, despite what they owe to the larger cultural shifts that occurred in early modern Britain. But in the eighteenth century, new understandings of laughter, of the distance between self and others, of the foundations of aesthetic and moral knowledge, shaped the idea of humor and made it more fully a part of an emergent bourgeois culture of sensibility and individualism. It is to those changes, and their import for the idea of the sense of humor, that I now turn.

TWO   # Humor, Laughter, and Sensibility

The meaning of humor, as we have seen, had become associated with laughter in new ways from the sixteenth century forward, and had joined a constellation of terms that helped define the meaning of laughter in the modern era. But the meaning of laughter in Anglo-American culture, and in European cultures in general, had not been static throughout the modern period. In fact, the appearance of humor as a new relation of laughter, as a category or object of laughter and the laughable, occurred at a fortuitous time in the history of laughter itself. The histories of humor and laughter were convergent, the changing meaning of each giving support and additional definition to the other. We can no more understand the concept of humor independent of the meaning of laughter than we can understand laughter in the modern era without the concept of humor. The histories of the two are inextricably joined.

The History of Laughter

Although there have been calls for a history of laughter, most notably by Mikhail Bakhtin,[1] no such comprehensive history has been written, and psychologists, philosophers, and others continue to treat laughter as an ahistorical phenomenon. This ahistoricity is most evident in the generally accepted classification system by which theories of laughter are divided into three analytically distinct and timeless categories: superior-

d relief theories.[2] Individual "theo-
respects from these categories, and
ore than one of the three theories,
to be comprehensive and definitive.
nter to a static and abstract system
ners, psychologists, and critics have
ahistorical categorization obscures
in the general understanding of
l how it affects the nature of social

of laughter theories obscures, in the
ovious to the historian: superiority,
nout exception, are modern in their
of laughter frequently appear to be
variants of the so-called superiority theory in the classificatory schemes
of present-day analysts, but that is largely because these analysts interpret
those understandings through the lens of the egoistic psychology of
the modern era. It would be more appropriate to call these premodern
understandings of laughter "deformity theories" rather than superiority
theories, because they focus on the deformed nature of the laughable
object rather than on the feeling of psychological superiority. In other
words, the historical perspective reveals that there has been a long-term
transition from a theoretical focus on the object of laughter and its
qualities—the thing laughed at—to a newer concern with the psychological causes of laughter.

From Aristotle through Hobbes, the tradition of thought about laughter can be characterized as of a piece. For Aristotle, and for most of those
who followed him, laughter was caused by ugliness or deformity in the
object laughed at, with the proviso that the object aroused no other
strong emotions such as pity or anger that might act to stifle laughter.
Ugliness was viewed, by and large, as an essential quality of objects that
were deemed risible, rather than a subjective evaluation in relation to
some equally subjective notion of beauty. Risibility was an inherent quality of objects apart from any particular response; the natural response to
a risible object, of course, was laughter. The cause of laughter could be
located in qualities of the object itself. Variations and additions to this
theory of the risible, such as Madius's sixteenth-century adaptation of
the notion of wonder, novelty, or surprise as essential to the risible,
while potentially subjectivist in their implications, did little to change

the general understanding of the causes of laughter advocated by Aristotle and Cicero.[3]

It was Thomas Hobbes, more than any other figure, who gave a new direction to the understanding of laughter. The coherent set of terms of laughter—ridicule, raillery, banter, humor, wit—that emerged in eighteenth-century England did so in a context that was heavily influenced by Hobbes's theory of laughter. Hobbes, who has been quoted time and again as the primary modern proponent of the so-called superiority theory of laughter, actually spoke of laughter only very briefly, but the felicity and terseness of his statements have made them eminently quotable. Here is the entire relevant passage from *Leviathan* (1651):

> *Sudden glory*, is the passion which maketh those *grimaces* called LAUGHTER; and is caused either by some sudden act of their own, that pleaseth them; or by the apprehension of some deformed thing in another, by comparison whereof they suddenly applaud themselves. And it is incident most to them, that are conscious of the fewest abilities in themselves; who are forced to keep themselves in their own favour, by observing the imperfections of other men. And therefore much laughter at the defects of others, is a sign of pusillanimity. For of great minds, one of the proper works is, to help and free others from scorn; and compare themselves only with the most able.[4]

The psychological orientation of this theory, with its emphasis on the comparison of self with others, puts it a great distance from the theory of the risible advocated in the Aristotelian tradition. However, Hobbes still retains the notion of a "deformed thing" as the object of laughter, even as he relocates the source or cause of laughter in the subject, as one of the passions. He also retains a characteristically medieval attitude toward laughter, condemning it as unworthy of those with pretensions to greatness or even civility; laughter was articulated by class differences, making it perfectly acceptable for peasants and "rustic folk," but unacceptable by courtly standards in which laughter was read as the sign of a "light mind."[5] Although rooted in traditional attitudes and viewpoints, Hobbes's theory of laughter was the first, and in some ways the most influential, psychologically based theory.

There are two points worth making given the subsequent treatment of Hobbes's theory of laughter as the main representative of the ahistorical type of the superiority theory. First, the egoistic psychology of self-centered passions seemed to present a far greater threat to a social order based on civility and liberty, rather than despotic rule, than did the Aristotelian object-based theory of the risible. The Aristotelian view of laughter, and of comedy for that matter, tended to reinforce a view of society as rank-ordered, hierarchical, and fixed; the objects of laughter were of the "lower" or "baser" sort by nature, and laughter as a consequence did no injury to its objects and posed no threat to the natural order of society. Hobbes's view of man's egoistic passions, on the other hand, seemed to demand strong government in order to preserve order. It was for this reason, among others, that the Hobbesian theory prompted such a strong reponse among the promoters of a rational liberal order in the eighteenth century. With laughter rooted in the subjective passions rather than in the nature of objects, laughter became problematic in a way that it had never been before.[6] Which is to say: a psychologically based superiority theory of laughter was controversial at its very inception in modern England in a way that the Aristotelian theory of the risible was not.

The second point that has become obscured in treatments of Hobbes's and other theories of laughter is that Hobbes never mentions humor. In the twentieth century, owing partly to the common psychological foundations of all theoretical formulations of laughter, theories of laughter and of humor have become conflated. Sometimes humor is treated as the psychological or emotional correlate of laughter considered as a form of behavior. Other times, the two are used nearly synonymously; where there is laughter of a nonabnormal kind, there is humor. No precise definitions are necessary, because we assume that humor and laughter have a close relationship to each other; any theory of laughter that would not discuss humor would seem inadequate. But for Hobbes, and for the seventeenth century in general, humor was not a primary category of the laughable as it is today. Hobbes's is a theory of laughter, not of humor; it was the eighteenth century that would introduce humor as one of the main designations for the laughable in an attempt to mitigate the destructive implications of laughter understood in Hobbesian terms.

Ridicule, Raillery, and Banter

The terms of laughter that were prominent in the first half of the eighteenth century derived from the same problematics of laughter suggested by Hobbes. The main terms were "ridicule," "raillery," and "banter"; all were virtually unknown in England prior to the second half of the seventeenth century. By the early eighteenth century, they were commonly recognized terms among the literate population. The sheer proliferation of terms for laughter during the later seventeenth and early eighteenth centuries suggests the extent to which the meaning of laughter had become problematic and was undergoing serious redefinition.

Hobbes's introduction of his theory of laughter, grounded in an egoistic psychology that elevated self above the object of laughter, was consonant with the emergence of these new terms of laughter, and of ridicule in particular, in the later seventeenth century. The word "ridicule" appears as a back-formation from the word "ridiculous," and the earliest usages of ridicule are to refer to the object of laughter itself; a ridicule was something that was ridiculous. The concept of the ridiculous, of course, accords well with the Aristotelian theory of the risible. The ridiculous is a quality of objects that makes them inherently laughable, while the early usage of ridicule refers to the objects themselves, and not to a way of regarding or treating objects. The concept of ridicule as a practice, a mode of representation, a way of regarding objects that mixed laughter with contempt and scorn, arose contemporaneously with Hobbes's remaking of the meaning of laughter; both signaled a movement away from the object of laughter and toward the subjective sources of laughter.[7]

From being a virtually unkown term in the early seventeenth century, ridicule became ubiquitous by the early eighteenth century. As one scholar of the period has remarked, "The age of reason could perhaps more eloquently and adequately be called the age of ridicule."[8] At one level, reason and ridicule became competing systems of logic and rhetoric, as well as threats to established institutions, as is indicated by the uproar and debate occasioned by Shaftesbury's "ridicule as the test of truth" argument.[9] The gist of this debate came down to whether or not ridicule was a mode of treatment that was capable of discriminating between what was objectively true or false, particularly in matters of religion. What was accomplished in the debate, above all, was the elevation of ridicule to a level of public awareness in discourse and, consequently, a new public understanding of laughter.

If laughter had been a passive response to objects that themselves possessed characteristics that created amusement, ridicule now put human agency at the center of laughter. Ridicule, in fact, was aggressive;

it redefined laughter along an axis of attack, of debate and contention. Laughter still came suddenly, but it came as a result of a deliberate logic of scorn and representation, rather than as a passive response to "the risible." By making attack central to the primary process by which laughter was to be aroused, the concept of ridicule did as much to define laughter in terms of the ridiculer as it did in terms of the object of ridicule. Even as Shaftesbury and others attempted to maintain a parallelism between objective states and their subjective representations by ridicule, they ended up with their opponents: defining ridicule as the process by which things are made ridiculous, rather than simply a response to the ridiculous. Ridicule heralded a new, active conception of the process by which laughter was created, a process that was person-centered rather than object-centered.

For the eighteenth century, particularly for the first half of that century, "ridicule" was to be the most general covering term for all representation that caused laughter and mirth, just as "humor" was to become an equivalent term in the later nineteenth century. This was so much the case that even those, like Francis Hutcheson, who sought to remove the stigma of contempt and scorn associated with laughter, could criticize Hobbes and others for failing to distinguish "between the words laughter and ridicule: this last is but one particular species of the former, when we are laughing at the follies of others." Even Hutcheson, recognizing that a distinction should be made, often used the word "ridicule" as synonymous with any laughter-producing phenomenon.[10] In some ways this was because no good alternative term existed, although the concept of "the ludicrous," which tied laughter to play rather than to scorn, achieved recognition in some eighteenth-and nineteenth-century writers, as did the continued use of the term "the risible."[11] But beyond the linkage of laughter to contempt and scorn, the concept of ridicule did what these other terms could not; it made laughter a consequence of action rather than something inherent in the nature of things, and so put it under man's control.

Within the universe of laughter defined by ridicule, the preeminent form of social and conversational laughter, as opposed to literary, dramatic, or other relatively formal modes of representation, was defined by raillery. As Stuart Tave has remarked of the eighteenth century, although not altogether correctly, ridicule was "the subsuming category of ill-natured wit, of which raillery was the social form and satire the literary."[12] "Raillery," as a recognized term, rose simultaneously with "ridicule." Prior to the second half of the seventeeth century English writers would not have been familiar with the term, nor would they have given laughter the central place in conversation and social life that is implied by the importance of the term "raillery" in eighteenth-century culture.[13] The rise of the term "raillery" is an important index of the extent to which the site of laughter in cultural understanding became social life itself, rather than merely the theater or other object-specific sites of laughter. Laughter was not simply something produced by a play or a poem, but was a substantive part of the give-and-take of social life, of repartee.

This is not to suggest that laughter had previously been limited to the strict sphere of static fixed objects, whether they be literary products, characters in "real life," odd events, or grotesque incidents. Laughter, of course, has always been a part of sociability, of what goes on when people gather in groups to meet, to talk, or simply to be together. What was new about the eighteenth-century terms of laughter, such as "raillery," was that they construed the active process of conversation as one of the primary arenas of laughter; they reoriented laughter along an axis of everyday social experience, whereas previously the understanding of laughter had structured social experience away from the ebb and flow of "ordinary life" and toward the fixed and static concrete objects that existed outside of the events of everyday life.

Two examples will suggest the nature of this shift, this bringing of laughter into "everyday life" as an embedded process, and away from the object-based ontology of laughter. The familiar image of the medieval court includes the indispensable jester or fool. The purpose of the fool was precisely to be an object of laughter, the butt of all jests. All laughter was concentrated on him and was the result of his presence. By the end of the seventeenth century, William Temple could complain that ridicule and raillery had become such common "virtues" that "the wits in vogue" had taken up that part of conversation "which was formerly left to those that were called fools, and were used in great families only to make the company laugh."[14] The diffusion of laughter away from the concrete personage of the fool and toward the general company of wits was based in part on a new understanding of laughter as something that did not entail its creator being its object.

George Campbell's analysis of rhetoric also revealed the new under-standing of laughter to be fully realized by the last quarter of the eigh-teenth century. According to Campbell, wit, humor, and ridicule were rhetorical precepts that were proper to "the eloquence of conversation," rather than "the eloquence of declamation." The former was a more distinctively modern brand of rhetoric, while the latter was characteristic of ancient rhetoric, and relied on sublimity, pathos, and vehemence as its tools.[15] The elevation of conversation to a level of prominence as an arena for rhetoric speaks of the general modern elevation of "ordinary life" over the life of "civic duty," of private speaking over public speaking.[16] That the modern terms of laughter were seen to be particularly appropriate to this level of speech suggests the extent to which the newer definitions of laughter were part and parcel of the modern movement away from fixed and static forms and toward a new understanding of active and creative life.

The concept of raillery, besides constituting one of the main terms in seventeenth- and eighteenth-century culture by which laughter was embedded in everyday social life, also went a step beyond the concept of ridicule in freeing laughter from the object-based theory of the risible. Raillery, unlike ridicule, had no objective correlate. One might accept ridicule as a "test of truth" because its objects were truly ridiculous; the ridiculous preceded the practice of ridicule. But raillery was pure practice. There was no such thing as a "raillerous" object, only raillery as a mode of action. Further, because raillery was conceived of as an oral mode, unlike ridicule which could take written form as well, its very being was transitory and context-specific rather than stable and relatively autonomous.[17]

Very much like "raillery," the word "banter" came to designate a species of laughter-producing practices specific to conversation. Of unknown origin, and often ascribed to "the vulgar cant" of the period, banter emerged in common usage in the late seventeenth century, perhaps a little after ridicule and raillery had appeared at midcentury.[18] The two terms were often used interchangeably, but the French origins of "raillery" and the "vulgar" origins of "banter" suggest the class differentiation of the terms. Even George Campbell, who made it his business to distinguish clearly between words, could find little other than class to distinguish the terms:

> The words *banter* and *raillery* are also used to signify ridicule of a certain form, applied, indeed, more commonly to practices than to opinions, and oftener to the little peculiarities of individuals, than to the distinguishing customs of usages of sects and parties. The only

difference in meaning, as far as I remarked, between the two terms, is, that the first generally denotes a coarser, the second a finer sort of ridicule; the former prevails among the lower classes of the people, the latter only among persons of breeding.[19]

Shaftesbury himself, always the promoter of style and refinement, saw in banter simply the extreme form of raillery, the point at which raillery became impolite.[20] The prominence of "banter" as a term denoting a practice aimed at producing laughter would seem to indicate that the emerging ontology of laughter was not confined to the "well-bred" elite, but was broadly shared throughout English society, even as the forms of ridicule were distinguished by class.

These three terms—"ridicule," "raillery," and "banter"—emerging simultaneously in the second half of the seventeenth century, heralded a basic reinvention of the meaning of laughter at a broad cultural level. As a cluster of terms relating to laughter and the practices that produced it, they attained unusual prominence by the early eighteenth century; no discussion of rhetoric, of manners, of social life, even of politics and religion, could be considered complete without some reference to the practice of ridicule or its subspecies. Given an early boost by the Restoration rejection of Puritan strictures against the dangers of laughter, this cultural reinvention of laughter did not simply replace a generally negative attitude toward laughter with a more positive assessment of its social role; rather, it changed the very meaning and nature of laughter itself. The new terms of laughter were indicative. They elevated creative practice over objective meaning, conversational style over content, the experience of everyday laughter over the abstractions of the theory of the risible.

Scorn and Incongruity

On the surface, the question that seemed to preoccupy eighteenth-century writers and thinkers was one of whether to view laughter as positive or negative. Was laughter ill-natured, scornful, and full of contempt, as Hobbes had suggested, or was it good-natured, harmless, and amiable?[21] Beneath this surface disagreement, however, Hobbes shared much in common with the general understanding of laughter in late seventeenth- and eighteenth-century Britain, despite the fact that the positive celebration of laughter was a fundamental reaction against Hobbes. The term "ridicule" and its relatives were to be fairly open in terms of the extent to which they encompassed different evaluations of laughter as good-natured or ill-natured. Even today, for instance, the term "ridicule" generally indicates scorn and mocking laughter, but its antecedent term, "ridiculous," is used almost synonymously with the word "absurd," and has little in the way of contempt associated with it. Similarly, raillery came to be associated, by Swift and others, with good-natured playfulness in conversation, rather than with the scornfulness and antipathy that was often linked to ridicule.[22] Yet, there was nothing fixed or static in the association of ridicule with a view of laughter as scornful, and the meaning of ridicule could and did change.

What was continuous in the notions of ridicule, raillery, and banter was what Hobbes had hit upon: that laughter arises out of social relations, practices, and the relative evaluation of persons and things, rather than the nature of things themselves. One might say that the shift from an object-based understanding of laughter to a subject-based one *occasioned* the debate over antipathy and sympathy in laughter; that debate was only possible in a framework where laughter was regarded as the result of a mode of representation or perception of an object rather than as a result of the inherent qualities of the object itself. Antipathy or sympathy required the positioning of the self vis-à-vis the object of amusement.

Given this essential continuity between Hobbes and eighteenth-century understandings of laughter, it is also true that the normative evaluation of laughter underwent a significant, if not quite so profound and abiding, change during the same period. Laughter, which seemed to occupy such a prominent place in the drawing rooms of "polite society," as well as in the coffeehouses and public spaces of English cities, came to seem less an expression of antipathy, and more a result of cleverness and gamesmanship. Although few would deny that contempt and scorn were sometimes present in laughter, most eighteenth-century writers on the subject came to regard the contemptful feeling of superiority as secondary or incidental to laughter, thus providing a justification for the practices of ridicule and raillery as part of amiable conversation. The key to this normative reevaluation of laughter, this sanitizing of the harmful and antipathetic elements, was the elevation of the intellectual causes of laughter over the emotional. If the emotional root of laughter was the feeling of superiority, the intellectual root came to be understood as the principle of incongruous ideas.

When Sydney Smith introduced the principle of incongruity as essential, beyond character, to humor in the early years of the nineteenth century, he was able to do so because that principle had become the generally understood cause of laughter in the eighteenth century. Smith summed up the eighteenth-century reevaluation of laughter in his own understanding, conceding that "the object of laughter is always inferior to us," but denying "that every one who is inferior to us is an object of laughter." Inferiority might be a necessary cause, but not a sufficient one. "The discriminating cause is *incongruity*, or the conjunction of objects and circumstances not usually combined."[23] This was simply to repeat the insistence on incongruity as the primary and necessary cause of laughter that eighteenth-century thinkers regularly made. Hutcheson's influential *Reflections upon Laughter* argued, *contra* Hobbes, "That then which seems generally the cause of laughter is the bringing together of images which have contrary additional ideas, as well as some resemblance in the principal idea."[24] Eighteenth-century Scottish thinkers, who were to become influential in American thinking, in the main followed Hutcheson on this point.[25] To early and mid-nineteenth-century writers, the connection between laughter and incongruity seemed just short of obvious. "The essence of the laughable," said Hazlitt, "is the incongruous."[26]

The principle of incongruity offered a means of "defanging" laughter, of domesticating it and making it acceptable as part of everyday behavior in a society that was growing increasingly leery about the dangers of personal attack, rudeness, and abusive behavior.[27] Although the idea of incongruity was not simply a response to tensions generated by the increasing presence of laughter in conversational situations and to the need for a new urbane and cosmopolitan style of politeness in a world grown increasingly commercial and "middle class," it certainly provided a means of resolving those tensions. The idea of incongruity as the foundation of laughter turned ridicule into a game, a matter of intellectual cleverness, rather than a species of attack and abuse; the abusive and scornful elements might remain in ridicule, but now they were subordinate to the purely intellectual elements involved in the relation of incongruous ideas. In line with the general movement away from object-oriented conceptions of laughter, the principle of incongruity helped focus attention away from the object or "butt" of laughter and toward the company of wits, and their escalation of the game of cleverness. Whereas the superiority theory of Hobbes had implied a potentially dangerous social relationship characterized by the inferior object and the superior subject, by the mid-eighteenth century the ubiquity of incongruity theory had diminished those dangers by stripping the relationship of its emotional force, by making laughter a result of abstract relations in the mind, by turning ridicule into a victimless game. Incongruity made laughter safe in company.

And yet, ridicule retained its relationship with contempt, and continues to do so to this day. Despite all those who used the term "ridicule" to refer to practices that raised laughter based on the incongruous relation of ideas, it was not easy for ridicule to lose its connotations of contempt and scorn. If the early eighteenth century saw an understanding of laughter defined by terms such as "ridicule," "raillery," and "banter," by the end of the century there was an increasingly difficult fit between these established terms and the newer understanding of laughter as based in incongruity. These terms were adaptable, to some extent, as is evident by those who used them in the context of discussions of good-natured laughter or incongruity, but they carried with them nagging reminders of mocking, scoffing, and ill-natured abuse. The changing meaning of laughter, in fact, left something of a vacuum in the terminology of laughter, for words such as "the risible" or "the ludicrous" were object-based, while "ridicule" and its relatives retained undesirable meanings. These terms were still used, but they slowly gave way to the terms that would come to color nineteenth-century understandings of laughter: "wit" and "humor."

Wit and Humor

The wit/humor distinction that was to become so prominent emerged in the later seventeenth century, as did ridicule and its relatives, but it was not until much later in the eighteenth century that the distinction became the main one for categorizing modes of laughable representation. By the nineteenth century, the wit/humor distinction was ubiquitous, filling the vacuum left by the changing meaning of laughter. Countless essays and books discussed "wit and humor," the two bound closely together, but always apart, as if in their union they accounted for the whole range of types of laughter. Although wit and humor are not so closely linked today, "humor" having become a predominant umbrella term of which "wit" is often a subcategory, the nineteenth-century linkage of the terms leaves its residue in the present. For instance, the main Library of Congress subject heading for material that today we would call "humor," is in fact "wit and humor," as if the implied union and distinction of the two terms were obvious, which they surely were to nineteenth-century librarians.

We have already seen the changes that drew humor into the realm of laughter, but as important as those changes were in giving definition to humor, equally important was the relationship of humor to wit. It was the opposition between wit and humor, in the context of an increasing subjectification and internalization of objective qualities, on the one hand, and a shift in the meaning of laughter, on the other, that gave form to humor, that provided a set of meanings and connotations that it could not have had on its own. In the long view, what is important about the distinction was not whether eighteenth-century thinkers elevated humor above wit, or whether nineteenth-century comic theory reestablished wit over humor as the more valuable mode of expression.[28] What was important about the distinction was the distinction itself; never fixed, always somewhat fluid, it provided the forum in which each term was defined against the other. Humor was not defined only by its changes through time, represented by an increasing abstraction from objective character, but also by its relationship to other terms in its sphere: ridicule, raillery and, above all, wit.[29]

The original wit/humor distinction emerged in the context of Restoration comedy, specifically the debate between Shadwell and Dryden. If comedy was to be based on character, in the Jonsonian tradition, than it was to rely on a concept of humor; if, on the other hand, it was to be based on manners and ideas, as advocated by Dryden and others, it would find its key in wit. The original distinction between wit and humor, then, was made along an axis that divided intellect from character; that division would have numerous ramifications in relating wit and humor to other oppositions: mind/body, form/content, artifice/nature, subject/object.

As soon as the terms of that original opposition were made, however, they began to break down. From the late seventeenth through the late eighteenth century, casual *and* critical use of the terms suggests they were used as synonyms as often as they were used as antonyms. There was no consensus on the meanings of wit and humor, although both were increasingly associated with incongruity and laughter. Humor was still related to character, and wit to ideas, but in practice that distinction was frequently blurred. What wit and humor shared was a notion of oddity or incongruity in representation related to laughter. While some thinkers were concerned with marking an absolute distinction between wit and humor, in the main the tendency was to see the two as forms of representation that shared a similar orientation toward their objects.[30]

Despite attempts to narrow the differences between wit and humor, and their often confused or synonymous uses in the wider English-speaking cultures of the time, the difference between the two terms was generally felt to be as important as the similarity, for the two words seemed to encapsulate two different sets of values, two conceptions of personhood and social relationships, two ways of life. Wit was associated with aristocracy, with the values of a "well-bred" elite; humor, on the other hand, in its modern formulation from the eighteenth century forward, was essentially a bourgeois concept, one in which naturalness, benevolence, and universality were primary elements. From the original intellect/character distinction associated with wit and humor flowed a number of other distinctions that gave substance to this division between an aristocratic and a bourgeois ethos. Wit and humor might share a relationship to laughter defined as a product of "incongruous affinity," but within that understanding the two terms expressed opposed conceptions of the social relations of laughter.

From the very beginning of the wit/humor distinction, this aristocratic/bourgeois split was present. John Dryden, arguing in support of comedy based on wit, as opposed to humor, claimed in 1671 that "to entertain an Audience perpetually with Humour, is to carry them from the conversation of Gentlemen, and treat them with the follies and extravagances of *Bedlam*."[31] If wit was "the conversation of gentlemen," based on cleverness, refinement, and a code of verbal conduct, then humor, grounded in the oddities of characters whose individuality pushed them outside such codes, could appear only as a form of madness. But from the bourgeois point of view, humor was infinitely preferable to wit, precisely because it elevated all the peculiar and concrete details of everyday life over the stylized conventions and intellectual elitism of wit.

Corbyn Morris, for instance, gave a list of reasons why humor was preferable to wit, in the process articulating the substance of the distinction itself. A quick perusal of that list reveals what is essentially a bourgeois worldview embodied in the concept of humor; the opposition of that worldview is given form in the meaning of wit. The values associated with humor, and advocated by Morris, are those of empirical realism, naturalism, character, everyday life, democracy, benevolence, geniality. They are opposed to the perceived intellectualism, abstractness, and antipathetic elitism associated with wit. According to him, humor deals sympathetically with the concrete details of "real life" character; wit emphasizes the superiority of the verbally astute and is evanescent rather than grounded in "reality."[32]

A century later, the American critic Edwin P. Whipple, lecturing before a Boston audience, would lay out the same opposition. In the intervening years, the distinction codified by Morris had become a general point of consensus, and humor had become a thoroughly middle-class concept. Humor, according to Whipple, "is a humane influence, softening with mirth the ragged inequalities of existence, promoting tolerant views of life, bridging over the spaces which separate the lofty from the lowly, the great from the humble." The Victorian middle-class sentiments of humor, dependent on "good feeling and fellow-feeling," were opposed to the "fierce and malignant passions" associated with wit. "Wit," said Whipple, "exists by antipathy; humor by sympathy. Wit laughs *at* things; humour laughs *with* them." And the reason wit could be antipathetic was because it was unrealistic, because "it cunningly exaggerates single foibles into character," while humor "represents the whole man." Realism and sympathy were thus allied in the concept of humor, as if the bond of benevolent "fellow-feeling" between object and subject were dependent upon, and a logical result of, the depiction of the concrete reality of character. "Wit cannot create character," because it finds its substance in abstractions, while "humor will have nothing to do with abstraction. . . . It hates all generalities."[33] The concept of humor, by the mid-nineteenth century, seemed to epitomize the bourgeois faith that to depict the real in all its concrete particularity was necessarily to treat it sympathetically.[34]

Even though wit and humor had come to share a common ontological foundation—both were understood as modes or styles of representation with an intellectual basis in incongruity—the contrasting historical roots of the two terms provided a continuing divide along which the modern distinction could be reworked. If humor originally signified the natural physical makeup of persons, and wit the intellectual faculty by which man was separated from nature, then for Victorians it was easy to see how the wit/humor distinction could be reproduced as a distinction between art and nature. "Humour," said Hazlitt, is "the growth of nature and accident; wit is the product of art and fancy."[35] This distinction was repeated countless times: "Wit is more artificial, and a thing of culture; humour lies nearer to nature"; "The distinction between wit and humour may be said to consist in this, that the characteristic of the latter is nature, and of the former art"; "humor is of nature and wit is of artifice."[36] And despite the bourgeois elevation of culture as an ultimate value, particularly in the post-Civil War United States where it became a way of solidifying a new class status, many members of the nineteenth-century middle class put their faith in a rosy view of nature over the suspect realm of artifice.[37] The latter seemed tied to a decadent and corrupt aristocratic elite, while nature was an open book, completely trustworthy, and resonant with the virtues of republicanism. The wit/humor distinction, in this context, offered a kind of shorthand for a new vision of nature consonant with the modern values of empiricism, realism, benevolence, and universalism over and above the intellectual cultivation, abstractions, deliberate artifice, and malignant elitism associated with Old World aristocracies.

This notion of wit as tied to a dessicated aristocratic ethos and of humor as alive and vital found its metaphors in humor's original signification. Humor was liquid, and was thus "the very juice of the mind, oozing from the brain, and enriching and fertilizing wherever it falls." Wit, on the other hand, was "as we often say, very dry."[38] The contrast between the wet and the dry, like that between the natural and the artificial, went deep into the history of the idea of humor itself, while at the same time encapsulating a specifically nineteenth-century set of values. Humor was a realm of rich, full natural growth, alive in all its particularity and diversity; wit, on the other hand, was a barren landscape of dry and dying abstractions. One referred to the progressive world of a burgeoning capitalist middle class, the other to the decaying world of idle and useless postfeudal elites. The recovery of the signification of humor as liquid, through its opposition to the dryness of wit, would play an important role in the idea of the sense of humor.

The use of such metaphors was one way of suggesting the terms of distinction between middle-class universalism and aristocratic elitism. This distinction was often made much more directly. As Samuel Cox said, humor "is one of the prerogatives of the fierce democracy and victorious republican, and has the right divine for its sanction. It disdains hauteur and pride."[39] Such was not the case for wit. The popular consensus of the mid-nineteenth century was that "wit is felt and understood by the best educated classes only, while humor appeals to the capacity of all classes."[40] By the early twentieth century, in the twilight of Victorianism, the distinction had become commonplace:

> Wit is the accomplishment of persons who are busy with ideas: it is the fruit of intellectual cultivation, and abounds in coffee-houses, in salons, and in literary clubs. But humor is the gift of those who are concerned with persons rather than ideas, and it flourishes chiefly in the middle and lower classes.[41]

Wit was now associated less with an aristocratic elite than with a purely intellectual one, but it was still seen as the preserve of the few, while humor was the possession of the many.

If wit found its place in the rarified world of ideas accessible to only a very few, humor was universal; for, as a writer to *The Nation* said in 1866, "humor deals with everyday life."[42] The sphere of everyday life was, of course, the kingdom of the bourgeoisie, the realm of the concrete particular, the common, the normal, of production and consumption. It was the realm of "everyman," in other words the modern abstract individual. Robert Kiely has remarked of the Victorian distinction between wit and humor, "The wit shows himself to be superior to other men through his ability to make quick and sharp distinctions. The humorist, on the other hand, is just like everybody else, only more so."[43] Just like everybody else, only more so: this is the definition of the modern individual, whose uniqueness and particularity is made to depend upon, and stand for, the common humanity of all people. The wit/humor distinction, then, helped to encapsulate the terms of difference not so much between two social groups, but between two conceptions of personhood and two valued realms of life. Wit offered a vision of a special class of people, located outside the mundane world of work and play that had come to characterize bourgeois society; humor offered a world of common inclusion based on individualism and everyday life.

By the end of the nineteenth century, the wit/humor distinction was a widely understood one. The opposition between wit and humor had come to be embedded in the popular joke books of the later nineteenth century, suggesting the extent to which the distinction was broadly shared and understood. For example, Melville D. Landon, the creator of a popular humorous character named Eli Perkins, could introduce his compendium of jests, jokes and anecdotes by casual reference to the difference between wit and humor. Although his distinction was not concerned with the critical analysis of the difference between the two forms of representation, he does go to the core of the opposition. Humor, according to Landon, is a representation of truth and reality; wit is an exaggeration, and thus untrue. For those who have seen humor, particularly American humor, as based on exaggeration, Landon's distinction seems initially to contradict the very substance of American humorous forms. But what Landon means by exaggeration is very much like what we might call abstraction: a remove from the concrete details of the real to a level in which ideas can be manipulated. The exaggeration characteristic of American humor, on the other hand, seems to reside in the accumulation of concrete details, as if to make reality even more real than it initially seems; such would be the case with the grotesqueries of southwestern humor, the tradition of tall tales, and other characteristically American forms. Although wit and humor could mean many, sometimes even apparently opposite, things, what Landon's casual use of the terms suggests is that popular consciousness associated humor with reality, understood in concrete and empirical terms, and associated wit with unreality, understood as abstraction and idea-based.[44]

According to Landon, irony, satire, and ridicule were all species of wit, because they were untrue.[45] The change in the use of terms is significant. In the later seventeenth century, ridicule had arisen as the general term for laughter-producing representations; by the middle of the nineteenth century, ridicule had become a subordinate term, only one among many. The wit/humor distinction had essentially supplanted ridicule as the primary organizing category structure for laughter. The shift in the meaning of laughter from object-based to subject-based, from deformity to incongruity, from the emotion of contemptful superiority to the intellectual surprise of the relation of ideas, opened the door for wit to emerge as a designation for laughter-producing representations, of which ridicule, with its associations of mocking contempt, was only one form. But wit was yoked to humor, because wit's association with the purely intellectual did not seem to cover the broad middle-class values of character, everyday life and, above all, the benevolence and sympathy associated with middle-class life from the eighteenth century on. Humor, with its foundations in characterology and nature, with its ambiguity with respect to the relationship between audience and character, was in a unique position to supplement wit in defining the meaning of laughter in the nineteenth century.

Unlike ridicule, wit was not associated primarily with an antipathetic understanding of laughter; but in its relationship with humor, wit assumed the position of the antipathetic to humor's location in the realm of the sympathetic. Because laughter was generally understood in the eighteenth and nineteenth centuries as rooted in incongruity, its expression was neither characteristically scornful nor benevolent; rather, it could be either, and the wit/humor distinction gave substance to this understanding. Sympathy and antipathy were seen as secondary characteristics of laughter, dependent on the mode of representation rather than inherent in laughter itself. The wit/humor distinction thus came to define the poles of antipathy and sympathy in laughable representation.

Humor and the Sympathetic Imagination

Laughter, in the European philosophical and critical tradition, had long been associated with a notion of distance from its object; there was nothing new in the general idea that the object of laughter was ugly, deformed, or inferior—that is, *unlike* the person laughing, distant from him. The modern form of this idea, the "superiority theory" of Hobbes and others, was psychologically based rather than object-based, but it shared the definition of the laughable object as other. The idea that laughter could be sympathetic, however, was something entirely new; it required a revolution in which the social and psychological space between persons was redefined, in which subjectivity was paradoxically elevated to a level in which the interiorized self could imagine itself in the experience of others. Laughter had always been directed at an object; to introduce sympathy was to create an entire category of laughter in which the laugher imaginatively engaged himself with the object of his laughter, in which he laughed "with" rather than "at." Under the pressure of a middle-class culture of benevolence, sensibility, and sympathy which arose in the eighteenth century, this new category of laughter was created. Above all, it was defined as humor.[46]

While the notion of humor as sympathetic had its antecedents in Jonson's idea of the relationship between audience and humor characters, it was not until the mid-eighteenth century that this understanding of humor began to take shape, and not until the nineteenth century that humor was characteristically associated with sympathy. The Victorian concept of humor took its cue from Thomas Carlyle, who gave the fullest expression to the notion of humor as benevolence. In a well-known essay, originally published in 1827, Carlyle claimed that "the essence of humour is sensibility; warm, tender fellow-feeling with all forms of existence." "True humour," he said, "springs not more from the head than from the heart; it is not contempt, its essence is love."[47] In America, Henry David Thoreau followed Carlyle explicitly, rejecting the idea that a "sneering, satirical devil" lay under humor, and claiming that "the secret of true humor" is that it "sympathizes with the gods themselves, in view of their grotesque, half-finished creatures."[48] Thoreau, characteristically, was able to have it both ways: to sneer at the "grotesque" and "half-finished" with vague contempt and to celebrate humor as the realm of sympathy. That the term "humor" was still used in ways that ran counter to the emerging centrality of sympathy is indicated by the need both Carlyle and Thoreau felt to use the term "true humor," and thus distinguish it from what others often called humor. As one writer said, countering Carlyle, "there is much humor that is by no means kind."[49]

Still, the middle-class use of the term, more often than not, invoked the kindly "fellow-feeling" of the sympathetic imagination. According to Whipple, "humour demands good feeling and fellow-feeling—feeling not merely for what is above us, but for what is around and beneath us."[50] A writer in the *Westminster Review* in 1847 defined humor as "the combination of the laughable with an element of love, tenderness, sympathy, warm-heartedness, or affection," and Richard Haywarde, writing in *The Knickerbocker* in 1850, concurred with that definition.[51] Many Victorians at midcentury seemed happy to accept a notion of "that genial humour which laughs with rather than at, its object."[52] Half a century later, this understanding of humor would continue to be prominent. "Humor," said a contributor to the *Atlantic Monthly*, "is not simply the sudden perception of a moral incongruity; it is the *sympathetic* perception of it. . . . [Humor] is laughing with the other man, wit is laughing at him."[53] Although the wit/humor distinction has ceased to have the resonance it held for Victorians, the distinction between laughing at and laughing with continues to be a popularly understood and accepted opposition.

In the twentieth century, the notion of humor as sympathetic laughter has, if anything, grown more common. No less an authority than Walt

Disney claimed that "people are often sympathetic when they laugh." Anita Loos, known primarily for her depiction of characters of limited knowledge and self-insight, with petty values of lower middle-class social ambition, argued that "in writing, my feelings about my characters and the harassing activities in which they get involved are not at all those of superiority or hostility but something very like compassion." According to Loos, the audience for the mass cultural comic figures of the 1930s— Charlie Chaplin, Donald Duck, Mickey Mouse—was "translating its own activities into those of the futile little souls on the screen and laughing at them with brotherly understanding and sympathy."[54]

The increasing association of sympathy with laughter in the twentieth century helps account for the generalization of the term "humor" to cover all forms of laughable representation. If humor was associated in the nineteenth century with sympathetic perception of the laughably incongruous, in the twentieth century laughter itself came to be seen as sympathetic; that is to say, humor gave its coloring to the entire range of laughter. One may, in fact, discern a trend from the eighteenth century forward in which the understanding of laughter moved from a general antipathetic meaning to the neutrality of incongruity, to the possibility of sympathy, and finally to a generalization of sympathy as a necessary, if not sufficient, element of laughter. Those British and American writers of the teens, twenties, and thirties who grappled with the theoretical problems of laughter tended to assume that sympathy was characteristic of most forms of laughter, even if their theoretical attention lay elsewhere. Both Boris Sidis and J. C. Gregory, for instance, were advocates of theories of laughter based on psychological relief, but both saw sympathy as characteristic of, if not all forms of laughter, at least all those save the "lower" forms.[55] Advocates of laughter as a form of play, such as Max Eastman and J. Y. T. Grieg, assumed not only that laughter as play was not hostile or antipathetic, but that it was good-natured and sympathetic.[56] Even those who advocated what are called "superiority theories," as if they reach in an unbroken tradition back to Aristotle, saw the superiority of laughter as tempered in some way or other by sympathy.

The understanding of laughter thus took place in a context where sympathy and sympathetic relations had become central to the understanding of society and social relations.[57] Adam Smith, whose *Theory of Moral Sentiments* (1759) was one of the central texts in the "sympathetic revolution," still preserved an antipathetic notion of laughter by making laughter an exception to the requirements of sympathy.[58] Alexander Bain, often held up as the nineteenth century's most important superiority theorist, seems to follow Smith in seeing laughter as lying outside the realm of sympathy, but the extent to which sympathetic relations have impinged upon his understanding is much greater. According to Bain, all laughter is based on degradation and malignancy, on "malevolent pleasure." That said, Bain's discussion of laughter seems to be oriented toward compiling a list of the means by which the sting is taken out of laughter, toward an evisceration of the Hobbesian essence of malevolence, in accord with notions of sympathetic relations. For instance, in explaining humor, the form most often associated with sympathy, Bain claimed that its "essence lies in the mollifying ingredients that appease the sympathies without marring the delight."[59] Bain's discussion is, in fact, one long act of appeasement of "the sympathies." The alternative, one suspects, would be to ban all laughter from middle-class society.

The Harvard psychologist William McDougall also offered a variant of the superiority theory, classing the disposition to laughter as an instinct that functioned to prevent excessive or unwarranted sympathy. McDougall's "new" theory of laughter assumed a world in which sympathetic reaction was the natural reaction, and in which man was in constant danger of expending too much sympathy on relatively trivial matters. This abundance of sympathy required an antidote so that energy was not spent in excessive and paralyzing emotional sharing of every trivial mishap. That antidote, for McDougall, lay in the instinct of laughter. Laughter was not only antipathetic, it actually functioned to prevent sympathy. In a strange (but in many ways appropriate) turnabout, humor, the form most often associated with sympathy, was converted by McDougall into laughter at one's self. Instead of laughing at others, as with most forms of laughter, humor allowed a person to sympathize with others as they laughed at him, thus preventing him from exercising excessive sympathy in his own direction. The "essential basis of all humor," according to McDougall, is laughter "at our own expense." Humor required sympathy because it demanded the subject see himself as others might see him, that he see himself, in short, as an object. Even in a theory of laughter that was designed to counter arguments for a sympathetic understanding, then, laughter could not help but be closely tied to sympathy.[60]

In McDougall and many of his contemporaries, the concept of humor had become precisely the opposite of its early modern characterological meaning. Where humor had once referred to the eccentricities of an objective character type, by the early twentieth century it had come to mean, for many, a mode of regarding the self as an objective character, while for others it meant a mode of regarding others as if they were oneself. The sympathetic imagination thus presented a paradox for the meaning of humor. Humor came to mean both a sympathetic laughing with others and a laughing at oneself. The imaginative capacity that could bridge the gap between the observer and the object of his observation, that could bar one from treating other persons as objects, was the very same capacity that allowed one to affect a detachment from the self, and consequently to treat oneself as an object. In the twentieth-century value scheme associated with humor, sympathy with others' mishaps was good; yet, in the common phrase, one shouldn't take oneself too seriously.

Bain's attempts to accommodate derisive laughter to the demands of the sympathetic imagination, and McDougall's image of laughter as an antidote in a world of abundant sympathy, suggest the extent to which derision or superiority theories of laughter had been engulfed by a larger context: the understanding of man as a sympathetic animal. The concept of humor provided the perfect link between the universe of laughter and the world governed by relations of sympathy. Humor, from the sixteenth century forward, had been about character, about the status of personhood, about how persons were to be perceived and converted into ideas. All the other terms associated with laughter, on the other hand, were linked to operations performed on others as a means of distancing them as objects in order to regard them in a different light; ridicule, raillery, and wit were all based on verbal practice, on the manipulation of concepts. Humor, however, asked the observer to measure the temperament, the concrete particularity and eccentricity of characters, to see in the details of character everything that was odd and peculiar, even incongruous, and then, having established the individualism of difference, to collapse the distinction between observer and observed through an act of abstraction by which those differences were dismissed. Humor both emphasized the differences between persons and acted as a solvent of those differences; it emphasized the distinctive, concrete peculiarities of the unique individual and the universal abstract sameness of all human beings. Humor thus brought sympathy to the world of laughter, and made laughter safe for the middle-class public.

Sensibility

The middle-class world of sympathetic relations, or at least the value attached to sympathy in that world, was part of a larger set of values associated with the burgeoning middle classes of the eighteenth and nineteenth centuries. Variously referred to as "sentimental culture," the "culture of sensibility" or, in a more active public form, the "humanitarian sensibility," this new set of values elevated emotional discrimination above the processes of cold rational thought and gave moral judgment a prerational basis in human sense.[61] The complex of sensibility, sentiment, and benevolence emerged as an alternative to the supposed rational calculus of the marketplace in an expanding capitalist society. These values assumed a more deeply interiorized self, with a host of faculties for making finer and finer discriminations, while at the same time insisting on the immediacy and transparency of natural sentiment. The rational man of the market, on the other hand, was clearly motivated by gain, but his motives seemed increasingly opaque and, unrestrained by sentiment, he was willing to treat people as objects in his unceasing quest for goal achievement. In valuing sensibility over rationality, sympathy over self-interest, sincerity over affectation, the new middle-class culture of the eighteenth century found a place not only for humor but for a new conception of sense.

The history of this idea of sense is long and extremely complex. In its many forms, the concept has referred both to intelligence or judgment and to perception of the external world through the physical organs. According to C. S. Lewis, the meaning of sense as judgment preceded its meaning as perception; the five senses and the notion of sense as a faculty of mind shared a common root in the Latin verb *sentire* ("to experience"), rather than one being derived from the other.[62] What seems to have distinguished premodern notions of sense from reason and higher faculties of judgment was its immediacy and particularity. Sense made an immediate judgment of the particular, while reason judged on the basis of abstraction and distance from the particular. In the Middle Ages, the subrational faculties of judgment were codified as the "internal senses," as opposed to the "external senses" of perception of the material world. The internal senses varied in composition, depending upon who was defining them, but they usually included fantasy, cogitation, memory, and sometimes the Aristotelian-derived faculty of common sense. They were, as David Summers says, "the particular intellect," "higher than sensation, lower than intellect, and uniquely human."[63]

Of the internal senses, the history of the idea of common sense is particularly instructive for the key role it comes to play from the eighteenth century forward. Aristotle's notion of common sense is radically different from the modern concept. The common sense, for Aristotle, was a central unifying faculty; what was "common" about it was not its universality or its transparent plainness, but its capacity to reduce the diversity of sense perception to a common basis. In Cicero's use of the term, it takes on an ambiguity that characterizes the further history of the concept. As Summers says, "It is not clear whether *communis* refers to a unifying sense or a sense shared in common by all people." The difference "is essentially a political question."[64] By the second half of the eighteenth century, common sense could become the rallying cry of a radical politics in the hands of Thomas Paine and, at the same time, the source of a socially conservative and stabilizing philosophy in the hands of the Scottish philosophers and their American followers. The idea of common sense had thus come to be generalized to include whole realms of opinions, values, and processes of thought and perception that were only hinted at in the more technical and narrow notion of the common sense as a unifying faculty. Common sense had not only come to be regarded as a universal faculty but, in its universality, had become one of the prime sources of authority for truths: moral, epistemological, and political.

The changes in the notion of common sense in the eighteenth century, its expansion as an internal source of authority shared by all, indicate something of the importance that was now attached to new meanings of sense. A proliferation of particular "senses"—a sense of place, a sense of honor, a sense of decency, a sense of the absurd—now so familiar as a linguistic convention, was made possible by the expansion of the meaning of sense in the eighteenth century. These meanings of sense denote, *contra* C. S. Lewis, much more than a generalized "awareness," or even a "perception," of the things to which they refer.[65] Rather, they refer to the capacity of persons to have that awareness or perception; they are internalized faculties, personal attributes, features of selves. They precede experience, structure it, provide the basis for immediate judgment of the particular. The growth of particular senses from the eighteenth century to the present day suggests the attempt to comprehend and codify the realms of particular experience by providing an ever-deeper image of the self. And the more senses people could be said to have, the more possible it was to discriminate between people on the basis of which "senses" they did or did not have, thus particularizing persons as objects of perception.

Perhaps the most important of the senses of the eighteenth century was the moral sense, for it not only provided a model for the proliferation of senses but was also central to the middle-class culture of sensibility. First developed by Shaftesbury, the idea became influential in the works of Hutcheson, and then received a much more general currency in the sentimental culture of the later eighteenth and nineteenth centuries. The basic notion of the moral sense was that man possesses a faculty, distinct from reason and emotion, that apprehends the moral goodness or evil of a particular action immediately; morality requires neither a rational basis nor a foundation in simple emotional reaction, but an immediate intuitive judgment of sense.[66]

If the judgment of moral values, of right and wrong, was dependent on a distinct sense, it seemed logical that the judgment of aesthetic values, of beauty and ugliness, was similarly constituted. Such at least was the logic that seemed to underlie Hutcheson's epistemology of values and that led to the formulation of the idea of the sense of beauty in the mid-eighteenth century. Hutcheson had inherited the fixation on sensibility from Shaftesbury and the Cambridge Platonists, and the new concept of taste as a faculty of judgment from seventeenth-century French critics. Writing in a context in which a newly distinct sphere of the aesthetic was being constructed, Hutcheson paralleled the moral sense with a sense of beauty. It is perhaps fortuitous that he chose the construction "sense of," rather than calling it simply the "aesthetic sense," for in doing so he opened the door to all the "senses of" that would follow—including, of course, the sense of humor. The sense of beauty was also different from the moral sense, and anticipatory of other "senses," in its constitution of the self as a consumer of aesthetic objects. The growing middle-class audience for art helped elevate a consumer-oriented concept of taste to critical status in the eighteenth century. Hutcheson's sense of beauty, as with taste, located aesthetic judgment in the protoconsumer rather than in adherence to objective formal standards.[67]

If, by the middle of the eighteenth century, a general middle-class culture of sensibility had taken form, and the meaning of sense had changed to allow for the proliferation of a host of new "senses," why did the sense of humor have to wait another century before taking its place in the English language? This apparent "lag" was partly owing to the shifting meaning of humor itself, an ambiguity about whether it referred specifically to character or had a more general meaning as it did in the nineteenth century. Humor in the eighteenth century still had too much of its older objective meaning attached to it. The expression "sense of humor" would undoubtedly have sounded odd and strained, as it would today if we were to speak of people possessing a "sense of temperament" or a "sense of character." The abstraction of humor from character, along with the shift in the understanding of laughter from object-based to subject-based, and the definition given to humor in its opposition to wit, helped define humor as something one could have a "sense of."

Most important, "ridicule," not "humor," remained the general term for laughable productions throughout the eighteenth century. The term "sense of ridicule" was, in fact, widely used in the eighteenth century. Hutcheson refers to it in his *Reflections upon Laughter* in a positive way, depite his rejection of ridicule as the sole or primary form of laughter. In his Latin treatise *Synopsis Metaphysicae, Ontologiam et Pneumatologium Complecteus* (1744), he also cites the *"sensus ridiculi"* as one of the internal senses.[68] Following Shaftesbury's logic of the moral sense, Mark Akenside supported ridicule as "the test of truth," because "the sense of ridicule always judges right."[69] Kames agreed: "No person doubts but that our sense of beauty is the true test of what is beautiful; . . . Is it more doubtful whether our sense of ridicule is the true test of what is ridiculous?"[70] According to Alexander Gerard, one of "the simple powers which constitute Taste" was "that sense, which perceives, and is gratified by the odd, the ridiculous, the humorous, the witty; and whose gratification often produces, and always tends to mirth, laughter, and amusement."[71] Gerard obviously sought a broader term than the "sense of ridicule," but was unable to find it in the language available to him; what he describes sounds very much like what we would call a sense of humor.

Well into the nineteenth century, as the wit/humor distinction supplanted ridicule as the primary organizing site of laughter, the "sense of the ridiculous" remained the term commonly used to refer to that sense which Gerard tried to describe. As late as 1836 an American advice manual for young middle-class women could speak of "a sense of the ridiculous" as "an original faculty of the human mind."[72] Similarly, Oliver Wendell Holmes, as the Autocrat of the Breakfast Table, warned against "the sense of the ridiculous" if not balanced by other senses, for "laughter and tears are meant to turn the wheels of the same machinery of sensibility."[73] Even Charles Dickens, who was known to the great Victorian middle-class public of both Britain and the United States as the exemplar of literary humor, with all its sympathy and richness of character, seems never to have referred to the sense of humor. He did, on at least one occasion, however, speak of his own "preposterous sense of the ridiculous."[74]

The sense of the ridiculous, of course, was somewhat different from what in the eighteenth century had been called the "sense of ridicule;" ridicule as a practice retained its association with scorn and contempt; the ridiculous, on the other hand, was only absurd or silly. The sense of the ridiculous tended to be more coherent with the Victorian middle-class public's appreciation of kindly and sympathetic laughter. It represented a move away from the sense of ridicule and toward what would come to be called the "sense of humor."

The roads that lead to the cultural formation of a widely used term such as the "sense of humor," then, as this chapter and the previous one have suggested, are rather complex. We take the concept of the sense of humor for granted, but in order for such a concept to make sense, for it to refer to anything, several fundamental cultural changes had to take place. The term "sense of humor" retains within it a set of changes that point to the development of a new concept of personhood, of a notion of the individual which yokes together an extreme particularity of self-hood and a hyper-abstraction of "everyman" and "everyday life." First, the meaning of humor itself moved from a physiological, to a character-ological, and finally to a discursive referent—in short, from an objective to a subjective meaning. Second, the understanding of laughter underwent a revolution by which the site of laughter production was relocated from the nature of the object to the activities of the mind, while at the same time humor was becoming newly associated with laughter. Third, an elevation of particular senses with the capacity to judge the particular in an immediate and unmediated fashion fed into a general middle-class culture of sensibility, creating a proliferation of internal senses. The convergence of these three long-term changes in the middle of the nineteenth century gave birth to the sense of humor. When we use the phrase today, the accretion of all these changes is present.

THREE

Bureaucratic Individualism and the Sense of Humor

The eighteenth century gave the Anglo-American world the cult of sensibility, the moral sense and the common sense, but not the sense of humor. It was the nineteenth century that formulated the term "sense of humor" and came to attach a significance and value to the personality trait designated by that term. If the sense of humor was a relatively late coinage to describe a character trait, it has compensated for that tardiness by becoming the most prominent of personality attributes in the everyday speech of the twentieth century. While we recognize all types of particular "senses" in describing the qualities of persons, none has become so universally understood and consequently so ossified and stereotyped as the sense of humor. More than a descriptive term by which a particular personality attribute is codified and given identity, the sense of humor has also become a value; to identify a person as possessing a sense of humor is invariably to make a positive assessment of that person.

Given the deep and abiding historical relationship between sense, humor, and individualism, the prominence of the sense of humor in nineteenth-and twentieth-century American culture suggests something of the cultural centrality of individualism over the past one hundred and fifty years. The sense of humor, in fact, provides a key to understanding the newer individualism characteristic of the twentieth century. This newer individualism stresses different elements than its predecessors. Instead of emphasizing the peculiarity and abnormality of the unique person, for instance, it focuses on the individual as a moderate and normal being; instead of celebrating the boundless subjectivity of the Emersonian self, it constructs psychological depth as an avenue to becoming objective; instead of offering individual freedom in opposition to social structures and institutions, it sees freedom as an act of adaptation to those structures and institutions. The history of the sense of humor provides a window onto this new vision of self and society, this twentieth-century bourgeois ethos of bureaucratic individualism.[1]

The End of Individualism?

"Individualism" is, of course, a problematic term in relation to the emergence of large-scale government and corporate bureaucracies in the United States of the later nineteenth and early twentieth centuries. An ethos of bureaucratic individualism would seem a contradiction in terms, at least in the terms of American social thought and in the more informal but popular American opposition between "conformity" and "individualism." European social thought, particularly the German historical sociology of the nineteenth century, however, saw no such contradiction; Ferdinand Tönnies's distinction between *Gemeinschaft* and *Gesellschaft*, as well as the many other community/society distinctions in this tradition, claimed that the bureaucratic and rationalized societies of nineteenth-century Europe *were* individualistic societies. Individualism was opposed to the static traditionalism of local agrarian communities, with their tight bonds of social relations and ascribed social status. Rationalized and bureaucratic societies, on the other hand, were meritocratic, based on contract rather than tradition, achievement rather than ascription. Rationalized corporate and government structures increasingly relied on a mobile, educated, and urban population; they were seen as freeing people from the rigid local traditionalism of the community. Even the emergence of a mass society in the twentieth century was seen as the extension of individualism to all persons, and consequently as a threat to values of order, stability, and meaning, rather than a threat to individualism itself. In short, in the main lines of European thought, there was no contradiction between individualism and bureaucracy; both were characteristic of a social order opposed to communitarian traditionalism, rather than of two types of social orders opposed to each other.[2]

In the United States, however, the community/society distinction was reworked in terms of American individualism. Instead of individualism being opposed to community, as it was in European social thought, it was made the basis for community. The "tradition" of America was the tradition of locally based small landholders and independent artisans, of Jacksonian proprietary capitalism, rather than the tradition of manorial landholding and hierarchical social relations. If European social thought expressed a romantic nostalgia for a preindustrial community of ascribed status, in the United States that nostalgia for community was transmuted into a longing for a world of face-to-face contacts between the autonomous individuals of an "old" middle class. The Jacksonian "island communities" described by Robert Wiebe, in his own American variation on the community/society transformation, as much as they are defined by localism and face-to-face relations, are at bottom composed of mobile, independent, autonomous individuals.[3]

The emergence of an industrial society based on extralocal and often national economic and political institutions in the latter third of the nineteenth century, a society of corporate and bureaucratic forms, of managerial rather than proprietary capitalism, then, was widely pictured as the antithesis of the "traditional" American community.[4] The most prominent social thought of the era viewed bureaucracy and corporate capitalism as threats to individualism rather than as embodiments of individualistic antitraditionalism. Coming out of the "crisis" of the 1890s, the first generation of American professional social scientists— men like Albion Small and Edward Ross—reaffirmed the individual as the foundation of the traditional antebellum American community at the same moment as they saw individualism in eclipse.[5] A generation later, sociologists such as Robert and Helen Lynd would see the 1890s themselves as a golden era of individualism, now eclipsed by the institutions of mass society.[6] Their lament for a disappearing order had deep roots in the American past, but from the 1890s forward that lament focused on the passing of individualism in particular.[7] The corporate society of the later nineteenth and twentieth centuries was pictured as a force overwhelming an imagined face-to-face community of autonomous producers.

The opposition between a disappearing individualism characterized by autonomy, self-direction, and the stability of the integrated self and an emerging corporate or bureaucratic culture in which character structure was fragmented and illusory, and the self a hollow shell, became a standard part of the popular social criticism of the twentieth century. David Riesman's popular distinction between inner-directed and outer-directed personalities as representative figures for two different historical eras seemed to sum up, for many, the midcentury understanding of this process of decline or loss.[8] Everywhere in post-World War II America, the social observer seemed to see a flight from freedom, a shallow conformity, a desire to fit in rather than stand out, an inability to achieve autonomous selfhood; and everywhere this trend was denounced in terms that reaffirmed a golden age of individualism and the ultimate value of the autonomous and integrated self.[9] The ritual lamentation for the loss of individualism, then, both affirmed the values of individual self-creation and insisted that modern corporate capitalism had destroyed those values. Individualism was supposed to have disappeared under the new corporate regimen, but its constant reaffirmation suggested just the opposite: the more individual autonomy seemed to have been crushed, the more important it became to reaffirm it.

Whether individualism takes the form of a description of empirical fact or a moral exhortation to return to lost ways, its ubiquity in the corporate capitalist society of the twentieth century suggests that it is not so much opposed to corporate capitalism as it is commensurate with it. Individualism is not a form of false consciousness that mystifies and obscures the lack of freedom and autonomy in twentieth-century society; rather, it is an integral part of that society. In opposing the autonomous individual to the bureaucratic machine, the social critics of the twentieth century reveal the way in which corporate capitalism has constructed a particular notion of the self. The opposition between two forms of self, or two types of personality—between character and personality, inner-directed and outer-directed, economic man and psychological man—is one of the ways in which the continuing prominence of the self is affirmed.[10] Nineteenth-century European social thought created a contrast between communitarian traditionalism and the individual self; twentieth-century American social thought prefers an absolute distinction between two forms of the self, both falling within the parameters of individualism. But the fragmented or "managed" self of a world of bureaucratic work and commercialized leisure, of a culture of consumption, is predicated on the autonomy and interiority of the integrated self of Victorian character and a culture of production. The reconciliation of the limited conflict between these two forms of self—an "inner" and an "outer" form—lies at the heart of the culture of bureaucratic individualism.

All this is to say that the concept of bureaucratic individualism is not the oxymoron it initially seems. The apparent paradox of bureaucratic individualism lies in its simultaneous affirmation of an ever-deeper interior self—autonomous, natural, and of its own making—and an infinitely adaptable exterior self—supremely sensitive to social circumstance and the mitigation of conflict. In fact, the road to the exterior self and its management lies through the capacities of interiority and self-control. Self-control as a nineteenth-century bourgeois virtue and self-expression as a characteristic value of the twentieth century are complementary values, not opposed ones. If control is a feature of the interiorized self or the "inner-directed" personality, and expression is a feature of the exteriorized self, it is equally true that the "managed" self of the twentieth century demands self-control and that self-control is also a form of self-expression. The point is not to deny the difference between an emphasis on self-control and one on self-expression, but to see that self-control largely *is* a form of self-expression, and that self-expression *is* a form of self-control. The two values—so often juxtaposed—are at root part of a common conception of the self; they assume an interiority capable of standing outside itself, of manipulating itself, an interiority that is the ultimate standard of value and source-of-action in the world.

A bureaucratic individualism unites a conception of autonomous and privatized selfhood with a range of interior capabilities that seek to abnegate any larger claims the self might make on the world. Those attributes of the self that are most highly valued in the bureaucratic world of American corporate capitalism are those that, paradoxically, diminish the self; the self is elevated and made more complex and interiorized in order for it to develop new modes of self-adjustment and self-control. Interiorization and valorization of the self go hand in hand with the disappearance of the self as a force in the world. Bureaucratic individualism is the union of apparent opposites: the individual self as the highest value, and the priority of rationalized institutions and social relations to which the individual must adapt.

The notion of such qualities as geniality, sociability, tact, tolerance, and adaptability as inherent attributes of individuals, rather than simply generalized social values to which persons might aspire, is characteristic of this new individualism. Social values exist not only as ideals, or even as prescriptive behavior, but have a localized existence in the self; they are not only standards of measuring behavior, but form the very substance of personality. Although characterology and the enumeration of the particular attributes of persons has a very long history, the intense concentration on the concrete particularity of the individual as a complex bundle of attributes and possessions is distinctively modern. By turning social values into personality characteristics, modern American culture focuses its attentions on the notion that the self is the source of all things. In particular, the notion of the self as the possessor of all manner of self-abnegating, adaptive, or self-objectifying attributes is at the core of the newer bourgeois ethos.

The sense of humor, in the nineteenth century, became one of the values by which the individual person was to be judged and, at the same time, one of those interior attributes that allowed for the dissolution of the self. As a term describing a value and a personality attribute, its common use tends to disguise its importance. Its ubiquity in everyday speech and its lack of formal codification as a central value make it seem both natural and invisible. It is trivial, taken for granted, not taken seriously in the serious business of arguing about social values by opinion makers. But, ironically, its power and representativeness as a valued personality attribute in the general ethic I am calling "bureaucratic individualism" is based on its mundane and ubiquitous existence. Today, no one seeks to challenge the value of a sense of humor, although it has had its critics in the past. A sense of humor simply *is*, and if pressed to understand why it should be a valued personality attribute, most persons would likely answer by saying that it is a good thing not to take oneself too seriously. To have a self with the capacity to not take itself seriously: this is the very definition of bureaucratic individualism.

Early Uses of the Term "Sense of Humor"

The commensurability of the concept of the sense of humor—as personality attribute and value—with the culture of corporate capitalism is strongly evidenced by the fact that they emerged simultaneously in the second half of the nineteenth century. And just as corporate capitalism did not become the dominant force in American society until after the Civil War, so the sense of humor, despite some earlier appearances, did not achieve its ubiquity until at least the 1870s. In fact, the spread of the sense of humor from its use as a relatively precise and infrequent term in literate middle-class circles to its generalization in the everyday use of virtually all Americans mirrors the growth and increasing intrusion of corporate and bureaucratic forms into every sphere of American society from the 1870s through the 1930s.[11] While the development of corporate capitalism was not responsible for the idea of the sense of humor—as the previous chapters detail, the concept was hundreds of years in the making—it certainly contributed both to that idea's prominence and to the cultural effectiveness of that idea's meanings. An examination of the early uses of the term—those prior to the 1870s—suggests not only the elements of meaning that were to be carried over into newer uses, but the differences between those newer meanings and uses and the older ones they supplanted.

It is never easy to date the emergence of a term; with rare exceptions, words are not coined at a precise instant, and one cannot usually declare a first use with any precision. Terms often circulate informally in speech before becoming prominent in print; sometimes they are not noticed as neologisms until they have achieved a level of frequency in circulation that may be relatively far removed from their original "first" use. As much as lexicographers and philologists seek the origins of words, it is often misleading to think of terms having an origin in a first use from which all other uses stem. Rather, it might be more appropriate to think of a gradual accumulation of instances in print that suggests the growth of a cultural currency. For the term "sense of humor," such a currency was apparently achieved in the late 1840s and early 1850s.

As I have indicated in the previous chapter, terms such as "the sense of the ridiculous" and "the sense of the ludicrous" were in common use throughout much of the nineteenth century. Edwin Whipple, for instance, speaking in 1845, made no mention of the sense of humor, even though his subject was wit and humor. Rather, he used the terms "sense of the ludicrous" and "the faculty or feeling of ridicule" in ways that suggest meanings that would later be associated with the sense of humor.[12] By the 1870s, Whipple himself would use the term "sense of humor" in a casual way, as if it had always been a part of his vocabulary, but in the 1840s it was relatively rare, even in discussions that seemed to touch precisely on it.[13] Many of the writings on wit and humor from the 1840s through the 1870s continued to refer to a sense of the ridiculous or the ludicrous, even though humor itself was increasingly prominent as the term under discussion.

In the 1840s the term "sense of humor" began to achieve a kind of cultural currency. Its earliest print appearances seem to be British. The first instance I have been able to find comes from the 1846 publication of Leigh Hunt's *Wit and Humour Selected from the English Poets*. Hunt uses the term only once, when he speaks of William Hazlitt's sense of humor.[14] Understood in this way, Hazlitt may be said to be the first person to have had a sense of humor attributed to him, at least in print. In William Makepeace Thackeray's *Vanity Fair* (1849), the term "sense of humor" is used four times: three times to refer to an attribute of the main character, Becky Sharp, and once to refer to a presumed quality of the reader.[15] The first American print appearance I have been able to discover is in Nathaniel Hawthorne's introduction to *The Scarlet Letter* (1851), "The Custom-House." There he contrasts the superficial "jollity of aged men" and the "mirth of children" with "a deep sense of humor."[16] The qualification of the sense of humor as "deep" sounds awkward, almost redundant, to twentieth-century ears, but it points to the relative novelty of the term. It had not yet achieved the fixed and stereotyped meaning that would overcome it in the later years of the nineteenth century.

What these early uses of the term have in common is the specifically literary context in which they occur; there is an important cultural reason for this common context. It was in the world of literature, especially in the novel, that a middle-class reading audience affirmed the centrality of character and the individualism of concrete particularity. One of the central events in the novel is the definition of character in terms of attributes, and one of its most important tasks has been to develop a language of character attributes that coheres with the readers' imagination of persons in everyday life. If the sense of humor emerged in print first as a character attribute—whether the "real" character of a Hazlitt or the fictional character of a Becky Sharp—it is no surprise that those types of writing concerned with characterization provided the sites in which those initial appearances occurred. Nineteenth-and twentieth-century American novels, in fact, provide numerous instances of characters defined as having senses of humor. From Hawthorne to Harold Frederic to Edith Wharton to Tom Robbins, the sense of humor appears throughout widely different genres and schools of American fiction, because writing in the novel has a common concern with character and its definition.[17]

The novel as a site for the definition of character attributes also differs from other types of writing concerned with character. Phrenology, one of the classic nineteenth-century forms of characterology, for instance, was more concerned with the analysis of all potential character traits as discrete units than with the definition of particular characters or the attribution of character traits to particular individuals. Phrenology defined itself as a more general "science" or typology of character, and so tended to treat individual persons as instances from which general principles could be drawn, or applied, rather than as the focal point of character attribution. The closest thing to a sense of humor for the phrenologist was what O. S. Fowler called the faculty of "Mirth" and what James S. Grimes conceptualized as the organ of "experimentiveness." Supposedly located in the upper and lateral part of the forehead, in close proximity to the faculty of Imitation, the faculty of Mirth was a member of what Fowler dubbed the "Self-Perfecting Group" of organs, which functioned as "a stepping-stone from the animal to the moral, and a connecting link between the moral and intellectual in man." Unlike the world of fiction, in which character attribution was concrete, particular, and individualized, the orientation of phrenology was toward an understanding of character in terms of schematic and abstract definition and ordering of traits. The faculty of Mirth was an abstraction, despite its supposed material reality; the sense of humor, on the other hand, although possessing no material substance or being, was readily comprehended as an attribute of particular persons.[18]

While the appearance of the term "sense of humor" in the novel from the mid-nineteenth century forward suggests something of the nature of the term and its use, by the 1860s and 1870s the term increasingly appeared in other forums. In criticism, for instance, a reviewer of James Russell Lowell's *Biglow Papers* in 1860 saw its setting as "most provocative to the sense of humor."[19] In social commentary, a writer to *The Nation* in 1866 claimed, in what would become an oft-repeated convention, that women "seldom show a sense of humor."[20] The *North American Review* of 1866 remarked that Americans had "a proper sense of humor," and in 1877 the *New York Times* described the Japanese people as possessing "a fine sense of humor."[21] In other words, one can sift through the publications of the 1860s and 1870s and find dozens of incidental appearances of the term, just as one might in the publications of today. What is notable about these appearances is the matter-of-factness of the "sense of humor" as a descriptive term. These uses indicate that the term had become so fully a part of the language that it called no attention to itself. Unlike the so-called keywords analyzed by recent historians—terms such as "capitalism," "individual," "liberal," "society," "alienation," "public" —terms such as "sense of humor" do not form the central focus of meaning and interpretation every time they appear in speech and print.[22] The casual or incidental use of the term "sense of humor" creates an impression of its ubiquity as a denotative term, neutral in its meaning, rather than as a value, which might make it a focal point of contestation.

What is distinctive about the early appearances of the term "sense of humor" from the 1840s through the 1870s is that they create a context in which the term is seen as primarily descriptive; there is little of the explicit promotion of the sense of humor as a value prior to the 1870s. Yet it is always dangerous to distinguish too sharply between the descriptive and the normative; although analytically separable, the two depend upon each other for their mutual existence. As Clifford Geertz has argued, every ontology implies an ethic, and vice versa.[23] The structure of reality, the kinds of things there are said to be in the world, has enormous implications for the values of the culture which subscribes to that reality. From the eighteenth century forward, the view of the self as a complex entity in which numerous "senses" existed as personality attributes emerged in the context of an elevation of sensibility itself. Such a transformation in the understanding of what a person is makes it impossible to see any of those new senses as value-neutral faculties or capabilities. To describe an attribute as a sense, in modern American culture, is to figure it positively. The ideas of the moral sense and the common sense were ways of elevating human nature, of refiguring the values associated with human capabilities. The only way to effectively denigrate or devalue a sense is to attach to it a qualifying epithet such as "sick" or "perverted," but to do this is only to suggest that the unsick or unperverted form of the sense is natural and good. Because individuals have senses of humor, to have a sense of humor is necessarily a good thing; even those who would come to criticize the sense of humor in the early years of the twentieth century always criticized the excessive value attached to it, rather than the thing itself.

The fact of the casual or incidental use of the term "sense of humor" as an act of personality attribution from the 1840s through the 1870s should not, then, be taken as a sign of a neutral or purely descriptive use. Nevertheless, there is a need to distinguish between the descriptive ubiquity of the term prior to the 1870s and the explicit elevation of the sense of humor as a value after the 1870s. Before the 1870s, the sense of humor was one element in an environment of terms available for personality attribution, character definition, and individuation; virtually no explicit attention was called to it in a manner that would single it out from other attributes. The value attached to it was purely implicit in the particular instances of its use, and it was granted no more value than other traits, such as a sense of beauty or a sense of honor. This was true even though the concept of humor had acquired so many positive associations with Victorian bourgeois values by the mid-nineteenth century.

From the 1870s forward, while the sense of humor retained these implicit valuations in its common use, it came to be singled out as a character attribute of particular value. Instead of being one element in a larger discourse of characterization, the sense of humor became the center of a discourse itself. An explicit recognition of the value and importance of the sense of humor, and an attempt to define what the sense of humor consisted of, characterized this emergent discourse from the 1870s through the 1930s. So, while the sense of humor retained its common use in attribution, as it does to this day, it acquired additional importance and meaning by becoming the focal point of a discussion in which its value was explicated.

"You Have No Sense of Humor": Emergence of a Value

In 1876, in a widely reprinted essay, Leslie Stephen wrote:

> A fashion has sprung up of late years regarding the sense of humour as one of the cardinal virtues. It naturally follows that everybody supposes that he possesses the quality himself, and that his neighbors do not. It is indeed rarer to meet man, woman, or child who will confess to any deficiency in humour than to a want of logic. Many people will confess that they are indolent, superstitious, unjust, fond of money, of good living, or of flattery: women will make a boast of cowardice and men of coarseness; but nobody ever admits that he or she can't see a joke or take an argument. If people were to be taken at their own valuation, logical acumen and a keen perception of the humorous would be the two most universal qualities in the world. . . . [E]verybody has shrunk like a coward at one time or another from the awful imputation, "You have no sense of humour." This phrase has become a commonplace: it is a kind of threat held *in terrorem* over the head of everybody who cares to differ from any accepted opinion.[24]

And so began a discourse in which the sense of humor was figured explicitly as a value, a discourse that would echo, in almost precisely the same terms, down to the present. The salient aspect of this way of talking about humor is not so much the naming of the sense of humor as a dominant value—or in Stephen's phrase a "cardinal virtue"—as it is the identification of that value in the context of an attribution of its lack. It is the horror of being named as lacking a sense of humor that has defined the value of its opposite. Whereas, prior to the 1870s, persons or characters had been occasionally or casually defined as having a sense of humor, there had been no attempt to define persons as *not* having one. But after 1870, the value of possessing a sense of humor was emphasized by the negative consequences that were associated with the absence of this most desirable of traits.

Stephen's rhetoric, in which a host of qualities, such as indolence or cowardice, are figured on exactly the same plane as the lack of a quality —the sense of humor—allows him to claim what is in effect a blank as an attribute of persons. Whereas some persons were once identified as possessing a sense of humor, there are now two classes of persons: those with a sense of humor and those without. There is no consciousness that cowardice might be something other than a lack of bravery, or indolence a lack of industry; the sense of humor has no other opposite than its lack, and the person without a sense of humor is therefore not simply unpleasant or bad company, but is literally an incomplete person. This logic of incompleteness is echoed in Max Beerbohm, writing in 1902:

> Perhaps the most effective means of disparaging an enemy is to [praise his virtues in every capacity] . . . and then to say what a pity it is that he has no sense of humor. . . . And what weapon could match for deadliness the imputation of being without sense of humor? To say that a man lacks that sense is to strike him with one blow to a level with the beasts of the field—to kick him, once and for all, outside the human pale.[25]

This is the logic of incompleteness taken to extremes, although it should be noted that it became increasingly common in the later nineteenth and early twentieth centuries to speak of the sense of humor, along with rationality, as one of the primary attributes that separated man from beast.

The way in which lack of a sense of humor was identified as a problem remained virtually the same throughout the twentieth century. Always couched in the language of social observation, of a kind of description of a social incident in which the imputation of a lack of a sense of humor is made, this discourse frequently presents itself as critical of social practice. But, as in Stephen, it always accepts as its own the descriptive terms and values it purports to be observing; for Stephen, for instance, the problem with those who are always accusing others of lacking a sense of humor turns out to be that they themselves are lacking the very attribute they fail to see in others. The psychologist H. A. Overstreet was less critical than Stephen, but the terms of his observation were fundamentally the same:

> [I]t is almost the greatest reproach to tell a person flatly that he has no sense of humor whatever. Tell him that he is disorderly, or lackadaisical, or homely, or awkward; he will bear up under these. But tell him that he has no sense of humor; it is a blow from which the best of us find it difficult to recover.[26]

Overstreet is here both social observer and one of "us" struggling to recover from the imputation of having no sense of humor.

Not surprisingly, the fear of lacking a sense of humor finds its way into Riesman et al.'s *The Lonely Crowd*, where it is imagined as a characteristic of the peer group of the other-directed. The passage in which the key event of attribution of a lack of a sense of humor, with all its attendant anxieties, occurs, is worth quoting at length. The authors are speaking of their interviews with young people:

> When we ask them their best trait they are hard pressed for an answer, though they sometimes mention an ability to "get along well with everybody." When we ask them, "What is your worst trait?" the most frequent single answer is "temper." And when we go on to ask, "Is your temper, then, so bad?" it usually turns out that the interviewee has not got much of a temper. If we ask whether his temper has gotten him into much trouble, he can cite little evidence that it has. What may these answers—of course no proper sample—mean? My impression is that temper is considered the worst trait in the society of the glad hand. It is felt as an internal menace to one's cooperative attitudes. Moreover, the peer-group regards rage and temper as faintly ridiculous: one must be able to take it with a smile or be charged with something even worse than temper, something no one will accuse himself of even in an interview—lack of a sense of humor.[27]

By the very act of saying nothing, the other-directed man reveals precisely how important the possession of a sense of humor is; no one describes having a sense of humor as his best trait, but to have a lack of one would certainly be his worst. Having a sense of humor is a tacit value, rather than an explicit one. Again, as in Stephen's writing seventy-five years previous, the lack of a sense of humor is figured on exactly the same plain as a quality—in this case, temper. Interestingly, the concept of temper seems to retain something of the older notion of humor, to which it originally referred, as an element of character beyond the control of the self. However, temper and lack of a sense of humor now find themselves together at the top of the list of undesirable character attributes.

The constancy of this discourse in which lack of a sense of humor is imagined as an inadmissible quality, as something an individual can be accused of, suggests that, contrary to Riesman, it is not simply part of a value structure associated with the post-World War II "society of the glad hand." Indeed, the terms of that discourse have remained essentially the same from the 1870s to the present day, and if the 1870s saw the effective removal of the "invisible hand" as the principle of political economy, the corporate capitalism of the later nineteenth century was still far from the "glad hand" of Riesman's day.[28] The constancy of the terms of this discourse surrounding the sense of humor suggest a cultural continuity over the past century and a quarter. The culture of corporate capitalism, as much as it has changed, is still of a piece. The discourse in which lack of a sense of humor is held to be a personal stigma, a sign of incompleteness, an imputation to be avoided at any cost, is part and parcel of the entire period associated with the dominance of corporate forms in American life. Cultural historians have insisted on a distinction between "character" as a Victorian model of selfhood and "personality" as a twentieth-century model of selfhood; the rise of the sense of humor, as a value defined by the problem of its absence, during the time period covered by the Victorian and the post-Victorian era suggests that this distinction is inadequate. Character and personality, rather than being fundamentally opposed to each other, have a great deal in common. To lack a sense of humor is to lack both personality and character.

If the value associated with possessing a sense of humor came to be defined against the problem of possessing a lack of a sense of humor, then the antithesis of the person who possessed that sense was the fabled figure or type: the man without a sense of humor. In order to define what was so valuable about the possessor of a sense of humor, the members of the literate middle classes created the stock figure of his opposite. Of course, given the universalism associated with humor in the nineteenth and twentieth centuries, many refused to believe that a person totally devoid of a sense of humor actually could exist. This despite the prominence of a discourse in which persons were continually being accused of lacking that sense. A good example of this refusal to believe in the man without a sense of humor is embodied in a piece of doggerel by Douglas Malloch, written in 1934 and entitled, appropriately enough, "No Sense of Humor":

> The funniest thing, beyond all doubt,
> is someone with the fun left out.
> A man without a sense of humor
> Seems like a myth, at most a rumor.
> I can't believe there can exist
> A person like a pessimist,
> Not here, not certainly hereafter,
> A man without a soul for laughter.
> . . . .
> It must be wrong, a myth, a rumor,
> This talk about no sense of humor.[29]

Nearly half a century later, and quite independently, Richard Armour produced the following verse:

> You've heard, no doubt, the vicious rumour
> That someone has no sense of humor.
> This can't be true, for all are born with it,
> And can endure both spite and scorn with it.[30]

If Malloch and Armour were light and irreverent, there were others much more in earnest about the impossibility of a man without a sense of humor. Leon Ormond, for instance, claimed that the sense of humor was "the property of all who call themselves human. When we designate someone as 'having no sense of humor' what we really mean is that it is not well developed, or more probably, that it differs in direction from ours."[31] Or, as Samuel Crothers put it, "Almost every one has some sense of humor, just as there is gold in sea water, though not enough to make its extraction commercially profitable."[32] The notion of the sense of humor as a commodity, a thing that can be measured and treated in quantitative terms, is here joined with an affirmation of its universality. The claim for the universality of the sense of humor as a human trait always took place in a context defined by the imputation of its lack; it was always a denial that there could exist a man without a sense of humor.

Who was the man without a sense of humor, and what were the characteristics that defined him as a negative being? Whether one believed that such a person could exist or not, the stereotyped figure of the man without a sense of humor provided an image of the incomplete, the deficient, the lacking, against which could be defined a more appropriate model of personhood. He was often described by examples: the ardent patriot, the fanatic religionist, the prohibitionist.[33] As Burges Johnson, onetime editor of the comic journal *Judge*, wrote, "The fanatic has no sense of humor. . . . The egotist gradually loses his sense of humor."[34] "A snob," said another writer, is "a typical example of the man without a sense of humor—that is to say, one who takes seriously things that are not serious on any broad view of human affairs."[35] Or, as Leo Markun put it, "When a man has a deficient sense of humor, we say that he is literal-minded. He finds it difficult to associate the same symbol with a variety of meanings, constantly shifting about."[36] James Russell Lowell, writing in 1884, described the man without a sense of humor as one "who, in old age, has as strong a confidence in his opinions and in the necessity of bringing the universe into conformity with them as he had in youth."[37] Even those, like the essayist Agnes Repplier, who saw the man with no sense of humor as one who "gets along very well without it," and who could to some extent appreciate the single-mindedness characteristic of such a man; even they sought to put distance between themselves and such a man. He was, said Repplier,

> apt to be a formidable person, not subject to sudden deviations from his chosen path, and incapable of frittering away his elementary forces by pottering over both sides of a question. He is often to be respected, sometimes to be feared, and always—if possible—to be avoided.[38]

Unlike later twentieth-century writers, Repplier did not pity the man without a sense of humor, but she characterized him in the same way as those writers did: fanatical, one-sided, rigid, oblivious to shades of meaning, and unsociable.

There were some writers, particularly in the twentieth century, who were willing to go further and lay virtually all of the world's problems at the doorstep of the man without a sense of humor. W. Béran Wolfe, in a psychological self-help book for a general audience, wrote that "men go to war, murder their wife's lover, suffer from nervous indigestion when the stock market goes down, or their golf scores are off, . . . kill each other because they disagree about God, religious rituals, or the ownership of a horse, pig, or political doctrine," all because they lack a sense of humor. "It is the saving human virtue," concluded Wolfe, only half facetiously, "without which there is little use in living."[39] While most people were not willing to hold the man without a sense of humor responsible for all the conflicts and ailments in the world, the fact that Wolfe could even joke about the problem in these terms, and on this scale, suggests the general disregard in which such a figure was held. To lack a sense of humor was to be the source of conflict, malevolence, or illness.

In the twentieth century, particularly from the 1920s forward, when psychological modes of analysis became increasingly prominent in American culture, the man without a sense of humor came to be seen not merely as incomplete but as mentally ill. One of the "outstanding characteristics of the psychoneurotic make-up," according to H. L. Hollingworth, was the lack of a sense of humor.[40] People who lack a sense of humor, said Donald Laird, a prominent navigator between the worlds of academic and popular psychology, "may be victims of a mental disorder, paranoia."[41] H. A. Overstreet defined lack of a sense of humor as a clinical problem, noting that in practically all cases of insanity the sense of humor "seems to be completely lacking."[42] The peculiar trait of the schizophrenic, according to William McDougall, was a complete lack of a sense of humor. Although laughter was often characteristic of madness, as it has been for many centuries, it came to be defined as abnormal laughter if it was not tied to the sense of humor; McDougall, for instance, saw "humorless laughter" as "a symptom presented by many schizophrenics."[43] The extreme form of the rigid, one-dimensional figure of the man without a sense of humor was the unstable, unbalanced figure of the psychotic.

If the virtue of possessing a sense of humor was defined against the problem of not possessing one, the figure of the man without a sense of humor suggests the meanings associated with the possession of that sense. Rigidity, literal-mindedness, one-dimensionality, fanaticism, single-mindedness, even insanity, were seen as consequences of lacking a sense of humor. A sense of humor, then, as Lowell described it, was a "modulating and restraining balance-wheel." [44] If the Victorian middle-class creed of high moral purpose often seemed to require an extreme adherence to a unitary code, the sense of humor as an element of that code pulled the self back from its implications. According to S. H. Butcher, "The sense of humor preserves sensibility from degenerating into sentimentalism; it keeps earnestness from becoming fanaticism; it helps a man to maintain his balance and sanity of mind in the complications of life." [45] Instead of seeing things from a single perspective, the man with a sense of humor had "a multitude of equally trodden brain-paths" that prevented any expression of fanaticism or extremism.[46] The sense of humor was constantly defined as an essential feature of the normal, the sane, the balanced, the healthy personality. In the value attached to the sense of humor, we find the typical bourgeois concern with moderation—a pushing away from extremes in favor of a "balance" in the middle—combined with the intense desire to see things in new, varied, and often contradictory ways. The self with a sense of humor is seen as both capable of internal regulation and checking of extremes and as an expansive entity capable of seeing from more than a single perspective. The limitless perspectives of "the extreme" are ultimately balanced by the moderating self. The sense of humor is both a source of unconventional and nonegoistic views and a check on them.

One of the central issues raised by the discourse surrounding the *lack* of a sense of humor, of course, had to do with the dominant gender ideology of the Victorian era. As Nancy Walker and others have noted, it was something of a cultural cliché that women lacked a sense of humor; we can find the statement made repeatedly, especially in the years around the turn of the century.[47] We might even say that for many men (and even some women) the image of the person without a sense of humor was codified in the image of woman. The man *without* a sense of humor was an anomaly; the woman *with* a sense of humor was the anomaly; the *woman* without a sense of humor, on the other hand, was typical of her gender. Just as the sense of humor was emerging as a value defined by the imputation of its lack, it came to figure in an important way in the drawing of gender distinctions in nineteenth-century America. It is clear, for instance, that the claim that some class of persons—in this case, women—lacked a sense of humor was a way of categorically excluding those persons from the social benefits that came to those who possessed the valued attribute. To lack a sense of humor was—and still is—to be outside the social circle where decisions are made, to miss out on the informal sociability that provides the basis for solidarity and social privilege, to be cast at a lower level by virtue of being socially inadequate.

It is fairly obvious that the sense of humor, like any valued personality attribute, has been a tool of social exclusion, and that the repeated and systematic insistence that women lacked a sense of humor had the result of reinforcing a fundamental gender distinction at the level of everyday life. Precisely because this is so evident, it is of little interest to the present discussion; I am concerned less with cultural constructs as instruments of social domination (or with the instrumentality of culture in general) and more with the specific meanings and content of those concepts.[48] What is of greater interest in the denial of the sense of humor to women in the late nineteenth and early twentieth centuries is how the specific cultural meanings of humor and the sense of humor intersected with the gender ideology of the era. According to Nancy Walker, denying women a sense of humor was a way of denying women intellectual capability. The ideology of separate spheres insisted that women were emotional and nonintellectual beings; they were seen as lacking the intellectual capacity to understand the incongruity of humor.[49] One of the problems with Walker's analysis is that she makes no distinction between wit and humor, a distinction fundamental to Victorian understandings of laughable representation. In fact, given the rootedness of humor in concepts of sympathetic understanding and emotional identification, as opposed to the antipathetic intellectualism of wit, we might expect a gender distinction that emphasized wit as a masculine attribute and the (passive) sense of humor as a feminine attribute. Such appeared not to be the case: why not?

The answer to that question lies in the cultural meanings of sympathy and their relation to the gender ideology of the era. To the extent that women, and some men, argued against the cultural truism by which women were seen as void of the capacity for appreciating humor, they tended to rely on the notion that women's sense of humor was "truer" because more bound up with sympathetic appreciation than that of men. The reason why men denied women a sense of humor, according to this perspective, was that men associated humor with ridicule and coarseness, and failed to see that women's sense of humor was sympathetic and "finer." The humorist Robert Burdette, for instance, writing in the early years of the twentieth century, claimed that "it isn't because her appreciation of humor is either atrophied from disease or has not yet been developed that she cannot enjoy the humor of ludicrously painful situations. It is rather because this sense in her is sensitive, delicate, sympathetic, refined to the highest culture. True humor delights her, while buffoonery, if it be brutal, shocks her."[50] And Elizabeth Stanley Trotter, responding to the charge that women lacked a sense of humor, argued that women simply rejected laughter based on mockery and ridicule: "they detest ridicule and deplore its effects upon both the user and the object, believing that it blunts the sensibilities of both." According to Trotter, "The rock that irretrievably separates the humor of men and women, then, is ridicule."[51] The answer to the insistence on women's absent sense of humor, then, was to distinguish between the sense of humor in men and women. Women didn't *lack* a sense of humor; rather, their appreciation of humor was *different* from that of men. "What it all comes down to," said Mary Austin, "is that women are more likely to be humorous about what they love, since it is all they can afford, and men about what they fear, as being the one thing they cannot afford not to laugh at."[52] And, it turned out, in rejecting ridicule, mockery, abasement, and laughing *at* others, and embracing sympathy, sensibility, and laughing *with* others, women put themselves on the side of the dominant bourgeois meaning of humor. What Carlyle had called "true humor," the humor of the heart rather than the head, the sympathetic engagement with the incongruous, was for many late Victorians, characteristic of the feminine imagination.

But if the view of humor as sympathetic was dominant, why were women repeatedly accused of lacking a sense of humor—of being "the sentimental and serious sex," as one claimant put it?[53] Sympathy was central to the definition of the moral nature of women in the doctrine of separate spheres. The bonds of sympathy lay at the foundation of domesticity. What distinguished the private household—woman's sphere —from the public life of men in markets and politics was that the former was premised on the subordination of self to the needs of others, while the latter was premised on the aggressive pursuit of self-interest. If the home was to act as a counterbalance to the ubiquitous spread of market principles—as a "haven in a heartless world"—it had to preserve an active principle in opposition to that of the market. It located that principle in the nature of women; woman's sphere and man's sphere were distinct and complementary because the natures of women and men were distinct and complementary. Men were aggressive, intellectual, rational, driven by their desires. Women, on the other hand, were emotional, sympathetic, benevolent, moral nurturers. They were concerned with kindness and the mitigation of pain over considerations of economic cost and long-term consequences. The attributes associated with women in this ideological gender system are, of course, those associated with humor in the nineteenth century, and they help explain why many supporters of the idea that women possessed a sense of humor could explain the presence of that female personality trait in terms of sympathy. What is more surprising, given the way in which women were so thoroughly associated with sympathy, is that they were so often categorically denied the possession of a sense of humor. If humor and pathos were said to walk hand in hand, it seems curious that "sentimental" should have been paired with "serious" rather than with "humorous."[54]

Sympathy and the sympathetic imagination, however, were not confined to the domestic sphere, and their operation in market society indicates how women, despite their putatively emotional natures, could be said to lack a sense of humor. One of the intellectual consequences of the sympathetic imagination was that it allowed for a breadth and expansion of the perspectives of the self, an engagement with multiple points of views and the operation of persons in their diverse social roles; in order to be successful in a society governed by the market principle of self-interest, men ironically had to be adept at seeing themselves from the viewpoint of others, of understanding the desires and interests of those with whom they sought to do business. The family and domestic life were seen to be self-contained, elements of a sphere built on relationships that were stable and fixed in nature; public life, on the other hand, was seen to be an ever-shifting terrain of strangers in pursuit of the main chance. In such a world, the sympathetic imagination allowed for intellectual breadth, an understanding of complexity, a guide to the motives of others. Sympathy allowed for at least the affectation of detachment from the narrow concerns of the circumscribed self. It was this idea of sympathy, as tied to humor, that was invoked when women were said to lack a sense of humor. An anonymous correspondent to *The Nation* in 1866, for instance, explained women's lack of a sense of humor in the following way:

> But humor deals with everyday life. It contrasts small things with greater. It is a good-natured comparison of the weaknesses of human

nature with a higher ideal—a kindly *reductio ad absurdum* of the trivialities of society. And the reason why women so seldom show a sense of humor is that they see nothing trivial in the doings and sayings of society. They believe in the importance of all that goes on in the circle about them.[55]

Or as Appleton Moran wrote in a letter to the *New York Times Saturday Review* in the debate that flourished around women's lack of the sense of humor in 1900: "The reason why women are less apt to be humorists than men is because humor is largely a sense of proportion. . . . [W]omen are more occupied with details, while men are obliged to grapple with results, which are the generalizations from or the crystallizations of details."[56] In this view, woman's sphere was closely circumscribed by the details of everyday domesticity, while the world of politics, business, and public life was boundless, fluctuating, and open. The sympathy of emotional identification that was characteristic of women's nature, then, was not the sympathy of intellectual and perceptual self-transcendence necessary for male negotiation of the public sphere.

The matter was never as simple as this, of course. Those who argued for or against the proposition that women lacked a sense of humor gave various, often contradictory, reasons for their beliefs. Some, in fact, claimed that women were witty rather than humorous, or that women were in possession of an unconscious vein of humor, or that their sense of humor was imaginative rather than perceptive, or that the difference between men and women with respect to the sense of humor was that women were content not to push a personal claim to the attribute whereas men were not.[57] What is significant about these arguments is that they reveal that the issue of women's lack of or possession of a sense of humor was a matter of debate within American culture; if we simply characterize nineteenth-century American culture as constructing a negative image of women as lacking a sense of humor, we put ourselves in the position of arguing with the past. Much of the scholarship on women's humor has adopted this stance; it has sought to show, through example, that women *did* have a sense of humor, rather than recognizing that the idea of the sense of humor itself was the historical product of a modernizing culture. Just as women were frequently denied such a sense, a counterargument by which they claimed that sense existed within American culture. My argument is not that the idea of the sense of humor was "contested terrain" or "negotiated" by women in counterhegemonic opposition to patriarchy; I leave such arguments to those who are not tired of them. In identifying the disagreement over women's sense of humor rather than the denial of humor to women as an important cultural fact, I wish to stress the conflict between the universalist orientation of bourgeois culture and its insistence on gender difference. "The sense of humor is universal" said Constant Coquelin in 1901, reponding to the ever-present claim that women lacked a sense of humor. According to an anonymous "literary man" in the same year, on the other hand, "It may be that women are deprived of the humorous sense in the same manner that a person may be born without sight or hearing or speech."[58] What both authors have in common, despite their fundamental disagreement, is the notion that the sense of humor is a natural human attribute. The tension between identification of the sense of humor as a universal attribute and the identification of some persons as "lacking" it reached its most pointed expression in the debate surrounding women and humor.

Echoes of this debate persist to the present, if only faintly. Rarely today is it categorically declared that women, as a class, lack a sense of humor. By the 1930s, the lingering traces of the Victorian gender ideology were on the wane, and it was less common to hear absolute distinctions between male and female "natures" in all things; the modernist reinvention of female sexuality and desire was only the most obvious reversal of Victorian views of women. When women moved into the professions, the arts, and the universities, not to mention the developing urban bohemias of the early twentieth century, the underpinnings of "woman's sphere" were eroded. As Nancy Cott has argued, the emergence of the idea of feminism (and the name) was premised on a broad understanding of women as cultural beings, rather than on the naturalist dichotomies of Victorian gender ideology.[59] In the later twentieth century the debate over whether women have or do not have a sense of humor has largely disappeared. In its place we have the repeated claim that *feminists* lack a sense of humor and, in opposition, the feminist claim that feminists do indeed have a sense of humor.[60] Here the image of the feminist woman, in the minds of those who would deny her a sense of humor, stands for the fervent moralistic reformer, the "politically correct" dogmatist, the stern-faced and inflexible ideologue. This is a far cry from what Victorians meant when they declared that women lacked a sense of humor. What the two meanings share, however, is the notion that to lack a sense of humor is to be single-minded, inflexible, committed to an absolutist morality.

The distance between the meaning of humor in sixteenth- and seventeenth-century characterology and the concept of the sense of humor in the later nineteenth and twentieth centuries is great. The person without a sense of humor is, in some ways, the direct descendant of the Jonsonian humor: possessing a single controlling viewpoint or motive, he is incapable of balancing himself and, as a consequence, runs to extremes. In the eighteenth century, this notion of humor as the foundation of character came to be celebrated in terms of the individualism of particularity and difference; the eccentricity of the humor or humorist was what marked him off from other persons, what made him distinctive. But in the later nineteenth and early twentieth centuries, the person who was single-minded and drawn entirely in one direction was viewed not as possessing or being possessed by a positive quality—humor—but as literally incomplete; that is to say, lacking a quality. And this lack was viewed almost universally as a negative, characterized by fanaticism, rigidity, and even insanity. The man without a sense of humor was a character not so much to be laughed at in a theatrical or fictive context, but one to be pitied and avoided in "real life." Those who possessed a sense of humor, on the other hand, were the precise opposites of the characterological humor of the previous centuries; balanced by a mechanism within the self, the man with a sense of humor was capable of seeing and acting from multiple perspectives without succumbing to the extremism inherent in any particular point of view. He was at once both the heir of the individualism of particularity and concrete difference—possessing an ever more complex set of particular attributes, qualities, and ways of thinking by which to differentiate him from other persons—and the antithesis of the extremism inherent in the characterological notion of humor. The more complex the individual became, the more capable he was of occupying a middle ground of "balance" and "normality"; the more he could be identified as different, the more he was the same.

Part of this revolution in meaning from the characterology of humor to the personality attribution of the sense of humor was rooted in a shift from active to passive understanding, from a concern with behavior to a concern with perception. To some extent this shift occurred in the meaning of humor itself, as the previous chapters document. But it was also embedded in the distinction between humor and sense of humor. Although many people used the two terms interchangeably, "humor" could always retain something of its objective meaning, while the "sense of humor" was necessarily a subjective faculty, and thus a mode of perception. As Brander Matthews of Columbia University wrote, insisting on the discrimination between the two terms, "Humor is positive, while the sense of humor is negative. A man with humor may make a joke, and a man with a sense of humor may take one."[61] In other words, the sense of humor was a passive faculty, a feature of the consumer rather than the producer, of the perceiver rather than the doer. For Matthews, as for most of his contemporaries, if asked to choose between the two qualities, the ready answer was that "the sense of humor is the more highly to be prized. . . . It is so good a thing that one can hardly have too much of it, although an ardent reformer might find that an excess of it chilled the heat of his resolution."[62] In other words, the passive capacity for perception, to the extent that it actually served to undermine action, was elevated above the active or creative capacity. The man with a sense of humor was a complex and valued figure of passive perception, while the man without a sense of humor was disparaged for his imperceptive demand that his action serve to define the world. But unlike the opposition between two concepts of humor—an older mode of being vs. a newer mode of seeing—the notion of the sense of humor as a passive personality trait turned the capacity for seeing into a mode of being; it transformed a perceptual ability into a source of personal and social identity.

Self-Objectification

The idea of humor had been colored by two fundamental changes occurring in the eighteenth and nineteenth centuries, as shown in the previous chapters: the notion that all laughter, including that arising from humor, was based on the perception of incongruity; and the idea that humor required a sympathetic imagination, a laughing *with* rather than *at*. The sense of humor was defined and valued primarily as a capacity for perception in terms of these two elements: incongruity and sympathy. The man without a sense of humor was rigid, dogmatic, incapable of seeing incongruity because his path of perception was one-dimensional, and incapable of sympathetic perception because he was so completely bounded by the interests of a narrowly defined self. But the complex self of the individual with a sense of humor was able to see the incongruity of his own interests in relation to those of others, because he was capable of thinking along many different pathways. As a consequence, he could see the contradiction between his own narrow view of himself and the view others held of him, and was able to redefine himself and his interests in terms of that perception. In other words, the sense of humor allowed for a perception of the incongruity between self and the world, through a process by which the sympathetic imagination conceived the self as if it were somebody else and measured its activities by the standard applied to others.

The sympathetic imagination, and the entire middle-class culture of sensibility of which it is a part, were at the root of the expansion of the self characteristic of what I am calling "bureaucratic individualism." The sense of humor was only part of a general redefinition of the self that began in the later nineteenth century. The tradition of American social psychology that began in the 1890s with William James's pragmatic concept of "the social self," Charles Horton Cooley's notion of "the looking-glass self," and even Franklin Giddings's formulation of sympathy as the basis for "consciousness of kind" cast aside the notion of the self as a unitary stable entity in favor of a new self defined by the process of social interaction.[63] The key to that process of self-definition by social interaction was the sympathetic imagination, for it allowed the self to expand outside its borders and to reflect upon itself as an object of consciousness. Cooley's looking-glass self, for instance, was a product of the reflection of others, defined by a perpetual navigation between the self as subjective center of consciousness and the self as object of consciousness. A constant process of viewing the self as others would see it, and an adjustment in terms of that viewing, created an ever-expanding self, closely attuned to the perceptions of others. This tradition of social psychology, and its definition of the self, became increasingly prominent in twentieth-century social thought, particularly in George Herbert Mead's analysis of the "Me" and the "I"—the self as object and subject —and Erving Goffman's figuration of the performing self.[64]

Before the sympathetic imagination could turn about and observe the self from the viewpoint of others, it had to achieve a kind of immediate emotional bond with others, a "fellow-feeling." This bond was both an expansion *of* the self and its capacities and an expansion *out of* the self. If humor, as Burges Johnson wrote in 1902, was "but a form of human sympathy," reaching outward in "an evident love for all mankind and his follies," it was also true that it was "an inherent possession, deep-seated, all-permeating, needing no contact with any outward thing to give it fire."[65] Although the sense of humor was not by any means the sole source of sympathy in the human makeup, it was characteristic in that it affirmed both a new and ever-deeper interiority and a dissolution of that interiority in the imaginative transcendence of the self.

Whereas in the mid-nineteenth century the association of humor with sympathy required a laughing with, a warm and tender fellow-feeling in the tradition that stemmed from Carlyle, by the early years of the twentieth century the object of sympathy was not always required for the avenue out of the self provided by the sense of humor. Mary Whiton Calkins, a psychologist and onetime student of William James's, defined the sense of humor on a parallel with the capacity for aesthetic appreciation (the "sense of beauty"), as an "impersonal emotion" to be valued as a personality trait precisely because of its capacity for self-transcendence. She did so, however, without the need to invoke an object outside of the self to which the sense of humor was sympathetic:

> Just as we are said to forget ourselves in our apprehension of the beautiful, so also we forget ourselves, that is, our narrow individuality, our special interests and purposes, in our appreciation of the humor of a situation. . . . It is because we have such need of pauses, in the arduous business of living, that we value the sense of humor so highly, and for the same reason we find the most estimable people, if devoid of humor, so inexpressibly tiresome.[66]

What is most interesting and characteristic in Calkins's understanding is the simultaneous affirmation of self-transcendence, of forgetting, of momentarily lacking a self, and the act of disparaging a lack of humor as indicative of an incomplete person. The idea of self-transcendence, in one form or another, has a very long history; what distinguishes this modern notion is the idea that the capacity for self-transcendence is a permanent attribute of the self in everyday life. The sympathetic imagination, the sense of humor, and other attributes of the self associated with bureaucratic individualism, thus contribute to an enlargement of the self at the moment they make possible a stepping outside of the self. Can anything be more modern than the idea that we enjoy and value the company of someone whose self is defined by its capacity at every moment to be not itself?

The simultaneous valuation of personality traits conceived of as deeply interior to the self and of self-transcendence points to one of the characteristic contradictions of bourgeois thought. The inflation of the self as the source of and consumer of all knowledge is coupled with an insistence on objectivity as the ultimate condition of knowledge; the desire to expand the self fades into the desire to expand *out of* the self. The line between subject and object becomes increasingly fuzzy, particularily when the subject itself becomes an object of consciousness, or, in contrast, when objectivity is itself defined as a personality characteristic— that is, when a person is described as being "objective" or possessing an "objective attitude" about a particular issue. To integrate objectivity into the self is to insist on then turning the self into an item or thing to be explored "objectively." Thus, a constant navigating back and forth between the self as object and as subject seems to be the requirement of a mode of thought that simultaneously affirms the values of self and of self-transcendence.

The emergence of the sense of humor as a prime value in the later nineteenth century is closely tied to the new definition of the self that began to appear in those years. Its history suggests something of why this should be so: the early modern idea of the humor as an objective character of eccentricity and concrete detail had been integrated into a newer understanding of laughter as rooted in subjective incongruity. An objective mode of being—the Jonsonian humor—had become subordinated to a subjective mode of seeing. In a very real sense, the man with a sense of humor was the man capable of seeing the objective Jonsonian humor within himself. The bourgeois contradiction between objectivity and subjectivity, self-transcendence and self-inflation, is reproduced precisely in the history of the idea of the sense of humor. The elevation of sense as a source of immediate intuitive knowledge in the eighteenth century, the relationship between humor and sympathy in the nineteenth century, the deep characterological roots of humor combined with the abstractness of the principle of incongruity: all of these elements of its history contributed to the distinctive role the sense of humor played in the valuation of self-objectification in the twentieth century.

The notion of the sense of humor as a capacity for self-objectification was first articulated in the 1890s and early 1900s in terms of the ability to laugh at oneself. If from the early 1800s humor had become increasingly associated with sympathy, it had also become tied to the notion of laughing *with* rather than *at*. The sense of humor was broadly understood as a capacity for sympathetic laughter, for seeing how "the other fellow" felt, while laughing with him. But from the 1890s forward, a growing number of people were to define a "true" or a "well-developed" sense of humor, not only in terms of laughing with others but also in terms of laughing at oneself. As Samuel Crothers wrote in 1899, "The coarse man, with an undeveloped sense of humor, laughs at others; it is a far finer thing for a person to be able to laugh at himself."[67] And eight years later, an anonymous contributor to *The Atlantic* echoed and extended Crothers's remarks: "One who has the sense of humor well developed can even laugh at himself, taking an external but sympathetic view of his own character, conduct, or circumstances. Without this sense, a man is liable to be deficient in self-knowledge."[68] The notion of self-objectification as it was formulated in relation to the sense of humor at the turn of the century tended to take the form of a simple valuation of the ability to laugh at oneself.

In the 1920s, 1930s, and 1940s this notion of the sense of humor as a capacity to laugh at oneself was given a more precise definition as self-objectification, particularly in the writings of those concerned with the psychologies of mental hygiene and personality. William Burnham, one of the early promoters of the mental hygiene movement, wrote in 1924:

> Among attitudes especially helpful in the attempt at self-discovery is a sense of humor. One who cultivates this attitude may often see himself as others do; and instead of seeing everything with the false halo of egotism, is able to look at certain experiences and mental attitudes as if they were in another individual. Thus one gets a wholesome form of the objective attitude, and an illumination and purification of one's mental processes and judgments of self which clarify one's whole mental apperception.[69]

The notion that one stands outside the self in an "objective attitude" in order to observe one's own behavior and ways of seeing "as if they were in another individual," and that such a stance is a sign of mental health and purity, is characteristic of the prevailing bourgeois ethos of the twentieth century.

Time and again, the sense of humor was invoked as one of the most important attributes in achieving this self-objectification. Twenty-five years after Burnham wrote the above passage, J. E. Wallace Wallin, also an advocate of mental hygiene, spoke of the sense of humor in almost identical terms. "Humor," he wrote, "helps us to see ourselves as others see us; it helps us to enter into the feelings and thoughts of others, and is an aid to objective self-study." Wallin concluded that humor and the sense of humor "should be cultivated in the homes and schools as prime characteristics of the healthy personality."[70] The converse of the idea that the sense of humor rendered the individual capable of "objective self-study" was the idea that the objective person necessarily had a sense of humor. According to Harry Emerson Fosdick, in his *On Being a Real Person* (1943),

> the person who has thus achieved a healthy objectivity has a natural and saving sense of humor. In anyone afflicted with abnormal self-concern, a deficient sense of humor is an inevitable penalty. The ego-centrics cannot stand off from themselves, look objectively and without undue partisanship at themselves and enjoy laughing about themselves.[71]

From being a means to achieve self-objectification, the sense of humor had become a necessary consequence of the achievement of objectivity.

Perhaps the clearest and most articulate invocation of the sense of humor as both a fundamental personality attribute of the individual and as an agent of self-objectification was made by the Harvard psychologist Gordon Allport, in his seminal work, *Personality: A Psychological Interpretation* (1937). The new personality psychology advocated by Allport was in opposition to the mechanistic empirical study of particular attributes common in the academic psychology of the 1920s and 1930s, and was antithetical to the social psychology of his day as well. For Allport, the individual was to be studied as a unique and irreducible totality, rather than as an entity to be broken down into units for the purpose of abstract comparison or treated as a mere consequence of social interaction. Personality, for Allport, although it could be shaped by society, was fundamentally the unique composition of the "biophysical" individual, considered as a whole. Allport's personality psychology was profoundly individualistic, concerned with the elevation and expansion of the self as a presocial whole, and with the preservation of the precious uniqueness of each person from the analytic attack of psychologists and sociologists who would reduce persons to types. In fact, Allport explicitly figured his own work in a long tradition of characterology that included the temperament analysis of humoral medicine. What unified this tradition was a concern with the person as a totality; what was distinctive about personality psychology was its elevation of the individual over the type as the mode of character to be analyzed.

But the individualism advocated by Allport, with its expansive self, was at root similar to that of the social psychologists; its expansiveness allowed for a kind of feedback that served to diminish its direct expression in the world. For Allport, what he called "the mature personality" was the fullest expression of this expansive self-regulating individual. And the cardinal trait of the mature personality was none other than the sense of humor. Allport, unlike many, sought to distinguish the sense of humor from what he referred to as the "cruder" sense of the comic. The latter sense was characterized by an appreciation of absurdities, puns, and the degradation of others and was possessed by all people, not just the "mature personality." The sense of humor, on the other hand, required a high level of intelligence and, most particularly, of "insight." Citing a study in which subjects ranked one another on a series of traits and in which insight and sense of humor had an extraordinarily high correlation of +.88, Allport concluded that the sense of humor and insight "are at bottom psychologically a single phenomenon—the phenomenon of *self-objectification.*" The man with a sense of humor "has the most complete sense of proportion concerning his own qualities" and, as a consequence, "is able to perceive their incongruities and absurdities in other than their customary frames of reference."[72] The "mature personality" in Allport's scheme is the one with the most highly developed capacity for perception of himself, rather than for action in the world. Allport, moreover, did not require the mechanisms of social psychology, with its constant navigation between the self and the other, to achieve self-objectification; the latter could be achieved by stepping outside the "customary frame of reference" into the no-man's-land of objective perspective.

Nearly twenty years later, the "mature personality" of *Personality* was to become the "tolerant personality" of Allport's *The Nature of Prejudice* (1954). The terms Allport used to describe the two kinds of personality were fundamentally the same; "empathy," "self-insight," and "inwardness" were characteristics of the tolerant personality, just as they had been of the mature personality. The latent liberalism of this concept of the self, however, was made explicit in the post-World War II battle against intolerance. The figure of the man without a sense of humor returned with a vengeance; there he was, sitting in "the meetings of agitators where grim-visaged auditors applaud intolerant utterances." He was a bigot, an irrational rabble-rouser, a narrow-minded ignoramus. The man who had a sense of humor, on the other hand, was eminently tolerant. According to Allport, "humor is a missing ingredient" in "the syndrome of the prejudiced personality," while it is "a present ingredient in the syndrome of tolerance. One who can laugh at oneself is unlikely to feel greatly superior to others."[73] The self-objectifying personality was thus established as the morally superior type; it was no longer the ardent reformer or the advocate of a narrow good that was imagined as lacking a sense of humor; rather, it was the intolerant bigot.

Only recently has the argument been made that the value attached to the sense of humor is at odds with that associated with tolerance. According to the anthropologist Mahadev Apte, there has been a key cultural conflict between two core values in the United States since the 1950s. The sense of humor has been esteemed as a "virtuous personality trait" at the same time as the ideal of cultural and ethnic pluralism has become a dominant force in American culture. For Apte, these two values are at odds with each other because the appreciation of ethnic humor presumably degrades ethnic minorities and is antithetical to the mutual consideration, respect, and tolerance required by the ideal of cultural pluralism.[74] While it is undoubtedly true that for some people having a sense of humor means degrading and laughing at ethnic minorities, it is in fact inconceivable that the sense of humor would be a "core cultural value" if this were its main or dominant meaning. In fact, to have a sense of humor more often requires that members of an ethnic minority learn to laugh at jokes about themselves; that is, to tolerate the stereotypes these jokes perpetrate. As one anonymous author put it in 1938:

> No negro was ever lynched, no Irishman beaten, no Jew persecuted, no Scotchman touched (forgive me!) because of what Mike said to Ike, etc. The dangerous, the seething nations in the world today, let us observe, are those that do not permit themselves the luxury of laughter. In Germany Charlie Chaplin is excluded. Jugoslavia bans Mickey Mouse. Brazil exiles Tom Sawyer.[75]

In the main, tolerance and the sense of humor are part of a common code, rather than in conflict; both aim to diffuse conflict by demanding that persons not take their own narrow identities and selves as the sole standard of measurement. As an advice writer to young women said in 1942, "One of the greatest ways to develop a charming sense of humor is to begin by realizing what a great variety of people, ideas and all manner of things there are in the world—by realizing that *nothing is absolute except the urge toward growth and life.*"[76] In a nutshell, the sense of humor in the twentieth century has been the personality attribute of the tolerant relativist.

The valorization of the sense of humor as an attribute of the self-objectifying personality was clearly not limited to the academic psychology in which it received its most articulate and technical conception. Popular psychology texts of the 1930s and 1940s advised their readers on the importance of having a sense of humor and laughing at oneself. "If you want to make people laugh," said Donald Laird, "and if your ego will stand it, deride yourself. Psychiatrists say that it is good for one's mental health to enjoy a joke at one's own expense. The mind specialist is more worried about the person with unbending dignity than the person who can take it—yes, even hand it out to himself."[77] And Donald McLean advised his teenage readers that "The *selfish* person does not really have a pleasing sense of humor, because he thinks too much about himself. . . . A sense of humor comes from having a sense of *perspective*. When we are able to forget our own importance, we can see the things that are funny."[78] Etiquette books and guides to manners for youth often stressed the importance of self-objectification through humor, although they rarely used that terminology. One published in 1942, for instance, advised its readers "to keep your sense of humor hitting on all eight. If you can laugh at things and at yourself, you will save many situations."[79]

There were, of course, those who rejected the possibility of self-objectification and laughing at oneself, and did so by maintaining an older egoistic psychology. The psychologist Knight Dunlap, for instance, concluded that "one does not laugh at one's self. Your own inferiority is not a comic matter to you." Although a very few people might possess the capacity to take a joke on themselves, "in the great majority of cases we laugh at ourselves in rather a mechanical fashion, in order that the joke shall not become any worse than it is."[80] For Dunlap, as for a distinct minority, laughter continued to be viewed as largely negative and based on the regarding of its object as inferior, rather than on incongruity. But Dunlap's challenge to the notion that the ability to laugh at one's self was not only a possibility, but a virtue, reveals the extent to which it was recognized as both an empirical fact and a widely held value. Dunlap seemed to feel the need to explain away what was an apparently common event—laughter at oneself—by arguing that it revealed a false conformity to the opinion of others, a kind of preventive against injury, rather than any "true" perception of the joke. But the difference between this "apparent" ability to perceive the joke and the "true" perception of the self as an object of laughter was, in fact, rather slim. Both required a sensitivity to the opinion of others, a willingness and ability to assume the behavior of others toward oneself, a willingness to recognize—if not to "see"—the self as the object of laughter.

From the 1890s forward, then, the personality attribute of the sense of humor was defined in terms of self-objectification, the ability to "take" or see a joke on oneself, the capacity to laugh at oneself. These terms of understanding, and the value attached to them, resonated throughout American culture—particularly from the 1920s through the 1950s, when they received frequent expression in both the academic and the popular psychology of the day and in the newly powerful mass media. That understanding drew heavily on the history of the concept, normally without acknowledging that history: the eccentric objectivity of the Jonsonian humor character was internalized as incongruity; the incongruity that came to matter was that between self-perception and how one actually existed in the world; the sympathetic imagination compelled the self outward to the perspective of others, and back inward to a concern with the self as other; the concept of "sense" allowed for both an expansion of the inner life of the self and an ever-increasing sensitivity to the external and objective world. This history did not need to be acknowledged by those who would value the sense of humor as a capacity for self-objectification; it was built into the very meaning of the term. Its rise to prominence as a value was built on the new concepts of the self that emerged in the later nineteenth century. And those new concepts of the self were fundamental to the definition of the ideology I am calling "bureaucratic individualism." The self-objectifying capacity of the sense of humor was specific to the individualism of a bureaucratic society; self-objectification removed the conflict between internal and external sources of authority and, in doing so, reconciled the ethic of self-determination with the demands of bureaucratic organization.

Inasmuch as the sense of humor was defined against its lack, and in terms of the significations it had acquired from the sixteenth century forward, it was also but one trait among many, particularly in the cottage industry of trait identification and proliferation that characterizes modern thought about character, personality, and self. True, it was often singled out as a particularly valuable attribute or possession, or held up as an example of the kind of trait possessed by the mature, insightful, or healthy personality. But it was also frequently tied to a host of other personality traits. Indeed, the sense of humor was defined as much by the other terms in its sphere of valued personality attributes as it was by its modern genealogy. Just as humor had been given definition by ridicule, raillery, and wit, so the sense of humor was given additional content by the traits of cheerfulness, tact, and sense of proportion.

The sense of humor was an integral aspect of that most valued of Victorian attributes, dispositions, or perspectives: namely, cheerfulness. Any glance at the multiplying self-help books, guides for youth, manuals of etiquette, and other forms of advice literature of the later nineteenth century reveals a common concern with "cheerfulness" as the foundation of character. Opposed to discontent, melancholy, morbid self-consciousness, and preoccupation with small concerns and worries, cheerfulness was a kind of code term for an entire Victorian ethic of joyful adherence to the rigors and duties of work, morality, and self-enrichment. It was necessary to cultivate cheerfulness as a perspective, as a "clear, bracing, sparkling atmosphere of the mind," in order to ward off the potential discontent which "tends to weaken and distort activity the moment it becomes a chronic disease of the mind." According to Edwin Whipple, "all healthy action, physical, intellectual, and moral, depends primarily on cheerfulness," and "every duty, whether it be to follow a plough or to die at the stake, should be done in a cheerful spirit." All of the values most characteristically associated with Victorianism— "industry, learning, genius, and virtue"—are "robbed of their greatest right and shorn of their most endearing charm" if lacking a foundation in the cheerful disposition.[81] For Edward Sisson a cheerful disposition was to be particularly valued because it was "so largely independent of circumstance: the cheerful man is happy in spite of troubles."[82]

The relationship between the sense of humor and cheerfulness was more than a bond based on a general disposition to be happy or to have a "positive" outlook. The ethic of cheerfulness was rooted in the notions of balance and proportion; the cheerful character recognized small worries for what they were, and balanced the minor concerns of the self against the larger duties demanded by morality and the Victorian creed. "Cheerfulness," said Whipple, "is a state or mood of mind consisting either in the equilibrium and harmonious interaction of the mind's powers and possessions, or in the sly infusion of humor into the substance of character. Its predominant feeling is one of inward content, complacency, and repose."[83] Like the sense of humor, then, cheerfulness at once led to a fuller, more expansive interiority, "independent of circumstances," and to a mechanism of compliance and contentment with whatever demands the external world might make. When C. Wright Mills imagined the white-collar worker as a "cheerful robot" some eighty years after Whipple, it was precisely this capacity for contentment and willingness to be manipulated that he disparaged. The cheerful character was passive, content, willing to take whatever was demanded of him without complaining, because he possessed, in Whipple's words, "that breadth and penetration of understanding by which objects are seen in their real dimensions and natural relations."[84] Cheerfulness shared with the sense of humor a capacity to see things "in their real dimensions" and a willingness to put the narrow concerns of the self in the context of the nature of things.

A twentieth-century counterpart to the Victorian character attribute of cheerfulness is tact. There is, of course, a great difference between cheerfulness and tact; at a basic level, the former is a mode of perception or a disposition, while the latter refers to a specific capability undergirding a mode of action. And tact has a specifically social content—its meaning makes sense only in relationship to sociality and dealing with other people, while cheerfulness seems to be independent of social circumstances. That said, tact, as an important character trait, has much in common with cheerfulness, and both were often mentioned as attributes possessed by persons with a sense of humor. Tact is derived from the term for the sense of touch, and in the nineteenth century came to be metaphorically applied to the sensitivity to the perceptions and motives of others; to possess tact was to be aware of what others would perceive as offensive, insulting, or unpleasant, on the one hand, and pleasing, complimentary, or inoffensive on the other, and to act in accordance with that sensitivity to others. The characteristic ability of the tactful person was the capacity to say potentially offensive things in ways that were perceived as complimentary, to turn the content of the thing said on its head by the fine manipulation of the form in which it was said. Tact came to be defined as the capacity to manage others through an understanding of proportion, fitness, and the requirements of the particular social situation. It became, in some ways, the characteristic virtue of Riesman's other-directed personality; tact, rather than the direct use of power, was the tool of the glad hand.[85]

Tact, or tactfulness, and a sense of humor were often mentioned together in the mid-twentieth century as attributes contributing to "personal attractiveness" or as elements of the "beloved personality."[86] For the social psychologists Emory Bogardus and Robert Lewis, writing in 1942, "tact and a sense of humor are closely related character traits," because tact "is primarily a sense of proportion," while a sense of humor "is a sense of the disproportion of things."[87] Both tact and a sense of humor, according to Bogardus, "involve the maintenance of objectivity. . . . Persons of tact and with a sense of humor do not allow self to get in the way of proper social perspectives."[88] Both tact and a sense of humor were undergirded by the sympathetic imagination; the opposite of tact was not simply bluntness or tactlessness, but a kind of narrow subjectivism in which the self lacked any window on the wider world and, consequently, was in the way of seeing outside itself. Tact, like the sense of humor, led out of the self into the objective world. In a way, it went beyond the sense of humor by converting a perspective or a mode of seeing into not only a mode of self-control but also a principle of human management.

The common element in the sense of humor, cheerfulness, and tact was what was often called a sense of proportion. All three were elements of an expansive self that allowed for the perception of the concerns of that self as relatively minor and for an adjustment of outlook in terms of the relative proportion of things. A sense of humor, said the authors of the 1951 self-help book *Live and Help Live*, is "a vivid sense of proportion that enables one to see big things as big and little things in their true littleness."[89] This ability to see things in proportion to one another was closely tied to the notion of objectivity as a perspective to be cultivated; the objective perspective, of course, was the one by which the true proportion of things was to be measured, even though "little" and "big" were relative concepts that had meaning only in relation to an evaluating consciousness. To possess cheerfulness was to see small concerns for what they were, and to measure them against the higher duties rather than allow them to become the source of discontent. To have tact was to understand the appropriate or fitting behavior in a given circumstance by measuring the larger ends to be achieved through the manipulation of that situation against the pettiness of the immediate reaction of the self. To have a sense of humor was to see the incongruity of imagining the concerns of the self as the greatest problems in the world, to measure the self by the yardstick of the perspective of others.

Yet the idea that the sense of humor was in some way a sense of proportion, and that such a sense was a valuable attribute, immediately raised a question: Was the self to be big or small? In order to have a sense of humor, a self had to be expansive, to reach outside of itself, to see things, including itself, in a broader fashion. But once this perspective was achieved, it meant an immediate contraction of the self as an object of consciousness; the concerns of the self were made to appear small, unworthy of the attention they had absorbed. The incongruity recognized by the sense of humor seemed in fact to be the incongruity of the self as both large and small at the very same moment. As the Danish psychologist Harold Höffding wrote, "In humour we feel great and small at the same time"; or, in the words of H. A. Overstreet, "what we call having a sense of humor *regarding one's self* is nothing more nor less than the power to switch from a contractive mood to an expansive." [90] This vision of the self as an entity capable of moving back and forth between an expansive and a contractive state, or perceiving itself as incongruous because both big and small, is characteristically ambiguous about the status of the self in the world. As much as the concept of a sense of proportion seemed to resolve the problem of the relationship between the self as both subject and object of consciousness, it concealed the ambiguity of the problem itself: What *was* the relative importance of the self in relationship to others?

A good example of that unresolved ambiguity, that walleyed willingness to see the self as both enormous and minuscule at the same moment, lies in the success writings of William Moulton Marston in the 1930s and 1940s. Marston's popular psychology texts promoted laughter as a kind of mind-cure; his writings were full of upbeat anecdotes about people whose lives were turned around through sheer mental power, including the power to laugh. The lives of the people who populated Marston's texts, like the lives of his supposed readers, were hemmed in by the petty concerns and machinations of office life, the routine of home and family, and the failures of love and marriage. Marston's task, like that of so much twentieth-century success literature, was to liberate the self from its concerns by counseling, on the one hand, acceptance of the conditions of life and, on the other, the power of the self to be larger than those conditions. The sense of humor was an important element in the therapeutic worldview offered by Marston because it involved the perception of incongruity and proportion; it made the self both small, in its acceptance of the priority of the world and its demands, and large in its ability to see the world as arbitrary and navigable by the expansive self.

In *Try Living* (1937), Marston introduced his chapter on laughter and the sense of humor with the case of "Brenda Upland," a distraught young woman saved from suicide by her sense of humor. Having discovered that her fiancé was already married to "a certain notorious night-club singer," Brenda was about to throw herself out the window of her hotel room when the house detective McCarty arrived. McCarty suddenly began to laugh at Brenda, who had forgotten to put her pants on before climbing out on the sill. "She too had a keen sense of humor and it saved her life. Darn it all—it *was* funny to jump out of a window without any pants on!" Laughter restored Brenda's "sense of proportion. . . . When she finished laughing she was sane again." When Brenda saw McCarty laughing, "Instantly her perspective changed. Brenda looked at her own body from the *outside*. She saw what McCarty saw, a ridiculous incongruity, a girl who had forgotten to put on her pyjama pants posing as the Queen of Tragedy." In other words, through the power of the sympathetic imagination, Brenda was able to adopt an objective perspective on herself and to see her behavior as incongruous; the concerns of the self were petty and ridiculous. Brenda then shifted her perspective to look at "her inner self," where "a curious transposition had taken place. The black monster created by defeat was still there but it had changed places and sizes with the real Brenda. The self was big and strong; it occupied now, the center of her mental picture. The monster was crouching way off in a corner, small, weazened, cowering."[91] By accepting the objective perspective of McCarty, Brenda had expanded her "real" self; all the concerns, problems and difficulties of the self became small and "unreal," while the power to perceive them as minor and insignificant was imagined as integral to the "real" expansive self. The message of Marston's instruction was that

> *you*, the individual, possess an unqualified power of final victory within your own self which nothing can or ever has defeated. . . . Try laugh-

ing. There's nothing like it for putting defeat where it belongs, in the position of an interesting, detached experience, awaiting the analytical attention of a self-confident, relatively gigantic you.[92]

The relatively gigantic you, however, was not so gigantic that it was not subject to another form of disproportion and distortion, the "exaggeration of the self to comic proportions." According to Marston, as he titled one of his subheadings, "TAKING YOURSELF TOO SERIOUSLY MAKES OTHERS LAUGH."[93] While the self is the source of all things and the most powerful entity in the world, it demands a diminution so that others will take you seriously; the self must be small in order to be large, and vice versa. Taking oneself too seriously means that others will not take you seriously; not taking oneself seriously means that others will. Or, as Marston wrote in *March On!* (1941), "When you have learned to laugh at your own solemnity you are no longer humorless and consequently no longer a laughingstock for other people. . . . Your laughing acknowledgment that you are ludicrous always makes you less so."[94] Even though the self is enormous, and rightly so according to Marston, it is not enormous to others, who perceive their own selves as larger than the concerns outside of them. To have a sense of humor is to enlarge the self by adopting the perspective of others toward the self; that is to say, by diminishing it. Marston, like his contemporaries, seemed uninterested in following this contradiction through to its final affirmation of the self as both all and nothing. Instead, he opted for a characteristic view of the self as possessing a sense of proportion that rendered it both big and small at the same time. In doing so, he allowed for an acceptance of circumstances and conditions while affirming the power of the self as more than simply an object of those conditions. Did the perception of proportion render the self big or small? Looking both ways at the same time, Marston simply avoided the question.

Self-Adjustment

In the hands of Marston and his contemporaries in the related worlds of applied psychology, mental hygiene, and popular mind-cure success literature, the sense of humor became more than a capacity for perception. The act of perceiving the incongruity of object and subject was a kind of therapy, an act involving the constant expansion and contraction of the self in terms of the circumstances, constraints, and expectations the world presented to that self. The sympathetic perception of incongruity seemed to prescribe a mode of behavior for dealing with the circumstances of the self. The detached self-analysis advocated by Marston was not merely a way of passively looking but was already conceived of as a way of being. The genealogy of the concept of humor from the sixteenth to the nineteenth centuries reveals a movement from humor as a mode of being to humor as a mode of seeing. In the world of twentieth-century psychology and its ancillary disciplines, the mode of perception defined by the sense of humor was refigured as a mode of action; in some sense, to see *was* to be. And that mode of action was understood primarily as a means of dispelling conflict and injury to the self through a process of mental adjustment. To have a sense of humor was to have a capacity for self-adjustment, to expand and contract at will, to navigate the rigid demands of a bureaucratic order by being inherently flexible.

By the mid-1920s the concept of "adjustment" was central to the problematics of the entire field of applied or industrial psychology. Within that field, developed as a handmaiden to corporate and industrial interests from the 1890s forward, there was a wide variety of theoretical perspectives; "adjustment" was a key idea in all of them.[95] By the 1940s and 1950s, virtually any high-school or college psychology textbook would espouse the importance of adjustment as both a value and a description of psychological fact.[96] The centrality of the idea of adjustment was not limited to the field of applied psychology; it received broad expression throughout twentieth-century discussions of the self. It is in some ways the most characteristic idea associated with the individualism of a bureaucratic order, for it imagines the self to be an infinitely complex and sensitive interior entity, a creator of itself, while simultaneously affirming the priority of rigid external structures to which the normal or balanced individual is capable of adapting.

Failure to make adjustment was the source of that most debilitating and dangerous state in a tightly organized society of hierarchical institutions: conflict. In order for such institutions to run effectively and efficiently, they created mechanisms for dealing with conflict. But given the generally negative light in which conflict was held, not only in business circles but within the culture as a whole, it is not surprising that the very notion of the person as an entity capable of infinite adjustment to circumstances was so widely held; the normal person adjusted to circumstances, while the abnormal or deficient person lacked the capacity for adjustment and was therefore a source of conflict, both within himself and in relation to institutional demands.[97]

The sense of humor was one of those attributes that contributed to the capacity for self-adjustment and, hence, helped to dispel conflict. William Mathews, writing in 1888, spoke of the sense of humor as a softener of controversy, an allayer of anger, a smoother of the "intercourse of life," and a guardian of the "minor morals" of society.[98] Ralph A. Habas imagined the sense of humor as "a vital factor in temper control," and "a *preventative* of anger or idle controversy."[99] Henry A. Bowman listed the sense of humor as one of the "factors in the individual" contributing to personality adjustment in marriage.[100] Because humor had a strong tie to sympathy, and sympathy was so often the foundation of adjustment and adaptation to others, the recognition of the sense of humor as a prophylactic against conflict frequently invoked sympathy, objectivity, perspective, and proportion as its partners. As the authors of *Mental Health* wrote in 1935, "Humor is bound up with play, sympathy, insight. It conserves the mental qualities which make for healthful plasticity."[101] The plasticity of the self, its capacity for contracting and expanding to meet the situation, its ability to "laugh off" its own failures and setbacks, served at once to protect the self from harm and also to diminish it as a force in the world.

In 1951 Charles E. Foster wrote in his *Psychology for Life Adjustment* a kind of summation of this notion of the sense of humor as a faculty of adjustment:

> One of the important things which each individual has to learn is how to "take a joke" or see the humor in a situation which may be pointed his way. This takes some training, effort, and experience.
>
> The person who "can't take a joke" has a long way to go before he can attain what the psychologist calls "social competence." . . . It is a skill which should be conscientiously worked for by anyone who hopes to be able to adjust satisfactorily to the stresses and strains of society.[102]

To have a sense of humor, in this view, is to possess a specific skill, acquired through "training," a kind of tool for the protection of the self through conflict removal in social situations. The notion of personality attributes as "skills," argues for a vision of the self as a package of uses, with "social competence" (meaning a liquidation of conflict in everyday life) as the end to be achieved. In some ways this utilitarian concept of the self is the logical outcome of the notion of perception as an active, rather than a passive, state; every personality attribute has its functional use in the business of living, and is simply wasted if not put to that use. The idea of the sense of humor as a capacity or an ability suggests a kind of broad potential for perception; the idea that it is a skill like other "social skills," besides requiring education, suggests it is to be used to accomplish a task. As Floyd L. Ruch wrote in 1937, "The person who actively seeks the element of humor in a trying situation is making use of an important procedure in emotional control. The ability to laugh it off has saved many an awkward situation in the classroom or in social life."[103]

It is no wonder that Leo Markun defined the sense of humor as "a true test of a well adjusted personality" or that, for another twentieth-century writer, a sense of humor "is now a thing to cultivate and achieve."[104] Given its use as an active "antitoxin" against "the microbe of egotism" or, conversely, against the feeling of inferiority, the sense of humor became a valued element in the sociable or gregarious individual.[105] Developing a sense of humor was seen as an asset because it involved learning "how to bend to [other people's] peculiarities without surrendering your own pet queerness." Reaching back into the early modern meanings of humor, John Erskine redefined them in terms of the twentieth-century values of adjustment and adaptation:

> Humor is the art of adapting oneself to another temperament. Every temperament, men used to think, is conditioned by the quality of moisture or "humor" in the individual's body. If you were melancholy, it was because you had a melancholy "humor." . . . To humor a person was to accommodate yourself to his characteristic tendencies. To have a sense of humor was to have such imaginative flexibility that you could adapt yourself to anybody.[106]

The definitions of humor and sense of humor offered by Erskine, of course, were characteristically modern despite his attempt to write them into the past; his logic, however, was to some extent the historical logic by which the terms were transformed to create their modern meanings. The infinite flexibility of the person with a sense of humor, his plasticity, was highly valued because of its social usefulness; as the external organization of everyday experience became increasingly rigid, the self was imagined as increasingly fluid and dynamic.

The modern value associated with the sense of humor reached back, once again, to humor's original signification as liquid. The difference between the nineteenth- and twentieth-century understandings of the metaphor of humor as liquid is telling. In the nineteenth century, humor was imagined as wet because fertile, rich, abundant, and expansive, as opposed to the dryness associated with death and decay. Time and again, Victorians sang the praises of humor in the same terms: "how it clears away the cobwebs from the brain," said William Mathews, "and keeps the wrinkles from the face! How it flows through the whole being, like a bubbling stream with perpetual verdure upon its banks! Without it, we are dry and parched."[107] To some extent these references to humor as a kind of fertilizer of growth continued into the twentieth century, but they were overwhelmingly subordinated to new understandings of humor—not as the water of life, but as a lubricant in the machinery of the social order.

At the foundation of the idea of adjustment, of plasticity and flexibility as capacities of the self, was the idea that the potential for conflict was omnipresent and that it lay in the power of the self to avoid that most dangerous of states. The sense of humor "is the best lubricator for the machinery of civilized society," said Henry Pritchett, for it "will take off the friction of [a person's] many-sided human contacts."[108] In a sermon entitled "How Can We Get Along Together?" delivered at Community Church in New York City in 1923, the Reverend Dr. John Haynes Holmes also declared the sense of humor to be "the best lubricant" to prevent friction in human relationships.[109] Arthur Bills's *Psychology of Efficiency* advocated the development of a sense of humor in a chapter devoted to "Friction and Lubrication"; according to Bills, because friction in everyday life leads to anger, worry and, most important, inefficiency, it is necessary to "lubricate" the people and situations responsible for it.[110] The idea of the sense of humor as a lubricant protecting against the constant friction of social life expressed perfectly the utilitarian notion of the self as a substance to be used by spilling itself out into the world; in doing so, it would not so much foster growth as ensure that the elaborate machinery of living continued to function in a regular way. Rather than a source of growth, the sense of humor could be imagined as a preventive of dysfunction. The self and its complex attributes made possible the functioning of the social machinery by providing the oil in the constantly moving gears of everyday social experience.

Friction, stress, and strain seemed to occur not as pointed conflicts separated from regular daily experience and elaborated as specific events, but as functions of the regularity of everyday life. Friction was the inevitable consequence of people working with people in highly organized and specific ways, rather than the result of conflicts over substantive issues. The sense of humor, given its history, was perfectly suited to dealing with the unspecified petty conflicts and irritations of everyday life. Humor, in the course of the eighteenth and nineteenth centuries, had become increasingly associated with the concrete details and particularities, first of character, and then of the whole realm of empirical reality. The valorization of the particular, of "ordinary life," that underwrote the bourgeois conception of humor made it ideal as a mode of perception of, and adjustment to, the minor, but persistent and regular, sources of conflict in everyday life. To acquire the "socially priceless" asset of a sense of humor, according to the author of *Living with Others* (1939), it was only necessary to develop "the habit of observing and remembering the interesting happenings of daily life." [111] And according to *The Book of Business Etiquette*, "Most of the causes of irritation during the course of the business day are too petty to bother about. . . . A sense of humor and a sense of proportion would do away with about ninety per cent." [112]

The sense of humor was the personality attribute most suited to dealing with the minor and the petty, because it viewed them as belonging to a realm worthy of attention. To have a sense of humor was to observe and record the small details and particularities of everyday life, to call attention to these details, and then to make them small and insignificant again by revealing the incongruity or lack of proportion in regarding them as significant. Even today, a favorite strategy of the stand-up comedian is to call attention to the small and insignificant—earwax, television ads, shoelaces, etc.—rendering it the object of attention, only to reveal the incongruity of regarding something so insignificant as worthy of the attention being bestowed upon it. It was not surprising, then, that, as one advice writer for young women said, "We are all grateful for persons who have a sense of humor. We like to have them in our group; we are glad to meet them in the daily routine." [113] The daily routine was the most suitable venue for the person with a sense of humor, because it was there, amidst the friction, stress, and strain, that the minor adjustments of the self took place, there that the machinery of society was lubricated.

All that was required was "the right application of a sense of humor" to ease "trying business or domestic situations."[114]

The self, contracting and expanding, laughing it off, easing tensions, lubricating the machinery of constant social contact, standing outside of itself, making constant adjustment in terms of how others might see it, applying itself to the business of mitigation of conflict, using itself to achieve ends through the concrete social situations of daily experience: this was the self of a bureaucratic society in which everyday life, with its routines, constraints, and rationalized discipline, was the primary level of reality.[115] This order, this discipline, was made compatible with, in fact dependent upon, the ever-expanding self. It was not simply a case of internalization of social rules, a disciplining of the self, as Norbert Elias and others have suggested.[116] Rather, the self was elaborated and expanded, made into the ontological basis for the possibility of discipline and control; it existed as a host of capabilities, skills, uses, mechanisms, and capacities embedded in its personality attributes. The sense of humor was a model of the personality attribute that contributed to this conception of the self and the form of individualism it supported. The culture of the bureaucratic society of twentieth-century America did not simply demand that the self adjust itself to a rationalized order; it actually imagined a self capable of making that adjustment. The coming of corporate capitalism did not spell an end to individualism; rather, it gave birth to an individualism of greater complexity.

FOUR   # The Commodity Form
of the Joke

The man with humor may make a joke, said Brander Matthews at the
end of the nineteenth century; the man with a sense of humor may take
one. This distinction was repeated more than once, although many people in the twentieth century have used "sense of humor" as a term to
describe both capacities.[1] What gets lost in the distinction is what floats
between the two personal attributes of humor and sense of humor: the
joke. In Matthews's expression, the joke is naturalized, taken for granted
as an item of exchange, understood as the given objective correlate of
the sense of humor. He can explain the difference between humor and
sense of humor as a difference in the relationship of persons to jokes
because he has assumed the entire structure of production and consumption—making, taking, and getting jokes—as the natural structure of
joking relationships. The humorist produces humor in the form of a
joke, and the vast audience of people who possess senses of humor con-
sume, and thereby "get," the joke.

   This metaphysics of joke exchange and circulation long antedates the
idea of the sense of humor. Swift, writing in the early eighteenth century,
could casually speak of the ability to take a joke,[2] and Shakespeare's
much-quoted lines from *Love's Labour's Lost* reveal a notion of the jest as
a commodity to be defined by its exchange:

> A jest's prosperity lies in the ear
> Of him that hears it, never in the tongue
> Of him that makes it.[3]

From the sixteenth century, when the term "jest" was first used to designate all manner of laughable stories, situations, and practices, to the later seventeenth century, when the term "joke" was introduced to refer to objects of the new practice of ridicule,[4] to the present and its overabundance of wisecracks and gags, Anglo-American culture has increasingly structured the laughable in terms of discrete, isolable units subject to manipulation and exchange, their value ultimately dependent upon the markets in which they are proffered. Even as laughter was increasingly figured as the product of subjective construction and practices, the objects of laughter were removed from the social relations in which they were embedded, and were then packaged as commodities—the objective expressions of individuals capable of producing and consuming humor.

The Joke and the Folktale

So naturalized has this idea of the joke as a discrete objective unit become, it is difficult to imagine an alternative to it. Every culture has jokes, we assume, and although their content might vary and the practices of exchange might be different in other cultures, there is little doubt that exchange is the appropriate metaphor for what goes on when humor is given objective form. An alternative way of envisioning the place of the laughable in social life could begin by looking to the folktake and the tradition of laughable narrative as rooted in community structures and practices; the meaning of the folktale, its form and its content, are circumscribed by the social identity of the teller and his relationship to his listeners—at least until the folktale is abstracted, catalogued, and typed by nineteenth- and twentieth-century scholars, at which point it takes on an identity similar to that of the joke. Yet this distinction between a premodern oral-narrative form, embedded in tradition and community, and a modern stripped-down entity, written and produced to appeal to a mass audience, is too stark, and not fully adequate to an understanding of the commodity form of the joke and its place in modern American culture. The distinction is helpful because it creates the contrast by which the definition of terms can take place: community vs. society; tradition vs. originality; the teller vs. the thing told; social relations vs. exchange value. We may know what a joke is, as a form defined by its commodity status, by knowing what it is not—a folktale.[5]

While there is some value to the absolute distinction between joke and comic folktale as two opposed forms of laughable representation, as a historical distinction it fails to comprehend the complexity of the relation between the two. The traditions of the raconteur, local storyteller, and community-based tale live on in the late twentieth century, even in commercialized and hybrid forms.[6] The commercialized joke, jest, witticism, and bon mot are not recent inventions; they have a long history, traceable through the jest books of early modern England and the classical ana and collections of facetiae that precede them. It is doubtful that a "pure" form of either the joke or the folktale has existed in the past and, if so, whether it would be historically recoverable. In addition, folktales often include what we would call jokes as elements of their overall structure, and many jokes take their structure and content from traditional folktales. There is no absolute dividing line between the two forms, even if we recognize a compelling and fundamental difference between them.

Nevertheless, we may see in the joke, as a readily identifiable and isolable unit of humor, a predominantly modern quasi-literary popular form, much as the novel is a distinctively modern literary form despite its similarities to and roots in other literary forms. The joke stands in historical relationship to the comic folktale as the novel does to the epic; the difference is that the novel aims to reproduce the detail of everyday life in language as a sign of the value of concrete, empirical, ordinary middle-class existence, whereas the joke aims at ultimate abstraction, condensation of detail, and exclusion of all elements not to the "point," so as to make it accessible as a product to an anonymous audience of consumers. Both the novel and the joke, however, are characteristically modern, one standing for the uniqueness of the individual work of art and the artist behind it, the other representing the interchangeability of parts, the techniques of mass production, the anonymity of modern life.

Jokes do not come with their authors' names attached to them, but neither are they the products of a ubiquitous folk culture, always already written, simply given. It was frequently observed in the later nineteenth and early twentieth centuries that there were no new jokes, that every joke had already existed for thousands of years, that jokes were universal things and their variations only elements to be explained away in the quest for the kernel of the "real" joke.[7] At the same time, a new professional class of joke writers emerged to fill the expanding demand for humorous material in the print and broadcast media, creating literally millions of new jokes. These joke writers also believed that there were no new jokes, even as they produced them by the score and in the process reshaped the very form and cultural status of the joke. It was under the commercial pressures of specialized joke-writing in the period from the 1860s through the 1930s that the form of the joke underwent a revolution; already an item of exchange, the joke was stripped of its extraneous elements, made into a consequence of new technologies of joke production, perfected as a union of the abstract principle of incongruity and the concreteness of the topical moment, and made purely objective to appeal to the sense of humor. Despite the fact that there was no simple historical transformation in which the comic folktale was reinvented as the joke-commodity, much of what we take for granted in the form of jokes, their existence in social life, and the ways in which they are told and retold was a product of the same era that discovered the sense of humor as a valued personality attribute.

The Cultural Status of Humor

The emergence of the commodity form of the joke was made possible by a transformation of the cultural status of humor in the second half of the nineteenth century. Humor was reconfigured, given greater cultural recognition, talked about in new ways, elevated to a position of respectability within bourgeois culture. In attaching an explicit value to the personality attribute designated as the sense of humor, Victorians reinvented the place of humor within their culture. But they did more than this. They defined the value of humor not only in intellectual terms, but in institutional and practical ones as well; they created a new space and status for this thing called "humor," and in doing so developed markets for the exchange of the new units of humor designated as jokes.

It has been difficult for historians to recognize this transformation in the status of humor. Scholars of American humor, since the subject was "discovered" in the 1930s and early 1940s by Franklin J. Meine, Constance Rourke, Walter Blair, and others, have tended to view humor as a relatively constant element of national life from the early nineteenth century forward.[8] This is partially owing to the understanding of humor as a literary or folkloric form; attention is focused on the texts conceived to be "humor," and their cultural status is assumed. In the tradition that stems from Rourke, humor is seen as a feature of "national character," and the argument over character is foregrounded in such a way that the status of the texts examined as humor is simply taken for granted. The sources are made to address the issue of national character rather than their own status as humor in American culture. Similarly, the classification of texts in terms of "schools" or "styles" of humor, characteristic of much of the literary scholarship on American humor, pushes the issues of genre and type to the fore by assuming a framework in which the larger category of "humor" is simply given.[9] Much of this interpretation of American humor is explicitly social or cultural in orientation, but it is concerned with the *content* of humorous texts and schools of writing, rather than the cultural status of humor itself. "Humor" is seen to be a given quality or feature of the texts themselves, rather than something constituted within the culture.

We can benefit by moving away from the analysis of humorous texts to an analysis of the culture in which those texts were produced and consumed. The existence of what we would call "humorous texts" in a society does indeed say something about the status of humor in that society, but not very much. Until we ask how humor was talked about in that culture, what values were attached to it, how it was structured and produced, we cannot begin to have an adequate understanding of its cultural status. Framing the issue in this way leads to a shift from a notion of humorous texts as cultural artifacts to a notion of humor as a value within a culture. This shift in perspective is significant, for it allows us to see what had been unseen for so long: the changing cultural status of humor, the new value attached to it, in the period from the Civil War to World War II.

As the previous chapter shows, it was not until the 1870s that the sense of humor was explicitly imagined as a valuable personality attribute. It was during this same period that a middle-class reassessment of humor elevated and separated it from the contexts in which it had been largely a secondary and subsidiary element. During the antebellum period, particularly in the 1840s and 1850s, American humor began to be recognized, both in the United States and in Britain, as a distinct literary genre.[10] During the same period, blackface minstrelsy was created as a distinctive American form that would provide the basis for both the comic monologue, representative of stand-up comedy in our own day, and the conversational or dialogue joke characteristic of vaudeville and radio comedy. But quasi-literary humor as well as theatrical humor lay partially buried in other forms during the antebellum years. The writings of the southwestern humorists—August Baldwin Longstreet, Thomas Bangs Thorpe, and George Washington Harris—were often confined to the pages of sporting journals like William T. Porter's *Spirit of the Times*, while the well-known Down East humorists—Thomas Chandler Haliburton, Seba Smith, and others—published most frequently in newspapers.[11] Quasi-literary humor, although selected and compiled by critics and scholars in the twentieth century as evidence of an antebellum profusion of "native humor" and "folklore," was produced as a journalistic endeavor by men whose main occupations lay elsewhere; humor was a sideline for its creators and for the editors who incorporated it into their publications. Similarly, in hindsight we tend to see in the origins of blackface minstrelsy the birth of a comic form; the overriding image of Sambo, the comic jester, and his incarnation in the early comic end-men, Tambo and Bones, seems the essence of the minstrel show.[12] But in the 1840s and early 1850s, minstrelsy integrated sentimental songs and depictions of plantation life with humorous sketches. Comic elements were subordinated to the values of sentimental culture that provided the main foundation of the minstrel show. Early minstrelsy may have been largely a working-class form of amusement, but it embraced the sentimental orientation of American bourgeois culture. It was only in the late 1850s that its comic elements began to predominate. As one historian of the minstrel show says, "By 1860 minstrelsy had been transformed. It had gone from . . . primarily musical to heavily comical."[13]

A comparison with Britain during the same decades is instructive. While the United States was unable to sustain a single periodical devoted primarily or exclusively to humor for more than a year or two, in Britain the long-lived *Punch* was established in 1841 and served to define a style of humor for the British middle-class public for several generations.[14] The editor of *The Nation*, E. L. Godkin, in the early postbellum years expressed dismay at the failure of the American reading public to support a comic paper in the vein of *Punch*, even as he saw around him evidence of an emerging appetite for jest among his countrymen.[15] The British middle-class public had an enormous taste for the kindly and benign humorous fiction produced by Dickens and his contemporaries in the mid-nineteenth century, while its American counterpart seemed primarily concerned with sentimentalism.[16] The distinction between the British embrace of laughter and the American suspicion of it was observed by Ralph Waldo Emerson, who on an 1848 visit to England noted in his journal that "the day's Englishman must have his joke, as duly as his bread. God grant me the noble companions whom I have left at home who value merriment less, & virtues & powers more."[17]

The newly emergent American middle-class public subordinated humor and laughter to the demands of sentimental culture, particularly to the cult of sincerity. According to the historian Karen Halttunen, it was not until the 1850s that sentimental culture began to open itself fully to laughter through the introduction of private theatricals in the middle-class parlor; that laughter recognized the incongruity of the sentimental ideal of sincerity and its necessary dress in conventional forms.[18] Increasingly in the postbellum years, the American middle class would make laughter and humor a central part of its social experience, but at midcentury sentimental culture, even as it incorporated humor, remained somewhat leery of laughter. As late as 1866, an author could promote increased amusement among the American middle class by insisting that "one of the great social faults of the American is, that he does not amuse himself enough, at least in a cheerful, innocent manner. We are never jolly. We are terribly troubled about our dignity."[19] The settled British public had no such compunctions.

A shift in the cultural status of humor began in the later 1850s with the reformulation of the minstrel show as a primarily comic form and the introduction of comic theatricals into the parlors of the middle-class home. But it was during the Civil War and the years immediately following that the comic and the humorous began to occupy a distinctive niche in national life, particularily in the life of the educated middle class. The major institutional change in the world of humor and the comic was the emergence of the professional comic lecturer. As one contemporary noted, "The United States possesses what no other nation does, several professed jesters—that is, men who are not only humorous in the ordinary sense of the term, but make a business of cracking jokes, and are recognized as persons whose duty it is to take a jocose view of things."[20] The most prominent of this small but distinctive class of professional funnymen included Charles Farrar Browne (Artemus Ward), Henry Wheeler Shaw (Josh Billings), and David Ross Locke (Petroleum V. Nasby). It was out of this milieu of the comic lecture that the Gilded Age's most powerful humorist, Samuel Langhorne Clemens (Mark Twain) emerged.

Like Twain, virtually all the new jokers had their origins in the margins of an expanding journalism. Browne was a migrant printer's devil and typesetter in New England and Ohio before creating the character of Artemus Ward for the pages of the Cleveland *Plain Dealer* in 1858. What began as a comic journalistic sideline, like so many of its antecedents in the world of American humor, soon required a performance quite separate from journalism; Browne assumed the identity of Artemus Ward and hit the lecture circuit, his newspaper appearances serving as advertisements for the comic performances he gave. The career of David Ross Locke followed a nearly identical trajectory. Beginning as a tramp printer's devil in New York, he worked for numerous newspapers in his native state and then in Ohio, until he created the comic character of Petroleum V. Nasby for the Findlay *Hancock Jefferson* and the Toledo *Blade* in 1862. Nasby, like Ward, soon became more than a part-time or incidental forum for his creator; Locke assumed the identity of his comic character. Henry Wheeler Shaw, who as Josh Billings had one of the longest and most successful lecturing careers, was also marginally involved in the newspaper business and other forms of on-again, off-again employment characteristic of the expanding economy of the mid-nineteenth century, before he had luck imitating the writings of Browne. The usual route for the new comic lecturers of the 1860s, including Twain, was through journalism; but unlike their predecessors who had also written their pieces for local newspapers, the new humorists were able to move beyond their subordinate position in the margins of the papers and appeal to a national audience by making humor and laughter their main purpose. Whereas Major Jack Downing, Sam Slick, and other antebellum comic characters existed and had an audience only by virtue of their newspaper appearances, during the 1860s newspapers became vehicles for the launching of careers in comic joking outside of journalism.[21]

In the 1870s and 1880s, humor attained a status altogether different from that of the antebellum years. Just as the sense of humor was elevated as a personal value, humor was elevated as a general social value. Humor and laughter began to appear as central features of middle-class life. William Mathews, writing in 1874, claimed that "the demand for humor is great among us [Americans], and the supply is not equal to the demand." "We have professional wits and humorists," said Mathews, "who furnish funny articles by the column,—mechanical jokers, who turn out jokes as the patent bread manufacturer turns out loaves," and yet there seemed insufficient humor despite all this labor.[22] E. L. Godkin looked at "the total annual production of jokes in the United States," was amazed by the quantity, and yet concluded that there were not enough jokes to furnish all the outlets for demand in the country.[23] Twenty years later, the Norwegian immigrant and realist author H. H. Boyesen was struck by "the jocularity which one encounters everywhere within the borders of the United States," and he observed that "all things, ourselves included," are "legitimate subjects for jokes." Boyesen bemoaned "the startling decay of eloquence in the United States" since the golden age of Daniel Webster, Henry Clay, and John C. Calhoun; in 1895 he had difficulty recalling "the name of any renowned American speaker of the last decade who is not primarily a humorist."[24] The most prominent national religious figure of the Gilded Age, Henry Ward Beecher, was himself widely recognized as a humorist, and a good deal of his popularity and success was said to rest on his sense of humor.[25] It is difficult to think of any in the long New England tradition from which Beecher came who could claim the same. In all spheres of life in the Gilded Age, humor was becoming a recognized good.

The era of the 1870s and 1880s is notable for the establishment of new middle-class sources of humor consumption. Whereas antebellum culture had no comic periodical of a stature to appeal to a regular middle-class readership, the Gilded Age produced three, whose longevity spans the critical period from the 1870s to the 1930s, when the modern commodity form of the joke was produced. *Puck* was founded in March 1877 and had a circulation of 80,000 within five years; it was to last more than forty years, going through a period of especially rapid expansion at the end of the 1890s. *Judge* was established in October 1881 and enjoyed an expanding readership into the 1920s: 50,000 in 1890, 85,000 in 1907, 100,000 in 1912, and 250,000 in 1923. After that, its circulation declined, and it expired in the 1930s. *Life* followed virtually the same pattern. Founded in January 1883, by 1916 it had a readership of 150,000, but by the 1930s it too went into decline. The title was sold to Henry Luce and *Time*, where it ceased to be a humor magazine altogether. Combining political cartoons, feature-length humorous articles, and assorted doggerel and jokes, these three magazines served to define humor as a distinct sphere of goods to be consumed in a growing market of middle-class consumers, rather than just a collection of ephemera or marginalia published in the spare columns of newspapers and periodicals.[26] The establishment of distinctively comic journals involved the separation of humorous from nonhumorous materials, but in making that separation such a premium was placed on humor that all kinds of periodicals expanded or created humor departments in the 1880s. The general expansion of the volume of periodicals in those years fed a heightened demand for humor in every publishing forum. Every newspaper had its columns of jokes or humorous writings.[27]

That this shift was largely a middle-class movement is suggested by the development of the college humor magazine in the same years. The university at the end of the nineteenth century became one of the primary agents of socialization for the youth of the American middle class as the bourgeois peer group took on many of the functions previously associated with family and community. A university education was one of the attributes by which members of the new middle class distinguished themselves both from their predecessors and from members of other social classes. Undergraduate life was greatly expanded by a host of extracurricular activities and organizations: varsity athletics, fraternities, social clubs, literary societies.[28] The establishment of college humor magazines was part of this general reconstruction of the American university and its purpose, and came to be one of the distinctive features of undergraduate life. Before the Civil War, there were no college humor magazines. In 1872, the *Yale Record* was founded, and in 1876 the *Harvard Lampoon*. By the turn of the century, dozens of colleges and universities claimed humor magazines; in the 1920s and 1930s, college humor was a well-noted and distinctive subgenre, and hundreds of college humor magazines were being published from coast to coast. After World War II, especially during the 1960s, with the development of the mass university and radical changes in undergraduate life, college humor was absorbed into the broader culture and the college humor magazine quietly disappeared; the *Harvard Lampoon* was in effect replaced by the *National Lampoon*. By 1980, fewer than two dozen humor magazines were still being published.[29] The heyday of college humor, from the 1870s to the 1930s, coincided with the growth of a general middle-class taste for large quantities of humor.

In the same month that saw the publication of the initial issue of *Judge*, October 1881, Tony Pastor opened the first "clean," "double-audience" vaudeville show in New York. Vaudeville was to be the dominant form of urban entertainment for the next fifty years.[30] The emergence of vaudeville as a predominantly comic form, characterized by "respectability" and a large middle-class urban audience, pulled the "low" laughter of what Elliott Gorn has called the "bachelor subculture" of the saloon[31] into the relatively genteel world of public amusement. The main sources of vaudeville humor lay in antebellum forms: the minstrel show, the circus, the dime museum, and what was often called "variety." In fact, Pastor always insisted that his shows were "variety," even while B. F. Keith and Edward F. Albee and other promoters attempted to distance themselves from the saloon associations of variety by adopting the name "vaudeville." [32] But the boisterous male-only audience for the variety show prior to the 1880s, with its association with marginal underworld figures, gamblers and gaming, hard drinking, prizefights, and various forms of "dissipation" and moral danger, rendered the comic laughter of variety suspect in terms of middle-class moralism. By stripping variety of its saloon context and of the "blue" humor or "jasbo," as it was known, that went with it, vaudeville was able to open the humor of the comic monologue, the two-act or conversational piece, and the comic song to a large urban public in a way that accepted the conventional gender strictures of the era. The Keith-Albee chain's explicit campaign to clean up vaudeville—to prohibit any jokes or material that could be considered offensive to "respectable" women, including not only jokes of a sexual nature but slang associated with saloons, blasphemous material, or questioning any of the conventional pieties of late Victorianism—represented at once a suppression and an elevation of variety. Vaudeville came to occupy the broad middle ground between "legitimate theater," which had itself only recently emerged from the realm of the morally suspect, and the dangerous "low" arena of the stag show and burlesque, which was increasingly marginalized in the later nineteenth century. [33]

Whereas variety in the 1860s and 1870s had been loosely organized, dependent on local circumstances for its character, and entirely subordinate to the commercial and cultural purposes of the establishments in which it took place, vaudeville in the 1880s and 1890s took on a distinct organization of its own at the regional and national levels. The establishment of local and national chains, the centralization of booking procedures, the development of the two-tier system of big-time and small-time, the standardization of the types and structures of acts within the show: all point to the thorough and rapid rationalization of vaudeville as a business enterprise and a cultural phenomenon. [34] The promoters of vaudeville, keenly aware of the rising status of popular comedy, sought to create and feed a national market for humor. As one contemporary noted, "The most serious thing about [vaudeville] is that seriousness is barred. . . . From the artist who balances a set of parlor furniture on his nose to the academic baboon, there is one concentrated, strenuous struggle for a laugh."[35] In the same way that the comic-lecture circuit of the 1860s had lifted the humorists out of the back pages of newspapers and periodicals into a relatively autonomous realm of comic performance on the national stage, vaudeville drew together the comic elements of various loosely organized nineteenth-century popular forms and elevated them to a distinct sphere.

Vaudeville represents the beginning of modern show business. The humor and comedy that lay at the heart of vaudeville provided the foundation for the major forms of popular entertainment in the twentieth century. Radio, television, and much of early film—before the dominance of standard theatrical conventions and narrative structure derived from melodrama—were largely comic media. Much has been made of the revolutionary nature of the mass media in the twentieth century, but rarely has it been recognized that the new popular-entertainment forms were heavily comic in nature. Whether fed by a new middle-class appreciation for humor in all its forms or by the appeal of physical comedy and comic characters to an ethnically diverse and multilingual urban audience, vaudeville sought a common ground in laughter. In doing so, it institutionalized comic forms as the foundation of a cross-class mass culture.[36]

It was not solely in the commercial forums of periodical production and popular entertainment that humor and laughter were raised to a new status in post-Civil War America. Many of the new joke books published in the later nineteenth and early twentieth centuries, although obviously commercial in nature, were aimed at nonprofessionals who sought easy sources for their own uses. The growth of the after-dinner speech as a bourgeois institution fueled the production of joke collections designed for the toastmaster and for all those who would be called upon to make addresses as part of the evening ritual. Once again, the comparison with Britain is instructive. While the English bourgeoisie firmly embraced the after-dinner speech as a venue for the reaffirmation of Victorian values, they tended to regard it as a serious, if not somber, occasion. The American postprandial talk, on the other hand, was generally comic in nature, and became more so into the twentieth century. Marshall Wilder, a sometime vaudevillian, noted gag thief, and private comic entertainer who plied his trade in London as well as the United States, observed that English after-dinner speakers "have little or no humor, but they are extremely earnest in their remarks. They incline more to argument than amusement." Wilder found this fact a peculiarity of the English, but only in contrast to the situation in the United States where humor often appeared to be the sole point of the after-dinner speech.[37]

What seems to have begun as the use of humorous stories to introduce a talk or illustrate a point soon became the main substance of the talk itself. Likely influenced by the prevalence of comic platform lectures in American culture, the after-dinner speech reproduced the structure of commercial comic forms. By the 1920s, guides to oratory had to remind their readers, in the words of one, that "the after-dinner speech is not a vaudeville monologue—a series of jokes strung loosely together," suggesting that many speakers gave precisely such a talk.[38] After all, as another instructor in public speaking put it, "The only important distinguishing earmark of the after-dinner speech is its emphasized use of the humorous illustrative story"; and if humor was the distinguishing feature, it was easy to see how it could become the main substance.[39] The lines between comic lecture, vaudeville monologue, and after-dinner speech were open and permeable. Sinclair Lewis's fictional Babbitt, preparing his convention speech with its requisite Pat-and-Mike stories, if not directly reflective of social practice, was at least indicative of the role jokes and humor had come to play in middle-class speech.[40]

The heyday of the after-dinner speech in the life of the American middle class lay in precisely the years that saw the rise and fall of vaudeville, college humor magazines, and the humorous periodicals *Puck*, *Judge*, and *Life*. From the 1870s through the 1930s, American business and professional organizations used the ceremonial banquet and its attendant speechifying as a forum for the consolidation of corporate, group, and professional goals and purposes. After World War II, the full-dress banquet with its series of speakers seemed increasingly antiquated. The after-dinner speech eventually came to parody itself in the present-day institution of the "roast," in which a guest of honor was humorously pilloried by a panel of luminaries on the order of Dean Martin and Don Rickles. But in its prime, the after-dinner speech was one of the fundamental ways in which humor was given recognition as an element of bourgeois life. One need only compare the practice of rhetoric and public speaking in the antebellum period with the overwhelming orientation of speech toward comic and humorous forms in the later nineteenth and early twentieth centuries to see that a basic shift in the way humor was regarded by the middle class had taken place.

Contemporaries were, in fact, quick to notice this change and to remark on the new status of humor. William Mathews summed up his impression in 1888:

> The present has often been pronounced the age of mechanical discovery, of great economical and political appliances, the age of steam, of free-trade, of reform; but a more appropriate title, it seems to us, would be the age of mirth or comicality. Certain it is that joking is carried to a height which it has rarely reached at any former epoch.[41]

The English humorist Jerome K. Jerome, certainly no enemy to the trade that provided him with a living, after visiting the United States could only remark, "I think the American indulges too much in humor. He really absorbs too much humor. It is like a man who has come to drink champagne for every meal. He drinks it every day and all day long."[42] It was often observers of the United States who had come from European countries—men like Jerome and H. H. Boyesen—who were struck to the greatest degree by the special presence humor seemed to occupy in the life of Americans in the later nineteenth and early twentieth centuries.

As shown in previous chapters, the concept of humor in the eighteenth and nineteenth centuries had increasingly absorbed other elements of bourgeois thought and values, such as the concerns with universality, sympathetic social relations, and the concrete experience of everyday life. What marks off the period from 1870 to 1930 from the two centuries prior to it is the institutionalization of the practice of humor and laughter as elements of middle-class life. Whereas many Americans in the 1840s might claim that humor was founded on sympathy and "fellow-feeling" they remained leery of it as a sphere of practice. But with the advent of the sense of humor as a valued personality attribute, the emergence of the "clean" laughter of vaudeville from the saloon culture of midcentury, the establishment of distinctively middle-class sources of humor such as the college humor magazines, and the newfound uses of humor in social experience, most of these misgivings were swept away. There were those who remained suspicious of what they perceived as a cult of the sense of humor and an overemphasis on joking and laughter in social life, but they were a small minority. In the main, laughter had become thoroughly acceptable by middle-class standards, not simply as a matter of principle but as a matter of practice. And the practical form that humor most often took, in this vast new market of middle-class consumers, was the joke.

The Joke as a Unit of Humor

In 1938, the Canadian humorist Stephen Leacock codified what seemed to him the nature of the joke:

> A joke may be defined as an item of humor reduced to a single point or particle. It represents the breaking up of humorous matter into its elements, so that we can examine and appreciate one little bit of it without any extraneous context. One might say that a joke is a self-contained humorous thought. Its essence is its isolation.[43]

Humor, as an object of study, rather than as a power of perception or mode of seeing, seemed analyzable in terms of scientific method; just like any object in the world, it could be broken down into its constituent parts, isolated from the contexts in which it appeared, abstracted, typified, and understood in terms of general principles. Humor, which in the eighteenth and nineteenth centuries had been figured as an evanescent quality, dependent on the specific concrete expression of character and everyday life, had become subject to the rational typology implicit in the principle of incongruity that undergirded all laughter. The joke was the incongruity stripped of all the details of language and context. Leacock was not alone in his desire to analyze humor into its discrete units; Max Eastman, Milton Wright, and others in the 1920s and 1930s discovered the joke as a fundamental unit of humor, discrete, self-contained, and subject to isolation for purposes of critical analysis. The movement to create a critical "science of humor" would reach its apex in the 1950s, in the works of Evan Esar, who sought a scientific typology of all jokes.[44]

This critical discovery of the joke as a unit of humor to be analyzed did not take place in an intellectual vacuum, fueled only by the application of scientific modes of thought to new objects. As has been suggested, the changing status of humor in the late nineteenth and early twentieth centuries was coupled with the expansion and rationalization of markets for humorous production. To market humorous products, it was necessary to break them down into units for the purpose of sale and consumption. While literary humor was often marketed to magazines and publishers in the form of the short "piece," story, or essay, the more popular forms of humor were increasingly reduced to their joke elements. By the 1920s and 1930s, when Leacock and others began to recognize the joke as an isolable, context-free element of humor, the practice of isolating jokes for the purpose of exchange was a fait accompli. The critical notion of the joke as a unit of humor served to confirm and provide an ontological status for what had become the primary form of practice in the new circles of professional humor production: joke creation and exchange. The practice of professional humor and the critical analysis of humor dovetailed in a shared understanding of the joke as humor reduced to its most elemental form.

The transition from a mid-Victorian construction of humor, as embedded in the relation of the humorist to his specific audience and the concrete detailing of character involved in the process of representation, to a twentieth-century understanding of the joke as an objective thing, free from the extraneous contexts of social relationships and manners of telling, can be observed in two essays from the period. In 1895 Mark Twain published a short essay entitled "How to Tell a Story"; in 1920, Thomas L. Masson, a longtime editor at *Life* magazine, wrote "How I Wrote 50,000 Jokes in 20 Years." Taken together, these two essays provide a window on the cultural invention of the joke as a unit of humor, specifically on the objectification of humor by a new class of professional humorists in the twentieth century.

The writing of Twain's "How to Tell a Story" was prompted by the author's sense of the corruption of oral forms characteristic of the antebellum Southwest of his boyhood and the comic platform lectures of the 1860s and 1870s. Not simply a primer for a younger generation of professional humorists, nor an attempt to pass on the accumulated wisdom of his years in the trade, Twain's essay is guided by the recognition that the very meaning of humor has been transformed by the introduction of newer oral forms. It represents an attempt to reestablish midnineteenth-century notions of humor in the face of the increasing abstraction and objectification of humor in the form of jokes. Twain's position, then, is less representative of the general understanding and practice of popular humor in the 1890s than it is of an older mode of humorous production coming into contact, and clashing, with the popular practice of the later nineteenth century. Underlying "How to Tell a Story" is a logic of instruction; however, the need for instruction lies not in the requirements of professional humorists for technical training in reaching a popular or mass audience but, rather, in the sense that humor cannot be rationalized and routinized—that, in an important sense, how to tell a story is something that cannot be learned.

The contrast between older and newer forms of humorous production is less than explicit in "How to Tell a Story." Instead, Twain seeks to distinguish forms on the basis of nationality: "The humorous story is American, the comic story is English, the witty story is French."[45] Yet the comic story appears throughout as not merely a representative of a national type, but as the contemporary form most at odds with the "American" humorous story. The comic story is, in fact, the joke, projected into the distant English past. And it is the form Twain finds most destructive of true humor; the telling of the comic story is "a pathetic thing to see," "makes one want to renounce joking and lead a better life" and, all in all, is "very depressing."[46] His description of the social instance of joke-telling is drawn not from a model of English social life but from the stock image of the loud and aggressive American, laughing at his own joke, eagerly seeking the approval of his audience, repeating the punch line to milk it for every possible laugh. "How to Tell a Story" identifies as its central problem the ubiquity of the comic story, even as it promotes the humorous story as the typical American form.

The heart of Twain's distinction between the humorous story, on the one hand, and the comic and witty stories, on the other, is that the former "depends for its effect upon the *manner* of the telling," and the latter depends "upon the *matter.*" The corollary is that "only an artist can tell" the humorous story, but anyone can tell the comic story or, in Twain's words, "a machine could tell the other story."[47] The problem with the comic story is that it exists independently of its teller, of the details of character, of the building of a relationship between narrator and author; its effect lies purely in its isolated, objective content. One of the central characteristics of the comic story is that it isolates its effects in what twentieth-century comics would come to call the punch line, and what Twain and his contemporaries referred to as the point, nub, or snapper. The comic story, or joke, is designed to build up to the point of a central incongruity, which is released in the final line; everything extraneous to that point is irrelevant and, if the form is to achieve its effect, must be eliminated. A machine can tell the comic story because the entire meaning of the story lies within its formal boundaries; it is relatively independent of elements that might detract from the snapper, or the formal condensation of the moment of incongruity. Twain's distaste for the comic story lies not so much in the democratic implications of a form equally accessible to all, requiring no special ability or talent to tell, as it does in his sense that the form of the joke is sterile and debased, emptied of the rich and explicable detail involved in the humorous story and its manner of telling. A sign of the utter difference between the two forms, for Twain, is his refusal to extend the term "humor" to the joke, and his alternative use of the term "comic."

The humorous story, on the other hand, embodies much of what the mid-nineteenth century had associated with humor: incongruity in the detailing of the concrete rather than the condensation of the point, the eccentricity of character, the self-conscious creator assuming the guise of the "objective" humorist. Twain's examples of the master storytellers in the humorous mode are not the popular humorists of the 1890s, but those of his young manhood in the 1860s, 1870s, and 1880s: Artemus Ward and James Whitcomb Riley. Because the humorous story depends entirely upon the manner of its telling, Twain finds it virtually impossible to identify it as a thing independent of the specific characters who have created it. While the teller of the comic story is pictured as an anonymous backslapping Anyman, the humorous story cannot be separated from the condition of its telling; it is utterly dependent upon the character of the humorist. The humorous story *is*, in an important sense, Riley "in the character of a dull-witted old farmer," narrating a tale in which "the simplicity and innocence and sincerity and unconsciousness of the old farmer are perfectly simulated."[48] The simulation of unconsciousness, characteristic of the eighteenth-century "man of humor" and his heir, the nineteenth-century "humorist," was one of the primary elements of Twain's humorous story. "The humorous story is told gravely," said Twain, and "the teller does his best to conceal the fact that he even dimly suspects that there is anything funny about it."[49] The apparently purposeless stringing together of incongruities, the rambling digression, the slurring or understating of the point, the unconscious dropping of a studied remark, the timing and use of the pause or non sequitur: these were the elements of the humorous story, and all were firmly grounded in the character assumed by the humorist. If the comic story was organized around the central incongruity of its point, the humorous story was designed to be pointless, its humor built on the negation, deferral, or understating of any goal. The comic story was utilitarian and efficient; the humorous story, art.

Twain's critique of the comic story was conservative in its attempt to restore a mid-nineteenth century idea of humor in the face of the emerging dominance of the joke. But it also looked forward to the emerging ideology of technique in twentieth-century professional comedy. "Comic timing," for instance, would come to be seen as a central technique by humorists, monologists, and stand-up comics, as would the emphasis on rhythm in the construction of routines. Twain's concern with the use of the pause can certainly be seen as of a piece with the technically oriented view of later comedians, but the difference between Twain's mid-Victorian view and twentieth-century comedy is fundamental. At the root of all twentieth-century comedy lies the joke; technical concerns focus on the means of delivering and routing that joke, on the maximizing of returns (in the form of "laughs") from it. Jokes, in short, are the building blocks of comedy routines, each one a discrete unit with its own "point." For Twain, alternatively, the humorous story existed neither as a building block of some other form nor as a collection of jokes. Rather, it was an integral whole, not a series of points, and as such was unanalyzable into its constituent parts. Stripping the humorous story from the context of its performance, as one might do with a twentieth-century comedy routine, was impossible because in a real sense the story only existed in its performance. There was no independent substratum of content to be analyzed. In other words, professional comedy's emphasis on technique, on "timing" and routing, went hand in hand with the emergence of the joke as a fundamental unit of humor. Twain was opposed to a technical conception of humor because he rejected the notion that jokes were humor and, as units of humor, were subject to technical manipulations.

"How to Tell a Story," then, is not simply a statement of preference for one historically neutral form over another, as if the comic story and the humorous story each had purely aesthetic reasons to recommend it. Rather, Twain's essay represents a point in the history of the idea of humor, a point in which the constraints of an older mode of production came into contact with those of a newer. Twain, as a member of the first generation of professional humorists—the platform speakers of the 1860s—lived through a period in which the expansion of the commercial market in humor both benefited his career and undermined the idea of humor as an ineffable substance, entirely dependent on character, manner, and detail, on which that career was built. Like many of his contemporaries, Twain saw the joke not as a new form but as an ancient one, stale, used-up, degraded. In *A Connecticut Yankee in King Arthur's Court,* for instance, he projected the practice of telling jokes into the medieval past, insisting that the common coin of late nineteenth-century jokes were old and "worm-eaten" even by sixth-century standards. This rhetorical universalizing of the joke as a form common to all ages was one of the ways in which Twain responded to the ubiquity of jokes in the humor market of the later nineteenth century. By portraying the joke as an ancient Old World inheritance, he was able to claim the humorous story as a new, creative, and progressive American form, even as it was being swamped by the dominance of the joke in American culture. But the universalizing of the joke as a transcultural form could cut both ways; in the eyes of the new professional humor writers of the 1890s, it meant that all humor could be reduced to the universal joke elements of which it was composed. "How to Tell a Story" was one of the last attempts to defend a mid-nineteenth-century notion of humor in the face of the requirements of professional comedy. That it shared something of the outlook of professional comedy suggests the cultural contradictions of that particular transitional era.

The generation that followed Twain's, those born in the 1860s and 1870s, came of age in an era when the commercial market in humor had created a host of new careers and practices for the professional humorist. Some, like Finley Peter Dunne, creator of the famed Mr. Dooley, and George Ade, author of the immensely popular "Fables in Slang," found a niche in the expanding urban journalism of the 1890s and the press syndicates that brought their distinctive products to a national audience.[50] Others, like John Kendrick Bangs, best known for *A Houseboat on the Styx*, occupied the genteel middle-class monthly magazines that had recently opened their pages to literary humor.[51] Although these figures, largely unread today, were noted as prominent humorists in their own time, perhaps more representative of the new careers in humor at the end of the nineteenth century were the anonymous joke writers and space fillers who were responsible for the columns of jokes, marginalia, and ephemera that overran the pages of newspapers and magazines. Many of these joke writers entered the trade through journalism; in the 1880s and early 1890s, editors of daily papers in cities as diverse as Philadelphia, Hartford, Yonkers, Danbury, Connecticut, and Oil City, Pennsylvania, either had staffers write jokes to fill space, or wrote the jokes themselves. Others got into the trade by feeding the new comic weekly journals in the 1880s. By the early years of the twentieth century, a regular "joke market" had long been established, dominated by fifteen to twenty men and women who anonymously scribed the vast majority of the jokes found in magazines and daily papers. In contrast to Britain, where jokes were often copied and recycled from American and continental sources, and where no joke market existed, in the United States a regular set of fees (often one dollar per joke, but ranging from twenty-five cents up to five dollars) and a routine structure for submission and payment were well established by the turn of the century.[52]

The career of Thomas L. Masson was at the center of the new market in jokes. A fairly well known minor humorist in his own day, Masson has been virtually erased from the historical record. From 1893 to 1930 he carved a middle-class literary career out of his daily work with "humor." Born in 1866 in Essex, Connecticut, Masson attended public school in New Haven, and as a young man moved to New York City to establish a career in the 1880s. After several unsuccessful starts, he became a traveling salesman, a fitting occupation, perhaps, for a man who would go on to become a joke-producing expert. While working as a salesman he began to submit short humorous pieces and essays to *Life*. His success led to a full-time job at the age of twenty-seven; from 1893 until 1922, during *Life*'s period of greatest expansion as a national comic weekly, Masson was managing and literary editor. His position as editor at one of the most prominent purveyors of humor for middle-class readers put him directly in touch with the anonymous hack writers, cartoonists, and jokesmiths that furnished the bulk of the material for *Life* and its competitors. He went on to write and publish widely in the field of American humor, editing a number of collections and writing several essays on the subject.[53]

Masson's career as an editor and an author reveals a kind of ecumenical reconceptualization of humor. For Masson, everything from the great literary masterpieces of Mark Twain to the most expendable one-line gag were of a piece; they were all humor, and as a business matter were of equal concern. Unlike Twain and the generation he represented, who drew a firm distinction between humor as an aesthetic form and the prosaic world of comic joking, Masson saw jokes as literary products, differing perhaps in aesthetic quality from the works of Twain, but inhabiting the same universe of humor. The jokes he crafted, he said, "are not masterpieces of humor. But then masterpieces of humor are very rare, as are masterpieces in other branches of literature and art." More important, his jokes were "saleable as the market goes, and serve to illustrate the mechanics of this more or less lucrative business."[54] The joke, if not a masterpiece, was at least, in the words of another editor of Masson's generation, "the most universal form of literature; it is protoplasmic, the simplest organized thing printable."[55] The literary editors of Masson's generation thus raised the joke to the level of literature as they reformulated it as the baseline of humor.

If Twain's "How to Tell a Story" served to warn its readers away from any notion that they could effectively learn to tell a humorous story, Masson's 1920 article "How I Wrote 50,000 Jokes in 20 Years" had an opposite intent; Masson's personal accounting of his years in the joke trade was offered as a model to be emulated by virtually anyone. Twain had disparaged the comic story by saying a machine could tell it; Masson elevated the joke by insisting that "joke writing is a trade which can be learned by any person of ordinary intelligence who has industry and application."[56] In fact, Masson offered himself as a prime example of the ordinary and average, and pointed to his own financial success as evidence of the universal access to the joke market available to the most talentless of his contemporaries. Quality and aesthetic issues are pushed aside in Masson's account by the focus on quantity of production and salability; the point of his essay, after all, is not how he wrote great jokes, but how he wrote 50,000 of them. It is the practical mechanics of production and marketing that concern him. Twain's "how to" was ironic, subverting its promise to reveal the practical secrets available to "Everyman"; Masson's "how to," on the other hand, delivered precisely what it promised—practical and technical rules by which anyone could become a "humorist."

Like any other field of industrial production, Masson warned his readers, the start-up costs in terms of time and effort would be relatively high; once, however, the techniques of joke-writing were mastered, volume could be increased and time and effort reduced. "In the beginning," said Masson, "I could never write more than fifteen or twenty jokes a day, and it took me nearly all day to do this." Through a gradually accumulated knowledge of the routine process of joke-making, he was able to increase his output to a hundred jokes in a single day. "It is comparatively easy for me now to write sixty jokes in two hours," he claimed, thus averaging two minutes per joke.[57] Compared to the techniques developed in the 1920s and 1930s by professional gag-writers in vaudeville and radio, Masson's practices were unsophisticated, but they show the extent to which a regimented set of practices had come to underwrite the production of humor in the form of jokes.

The form of the joke in Masson's commercial print world was borrowed from the world of vaudeville and its popular predecessors. "A joke," according to Masson, "is almost always a dialogue between two characters."[58] Whereas the older traditions of jesting had tended to favor a longer narrative form, in which dialogue between characters was embedded, and the voice of the narrator defined the interaction between characters as elements of a story, the practice of joke-writing for the comic periodicals and newspapers stripped the narrator from the interaction, and replaced him with the shorthand of easily identifiable characters in dialogue. In place of the detailed setting up of characters and situations, the vaudeville-derived joke used a basic form of straight line as set-up followed by punch line as payoff. Many of the jokes Masson used as examples seemed to come directly from the two-piece act on the vaudeville stage, such as the following:

> THE FARMERETTE: Do you think I can learn how to milk this cow in a
> week?
> THE FARMER: I hope so, miss—for the sake of the cow.[59]

One can almost hear the rimshot marking the punch line, a convention also derived from vaudeville.

By turning the joke into a dialogue form, Masson and his generation of literary editors removed literary style and manner, narrative voice, and other potentially idiosyncratic elements from their product. The joke was viewed as an objective representation of a moment of dialogue, accessible to all without the intervention of a mediating narrator. The difference between Twain's construction of humor and Masson's is thus not merely the difference between an oral and a written form, between how to *tell* a story and how to *write* a joke; rather, there is a difference between two models of orality, one narrative and the other theatrical, and their representation in writing. Twain's most famous stories, like "The Celebrated Jumping Frog of Calaveras County" and "Jim Baker's Bluejay," are, after all, written representations of the oral mode defined in "How to Tell a Story"; they are utterly dependent upon the manner in which they are narrated. What the joke editors of Masson's generation sought was a form independent of the manner of telling, and they found their model in theatrical dialogue abstracted from its performance. To rely on the idiosyncratic narrative was to personalize the joke, to make it much more difficult to mass-produce, and to create problems in marketing and distributing a nonuniform product. The uniformity of jokes in which there was no narrative intervention, and only the simplest representation of a single incongruous idea, best served the joke market of the later nineteenth and early twentieth centuries. The dialogue form was ideal because it removed the irregularities associated with individual authorship, while providing a condensed narrative through immediately recognizable stock characters and situations.

One of the greatest benefits of the dialogue joke to the joke writers and editors of that era was that it made jokes all that much easier to produce. As Masson put it, "There are only two ways of writing it. The first way is to get an idea that is worth joking about and then to have two characters make the joke. The second way is to have some character say something, and then get another character to reply in such a way that the joke is made." In other words, one could approach the joke via the punch line or the straight line, and those were virtually the only ways to approach it. The simplicity of the form allowed for infinite variation within an extremely limited framework. "As long as you have the architecture of a joke firmly fixed in your mind," advised Masson, "newer conditions are always arising to which the old form can be adjusted."[60] This idea of the joke form as a kind of template on which new jokes could be struck would receive more sustained treatment in the hands of the radio gag-writers of the 1930s, who came to depend upon it for their livelihoods. By insisting on the structure of the joke in vaudeville dialogue form, joke writers and editors were able not only to limit the irregularities of individual authorship but also to create a set of components that were geared toward mass production. In the age of Henry Ford and Taylorism, joke writers discovered the benefits of the simplified impersonal model as a productive tool.

If the dialogue form fixed the parameters of the joke on the "architectural" level, the use of stock characters provided a condensation of content and situation that made the dialogue form accessible to its audience without use of extraneous narrative detail.[61] The virtue of such character types, for the writer, is that they present an immediate entrée to the situation he seeks to describe because they are familiar, easily recognized, and condense an entire realm of associations for his audience. Knowledge of the range of character types was thus key for the early twentieth-century joke writer. "The first thing necessary," said Masson, "was to learn the old characters." Among these he included the mother-in-law, the tramp, the barber, the landlady, and the beleaguered husband and father, each of whom defined a set of behaviors, expectations, and situations. The husband, for instance,

> is a tired business man; he is supposed to be making constant love to his stenographer; to be always coming home late at night; to be worn out with his wife's efforts to drag him into society. If he lives in the suburbs, he is loaded down with bundles. The only real opportunity he has to assert himself is in his relationship to his daughter's lovers.[62]

Although this character was not as old as Masson suggested, dating from the 1890s as the "little man" characteristic of much twentieth-century literary and cartoon humor, by 1920 he had become so thoroughly stereotyped that the simple mention of husband or father conveyed the whole range of associations listed by Masson.[63] Character shorthand for situations and actions within the dialogue form of the joke thus freed the joke writer from the narrative requirements of other forms of writing.

The difference between the use of stock characters in twentieth-century joke production and in the forms of jesting that preceded it lies in the way the joke writers of the modern era yoked the typical to the topical in the definition of characters. As bourgeois characterology, particularly in the novel but also in personality psychology and other areas, moved away from the fixed typology of early modern thought to an individualism based on the union of the particularity of persons with a universal humanity, the joke moved in a parallel direction. But instead of abandoning typology of character, a move that would have been impossible within the condensed form the joke took, the joke came to rely on the constant creation of new and topical characters as expressions of the diverse range of persons. "A joke," said Masson, "in order to 'get over' with the public, must deal with a subject with which the public is thoroughly familiar." The joke writer "must depend upon the old forms, the old characters, as a basis," but he must also constantly adapt those characters to newly emerging topics. The range of characters must be expanded to include "the golf fiend, the motor fiend, the fresh-air fiend, . . . bohemians, New Thoughtists, high-brows, futurists and cubists, all kinds of social reformers and cranks."[64] Character types have had immediate social content, of course, in all cultures. The difference between preceding eras and the twentieth century is a difference in the mode of production; the new mode of character production required a constant revision and reinvention of character types in accord with a notion of topicality. In order for the joke to be mass-produced, new character models had to be constantly introduced while the formal structure and typology of character and situation were retained. The union of typicality and topicality in character definition made this possible. Joke characters were both easily recognized types and up-to-the-moment representatives of new social trends.

The use of the dialogue form and topical character types allowed for a kind of condensation of meaning in the individual joke. Jokes relied at once upon the contexts in which they were produced and upon their audience's familiarity both with the forms and with the characters they offered as shorthand, but they also stood as independent objective units. It was, in fact, the very condensation of external factors and meanings that made the joke appear as an isolated object, free from the explicit contexts of authorship and audience. In its published form, the joke stood alone, bearing no particular relationship to its author, who was anonymous, or to its audience, who might read it in a magazine or newspaper often several removes from the original place of publication. The very practice of submitting jokes for publication underscored the conception of the joke as an isolated unit. Each joke was submitted on an individual slip of paper; joke editors commonly received envelopes with packets of fifty or a hundred jokes, each written on a separate piece of paper in a uniform fashion. The joke editor could then choose only those jokes he saw fit to publish, and return the remainder to their author.[65] Every joke was considered on its individual merits, separately from all others, even as the submission process stressed the importance of mass production. The idea of submitting a single joke, rather than a quantity of at least a dozen, was considered absurd; the more jokes submitted, the more likely that *individual* jokes could be sold. The status of jokes as individual isolated units, stripped down to their bare essentials, was thus dependent upon their status as mass-produced goods.

Masson's guide to joke-writing reveals a set of assumptions and understandings about humor, its structure, and its practice that are antithetical to those expressed by Twain in "How to Tell a Story." Masson's position at the center of the twentieth-century joke industry gives his account an authority perhaps not otherwise attainable, but it also sets the limits on his understanding of humor. It may be objected that Twain and Masson were concerned with entirely different matters, that a comparison of the two serves to highlight not so much a historical transformation as a difference between two realms of production and the place of two historical actors within those realms. To some extent this is a valid point. Would it not make more sense to compare Twain with a nationally popular humorist such as Will Rogers or a well-known literary figure like Ring Lardner, rather than with a literary functionary like Masson? The simplest answer is yes, if we were in fact comparing the two as representatives of popular or literary humor, of celebrity, of public representation of character. But what I have sought is not so much a comparison between two men, but a comparison of the dominant forms of humorous production during two historical eras as experienced and understood by the historical actors at the center of those forms. The point is not that Masson is Twain's twentieth-century equivalent, but that a figure like Masson would have been an impossibility in Twain's generation, and that the kind of humorous story advocated by Twain was increasingly marginal in the world of a market-oriented editor like Masson. A comparison of Twain with Will Rogers would reveal essentially the same thing, although Rogers was less explicit about joke production and marketing technologies than Masson; still, what Rogers did was tell jokes, short and simple, one after the other.[66] The limits of Masson's understanding of humor, like the limits of Twain's, is a function of the language of humor, the dominant mode of production in a particular historical era, and the particular way in which Masson was situated in relation to that language and mode of production. In an important sense, Masson was not able to see beyond jokes as the essential units of something he called "humor," just as Twain was unable to grant jokes the status of something he called "humor."

The Universality of Jokes

If the late nineteenth- and early twentieth-century market in humor came increasingly to depend upon the topicality of jokes, their relationship to a specific and immediate set of social characters and situations, it is also true that jokes were increasingly held up as universal things, unchanging in their essentials and common to all ages and all peoples. In some ways this contradiction is mirrored in the bourgeois understanding of literature in general. Literary work was valued to the extent that it spoke of "universal and timeless truths" at the same time as an increasing realism and specificity in describing social, psychological, and moral situations came to characterize the major forms of writing: novel, short story, memoir, biography, essay. The universality of a piece of literature was seen as a function of its attention to the nuanced specifics of the unique and particular situation it sought to depict and the original and distinctive way in which it made that depiction. The "truths" literature revealed were at once strikingly specific and heroically universal; the particularity of content and mode of expression served as a kind of gateway to the realm of the universal, a realm unobtainable through "empty" abstraction and "vague" generalization. The particular and the universal were joined together in the understanding of literature, just as they were in the understanding of personhood that is characteristic of modern individualism.

The conceptualization of the joke as a unit of humor partook of this understanding, but with a fundamental difference. Jokes were not original forms of literature providing new insights into universal truths. Truth, in fact, often had little to do with the matter. Rather, jokes were understood to be universal objects in a literal sense. While the exterior dress of the joke, its specific wording and expressive form, might be subject to change, the essential underlying joke itself was deemed to be timeless and universal. The particularity of the joke's mode of expression, unlike other forms of literary expression, was not seen as an avenue to some general truth; rather, the joke was the concrete form of a universal "thing," reworked in new dress but still the same object. No one in the nineteenth and twentieth centuries would claim that the novel, or any particular novel, was a universal form of expression, no matter how "universal" its meanings were held to be. Yet this is precisely how the joke, and indeed every particular joke, was conceived. The reobjectification of humor in the form of the joke-commodity was thus accompanied by a tendency to universalize the joke as an object common to all times and places.

As early as 1868 the claim was made that there were no new jokes because every possible joke had already been made, not just recently but hundreds and even thousands of years in the past. According to one author, even the exclamation "Joe Miller!" in response to a joke as a way of indicating its antiquity was of ancient derivation, even more "in sense" than "in sound." [67] All jokes could be traced back at least as far as ancient Greece and the Athens wits' "Book of Sixty," the supposed model for all later joke books. Prior to being written, it was assumed, these "jokes" circulated orally and were of a preliterate nature. Disregarding any differences in form and content between the anecdotal tales of ancient

collections and the modern joke, writer after writer in the later nineteenth century insisted on the fundamental sameness of jokes at all times
and places as a sign of their origins in a common human nature. As
William Mathews put it:

> Clever jokes, in confirmation of the Pythagorean philosophy, never
> die, but simply pass through a thousand transformations, and reappear
> in new and brighter or less attractive forms. . . . Appealing to the same
> sense of humor as of old, tickling the human midriff as in the days
> of Troy, Nineveh, or before the Flood, they prove the oneness of
> humanity.[68]

Just as the sense of humor was imagined as a universal human trait, so
the joke was imagined as its universal objective correlate, a proof of the
essential sameness of persons and their capacities regardless of time and
place.

The idea of the universality and antiquity of all jokes served to fix the
commodity form of the joke as continuous with forms in the past, rather
than as an abrupt departure. This idea was born in the nineteenth century, when the market in humor aided the creation of the joke as a
discrete objective entity, and soon found a place in the stock ideology of
the professional humor writers and gagmen of the twentieth century. If
all jokes were of ancient pedigree, the job of the jokewriter was simply
to update the "classics" for a modern audience. In 1939, on the two
hundredth anniversary of the publication of *Joe Miller's Jests*, L. H. Robbins, citing Joe Miller as "the Adam of gag men," advised the neophyte
joke writer to "roast the tried and true chestnuts once more, streamline
them in 1939 words, pare them down to the split second, and they seem
as fresh as ever; or if they don't, they will be welcome anyway."[69] Milton
Wright claimed that the essentials of the joke hadn't changed at all since
at least the Middle Ages. "Today, however, we do it better. . . . We are
snappier now and more alert. Our stories must move at a quicker pace.
There are rules to be followed, if the tale is to be appreciated."[70] By
insisting on the "essence" of the joke as an unchanging substratum upon
which could be imposed the superficial differences of language, style,
form, and "rules," the gagmen of the 1930s and 1940s were able to see
their profession as continuous with the past, and to see the past as a
repository to be mined for material they could "update."

There were, of course, those who challenged the notion of the antiquity of all jokes as a truism. One such challenge took as its starting point the necessity of topical reference in any joke. "The reason that a worth-while joke is ever new is because it is a reflection of some current fad or fashion," said Frank J. Wilstach in 1922.[71] From this perspective, the "essence" of any particular joke lay in its particularity, its relationship to the transitory ephemera of social life; every joke was a new joke because the fads and trends that provided the content of jokes were constantly appearing and disappearing. By emphasizing the topicality and particularity of the joke, this argument only succeeded in making jokes appear all the more discrete, unconnected to any larger framework, and ultimately as individuated units of production and consumption. Another argument against the ancient pedigree of jokes was based upon a consumer-oriented (or, as it might be called in some circles today, a "reader reception") perspective. According to the well-known radio comedian Edward ("Senator") Ford, writing in 1944, "If you haven't heard a certain joke, it's new—at least to you. Consequently, there is no such thing as an old joke. If you haven't heard it before, it's new."[72] This argument is a bit disingenuous, particularly given Ford's support for the idea of the ancient derivation of all jokes, but it highlights the way in which an increasingly subjective idea of humor and the sense of humor was coupled with joke production. For Ford and his contemporaries, the use of what they regarded as "old jokes" in a world where emphasis was on constant novelty was acceptable because, by the standards of many of their listeners, those old jokes were new. The argument did nothing to challenge the notion of an objective antiquity but, rather, reoriented the criteria of novelty to the realm of the consumer, thereby making the "objective" pedigree of the joke irrelevant to its status, if not to its use in production.

In either case, the rejection of the notion of the antiquity of all jokes did not challenge, but rather reaffirmed, the idea that the joke form itself was universal. Those who argued that all jokes were of ancient derivation and those who insisted on the newness of jokes both assumed that the modern joke form, with its built-in metaphysics of exchange, production, and consumption, was a form common to all ages. The reason why there could be new jokes, for someone like Wilstach, was not because jokes themselves were a relatively new phenomenon, but because the universal form of the joke was always amenable to new situations and characters. Those who argued for the antiquity of all jokes, on the other hand, assumed that the various operations they performed on the "classics" in order to "update" them did nothing fundamental to change the joke status of the originals; in the source materials they used, they saw the joke form as they understood it, and the changes they made were seen as only superficial ones.

Even if one accepts the idea that the joke as a discrete objective item of exchange was common in all cultures, the particular jokes that twentieth-century writers deemed universal seem highly specific to a particular era and society. Ford's examples of ancient jokes included "bride's cooking," "whiskers," and the mother-in-law joke.[73] In fact, the mother-in-law joke regularly appeared on lists of the oldest and most "worm-eaten" of jokes; yet there are no mother-in-law stories in *Joe Miller's Jests* or any of the early modern Anglo-American jest books. Indeed, one scholar has suggested that the mother-in-law joke was purely a Victorian invention.[74] Similarly, Milton Wright claimed in the 1930s that a consensus among gagmen on the most ancient of the tried-and-true jokes was: "Who was that lady I saw you with? That was no lady. That was my wife."[75] By the 1930s, this joke had come to stand for the proverbial "oldest joke in the book." And yet, even if we were to dismiss its obvious vaudeville two-act dialogue form and its terse and snappy delivery, it is fairly obvious to the historian that this gag cannot possibly predate the mid-nineteenth century. Its entire content is dependent upon a shift in the meaning of the word "lady," and the ambiguity of that shift in a democratic culture, as well as upon a rather cynical view of domestic relations characteristic of the first half of the twentieth century. What level of abstraction would be required to render such a joke "universal"? If we labeled it a subspecies of the mistaken identity joke, we might be on the way toward such a goal —but at the price of emptying the joke of both its form and its content.

The joke was increasingly held to be an objective, concrete "thing," a product detached from the social condition of its creation; however, the idea of the joke as a universal object also meant that it was viewed as an abstract model rather than a concrete particular item. By insisting that jokes were somehow "given" as universal objects, rather than being the products of quasi-literary labor within a particular society, the ideologists of the gag could see jokes simultaneously as concrete items of exchange to be marketed in a world of corporate media and as divorced from the conditions of production characteristic of corporate capitalism. The abstraction of the joke as a universal form was thus part and parcel of its commodification. The way this abstraction was accomplished was through typology; individual jokes were held to be representatives of a finite number of types, while those types were then held to be literally the jokes themselves. If it was argued that there were eleven types of jokes, for instance, it was then simple to blur the difference between category and object by claiming that there were literally eleven jokes. This, in fact, was the standard logic of abstraction made by those who sought to categorize jokes into types: the categories came to be the very objects they represented; the eleven *types* of jokes were understood as the eleven *jokes*.

The number of categories could vary. Beginning in the late nineteenth century, numerous people connected to professional comedy and humor attempted to consolidate all jokes into set typologies. Carolyn V. Wells, a prominent journalist, cruciverbalist, writer of mystery novels and children's fiction, and sometime humorist, claimed that there were only fifteen jokes; the fifteen included the mother-in-law, marriage, whiskers, death, and goldbricks.[76] Agnes Repplier, who wrote widely on humor from the 1880s through the 1930s, argued that there were only eleven original jokes; Joseph Choate insisted that there were at least twenty-two.[77] Others went so far, as did one anonymous "Humor Expert" writing in 1909, as to claim that all jokes could be boiled down to one original "Ur-joke" from which all others were derived—"And that one is covered by the simple word deformity."[78] Milton Wright, more than twenty-five years later, would argue that from the perspective of there being only one joke, it would have to be covered by the idea "Surprise! Surprise!" All other jokes would be variants.[79] The overwhelming desire to create a typology of jokes is evidenced by the fact that neither "deformity" nor "surprise" was, even in the viewpoint of those writing, a joke, but was rather a shorthand for a general theory of humor and laughter; and yet each of these theories was made to stand as an object, a joke. There was little in the way of rigor or consistency of thought in any of these attempts to categorize jokes. What is important, however, is not the consistency of thought within any given typology of jokes, but rather the way in which the very idea that all jokes were subject to a finite set of categories—whether the "magic number" be fifteen, eleven, twenty-two, three, or one—became part of the common way of thinking within professional and humor criticism circles.

The most frequently cited figure for the number of possible jokes, from the early twentieth century forward, was seven. Most of those who referred to the seven original jokes throughout the twentieth century were at a loss to describe the seven, and even those who were able to reduce all jokes to a list of seven were not in agreement on what those jokes were. One writer, for instance, claimed that the seven were as follows: (1) deformed truth; (2) deformed man; (3) deformed spelling; (4) deformed construction of language; (5) deformed ideas; (6) deformed pronunciation; (7) double entendre.[80] Another listed these seven jokes: (1) the pun; (2) the insult; (3) sex; (4) family life; (5) the turning table; (6) the odd combination; (7) news.[81] Any particular list of the seven jokes could apparently refer to a combination of general subject matters, comedic devices, or joke forms. The fact that "the pun" and "sex," for instance, referred to different orders of reality—one linguistic *within* the joke, the other a class of behaviors or subject matter to which the joke *referred*—seemed to bother no one. Rather, it was the magic number seven, reappearing as a kind of mantra in twentieth-century discussions of jokes and joke-making, that seemed to possess an allure for professional comedy writers and critics. If all jokes could be reduced to a list of seven, it seemed, then a system could be established for producing "new" particular jokes from the template of the universal seven. That such a system was never erected speaks less of the failure of categorical thinking than of the inability to reach a consensus on which seven jokes would make the system possible. Professional comedy writers turned to other techniques, but never abandoned the idea that there were seven universal jokes that could be the foundation of all others.[82] The search for system, for new technologies of production, was central to the emerging world of twentieth-century professional comedy.

Technologies of the Joke in Vaudeville and Radio

The idea of the joke as the elemental unit of humor in objective form, it should be clear, was not independent from the practice of professional comedy. In fact, much of what I have been characterizing as the ideology of the gag was a set of ideas about the practice of humor; the very notion that humor was something to be practiced or produced was ideological at its root. The old notion of a division between society and culture, "base" and "superstructure," breaks down when ideas are seen as the forms and foundations of organization rather than as "reflections of" or even "influences on" an analytically prior material form. The restructuring of the joke, its form and its constitution in the mind, was part and parcel of the process of its production as individual units; every "material" joke bore the mark of an ideology of production, an understanding of what a joke was and how it was to be produced, even an understanding that it was to be a "product." This is not to substitute an "idealist" metaphysics for a "materialist" one, but simply to argue that the division between "mind" and "matter," long a fruitful one in Western thought, seems particularly inappropriate to a field in which the commodities produced are intellectual and linguistic, rather than material. The technologies by which the new jokes of the twentieth century were produced were ideological constructions, systems that defined, at some level, what jokes were. Built into the process of joke production was the idea that jokes were at once concrete, topical, objective entities *and* abstract universal forms. The idea of the joke and the joke form itself are inseparable.

The new technologies of joke production arose in a context where humor was seen and organized as a sphere of rational and professional production. That organization was accomplished through a series of divisions of labor in the world of professional comedy. The advent of vaudeville in the 1880s, with its specialized acts, led to the separation of the monologist from other comic performers; in mid-nineteenth-century variety, performers were usually responsible for a combination of song, dance, costumed character, and comic speech. Drawing on the forms of the comic platform lecture of the 1860s and the minstrel show's stump speech, vaudeville institutionalized the comic monologue as a form separate from other forms, requiring a specialized performer known as the monologist.[83] As Robert Allen has pointed out, late nineteenth-century burlesque did essentially the same thing: what had once been a form that integrated the comic into its depiction of female sexuality increasingly became a form in which those performers responsible for the display of sexuality and those responsible for joking were separated from one another in the structure of the show.[84] A class of specialized jokers who didn't dance, perform tricks, sing, play the banjo, or engage in physical or sketch comedy, but who simply spoke alone on stage directly to the audience, was one of the fundamental novelties of the vaudeville division of labor. In that division and its elaboration of the comic platform lecture lie the roots of modern stand-up comedy and what David Marc has characterized as the "presentational style" of modern comic performance.[85]

Brett Page, in a guide for aspiring vaudeville writers published in 1915, at the peak of vaudeville's popularity, described the monologue as a vaudeville form characterized by what it was not. According to Page, the monologue was not a soliloquy, because the performer speaks directly to the audience rather than to himself; it was not an entertainment involving performances such as impersonations or magic tricks, because its substance lay in speaking rather than performing; it was not a string of disconnected stories, because it required a narrative unity derived from character; and it was not a string of stories interspersed with songs, because it involved speaking and speaking only. Rather, according to Page, there were eight characteristics by which the monologue as a specialized form of presentation, undertaken by a specialized class of performers, could be defined. The monologue must (1) be performed by one person; (2) be humorous; (3) have unity of character; (4) not be combined with any other type of performance; (5) be ten to fifteen minutes in length; (6) be marked by compression; (7) be distinguished by vividness; and (8) follow a definite form of construction.[86] By the time of Page's analysis of the monologue, the work of the monologist had come to be seen as a distinct sphere of comic performance amenable to a set of rigorously defined rules that separated it from all other entertainment forms. Those rules would allow for systems and principles by which "material" could be produced.

It was, in fact, in vaudeville that the modern notion of comic material was first invented. Unlike in any other field of literary or quasi-literary production, the idea of material referred to the actual products created and presented to audiences. In literary production, the term "material" referred to the raw sources—whether they were "experiences," documents, or historical or social "situations"—from which the writer sculpted his art; the writer's material would be the subject matter that required "treatment." It would seem odd to think of a novel, for instance, as the writer's "material," except in the postmodern sense of it being a source to be "treated" by yet another novelist. Yet, in the world of professional comedy, this is precisely how the term "material" was used. Jokes and gags were not designed to "treat" material; they literally were the material itself. This use of language is in line with the general ontology of the modern joke-commodity as defined here: because jokes are autonomous objective things, they can be seen as having a material existence independent of their creation.[87]

The second major division of labor in professional comedy occurred in the years of vaudeville's widest success, from the mid-1890s through 1920. The emergence of the monologue as a separate sphere of production and performance was followed by a division of labor between writing and performance. In variety and early vaudeville, the comic performer's material tended to be derived from earlier performances or written by the performer himself. Acts tended to use the same material over many years, and when they did add new material to their performances, it was often picked up from other acts on the circuit and adapted to the requirements of the particular performer. There was little need to create new material in a world where local audiences would greet the old comic performance as if it were a novelty; many vaudevillians were able to make entire careers out of repeating the same act night after night for decades. Material also circulated through the activities of "gag thieves," who might "steal" the work of other performers that happened to be on the same bill for an evening, adapting it to their own acts. The early monologists were largely responsible for creating their own material, although much of it was undoubtedly lifted, and adapted to the monologue form, from performances they had seen. There was little emphasis on novelty and topicality in early vaudeville. In fact, the system of playing on circuits to local audiences probably discouraged the introduction of new material: topical issues varied from locale to locale, and so novelty represented a risk, whereas the "tried and true" material guaranteed success.[88] The most appropriate way to think of the status of material in variety and early vaudeville is in terms of circulation within a relatively closed system; in late vaudeville and twentieth-century professional comedy, the emphasis would move away from an idea of circulation and toward an ethic of production for an ever-expanding system.

The separation of writing from performing began in the late 1890s, although many vaudeville performers would cling to the old ways or make adjustments when required by writing their own material throughout the vaudeville era. The earliest form of the division between writer and performer was based on the "wholesaling" of jokes to performers; the writer functioned as an independent craftsman. Later, writers would be hired as staff members to produce jokes for comedians; they would come to sell their labor rather than the products of it, although their success would still be gauged by the quality and number of jokes produced. The most prominent of the early gag-writers was James Madison, a onetime performer who gave up performing to specialize in writing material. From 1898 to 1918 he published *Madison's Budget*, sometimes referred to as the comedian's Bible, a serial of new jokes which was similar to the subscription services that today provide gags and topical jokes to radio announcers and entertainers. Madison also provided specialized services to particular performers, most notably Nat Wills, the "tramp" monologist, who was one of the first vaudeville performers to make topicality the foundation of his act. His monologue required new jokes every week; the advent of topicality as a common feature of jokes meant that stress was placed on production and the role of the writer, rather than on circulation and the role of the performer.[89]

In the world of late vaudeville in the 1920s and early radio in the 1930s, yet another specialization was introduced within the ranks of the gag-writer. If the gag-writers of Madison's day worked alone as independent producers and wholesalers, the most prominent writers of the 1920s and 1930s—Dave Freedman, Hal Horne, and Eugene Conrad—presided over staffs of low-paid workers responsible for the collection and organization of material. It was within this milieu that the professional comedian's reliance on what was called the "joke file" came into being. Usually organized by subject matter, and often cross-referenced, the joke files of the radio gag-writers represented the extensive compilation and collection of the entire historical record of humor, wit, and the laughable reduced to common joke form.

Hal Horne, for instance, spent three years and $25,000 compiling his joke file of three million entries. At one point in the process he had twenty women in his employ, copying jokes out of collections in public libraries, ransacking used-book stores, digging through old humor magazines. Anything that could be considered in any way a joke was fair game and could be reduced to the same status as all other jokes, ending up on a file card under the most appropriate heading. Horne then wholesaled his jokes, on whatever subject a client might request, at the rate of $10 per forty jokes; all the jokes might not be usable, but the bulk rate guaranteed enough usable jokes to make it worthwhile to his customers. Eventually Horne decided to sell his entire collection; and Walt Disney, in a move perhaps designed to corner the market in jokes, bought Horne's files. In the late 1920s and early 1930s, as the high-powered gag-writers made the transition from a declining big-time vaudeville to radio comedy, with its built-in national audience and insatiable demand for new material, the organizational form of the joke file became the dominant one in professional comedy.[90]

The joke file was not merely the product of collecting and transcribing previously existing jokes, but should be seen as a technology for the organization and production of jokes. Built into the organizational form of the joke file was a notion that all humor could be reduced to its joke forms, catalogued, and then reproduced for mass consumption. If a particular radio show was to deal with lawyers one week, for instance, the gag-writer was able to go to his files, examine all the jokes listed under "lawyers," and construct a script based on the organization of those individual jokes.[91] Each joke was conceived of as an independent unit, already written, simply in need of adaptation to a particular circumstance. The professional practice of using joke files to produce radio comedy, then, was not independent of the idea of the joke as a commodity or an elemental unit of humor; in fact, it is impossible to conceive of the practice of joke-filing without the idea of the joke as part and parcel of that practice.

The abstraction of the joke from its earlier contexts, its treatment as an individual unit to be catalogued, found its mirror in the academic world of the 1920s and 1930s. The joke file of the professional gag-writer and the folktale index of the academic folklorist have much in common, including the restless search for "material," the ransacking of sources such as jest books and almanacs, the system of universal reduction to a finite set of common themes or elements, the voluminous attempt to be comprehensive, and the notion that, while there are endless variations on jests and jokes, all jokes are really thousands of years old. While the development of folklore indexes was given the imprimatur of European scholarship, with all the prestige that entailed, the professional comedy writer's joke file was envisioned by its creators as simply a master tool of the trade, a necessity for large-scale production. Despite the fact that the joke file and the folklore index seemed to occupy different worlds and have different meanings and purposes attached to them, they shared an underlying organizational and conceptual imperative: the comprehensive collection of all particular jokes/folktales and their reduction to a common status as types. A glance at a latter-day index indebted to the European scholarly tradition, such as Gershon Legman's *Rationale of the Dirty Joke* (1968), reveals what is essentially a joke file dressed up in academic garb.[92]

The joke file and its requisite division of labor was part of a larger system of joke production that began to emerge in the early years of the twentieth century and reached its pinnacle in the mid-1930s. As early as 1908, observers recognized that "humor is essentially a commercial production" and, while mocking the notion of its reliance on typical corporate-organizational forms and technologies (time management, telephone banks, secretarial control, mechanical recording), gave credence to the establishment of new forms of production.[93] By 1936, those early organizational forms had become the more highly elaborated norm. As the *New York Times* editorialized:

> Writing "gags" or jokes for radio comedians is on the way to becoming Big Business. It goes beyond the radio star who hires some one to do his funny lines. The gag purveyor in turn runs a factory. He has a filing system which covers all the jokes in history and he employs a staff of writers. In the handicraft age poor Jack Point handled all the available lines of humor, but now in the mass-production age there are probable experts in direct statement, in suggestion, in inference, and in innuendo. The finished goods go to all markets. . . . The radio is a vast consumer of humor. In the old days a comedian's gags were good for the run of the show. Now he must have a new routine perhaps twice a week.[94]

The result of increased demand, as another writer remarked in 1938, was that "no longer does one say 'A joke's a joke.' A joke is now a valuable piece of property, no matter how thin you slice it."[95] Or, as an editorial summarized thirty years earlier, "The organization of humor is in line with modern progress."[96] "The comic," said Clifton Fadiman in the 1950s, "is an efficient machine for distributing a certain standard manufactured product."[97] The transformation of professional joke production in the first half of the twentieth century, then, was widely recognized as an extension of capitalist mass-production principles to the field of humor.

The three major technologies of humor production in vaudeville and radio comedy were refining, routining, and switching. The first two arose out of the writer's milieu of late vaudeville, as the new class of specialized joke writers created material for the monologist. The third technology, switching, was devised by the gag-writers of the radio era and relied on the joke file for its being. In the idea of "the switch" we find the purest expression of the notion of the joke as both an abstract, universal form that is simply given and a concrete, topical entity designed to deal with the particulars of a specific context; in other words, the switch represents the union of the typical and the topical in the form of the joke. This notion, of course, is present in the practices of refining and routining as well, but in a somewhat less developed form.

The process of refining jokes for production was based on the notion that every joke has its most perfect form of expression. While there might be several ways to tell a joke, the writers of late vaudeville concurred that there was always one best way.[98] The job of the writer was to find that perfect form. The first step, in the words of a later gag-writer, was "to bear in mind that in each gag, only one joke idea must be established. All confusing elements and unnecessary wordage must be discarded."[99] Refining, then, became a process of stripping the gag of extraneous material, separating the "true" joke element from the dross of its expressive form. A gag with more than one idea was impure and imperfect. The secret of the refined gag lay in its brevity, its lack of relation to anything outside itself that might undermine its sole meaning. As the vaudevillian Frank Fogarty, who still wrote his own material in 1915, put it, "There's only one right way to tell any gag and that's to make it brief." According to Fogarty, "You can kill the whole point of a gag by merely an unnecessary word." The vaudeville gag-writers made an obsession of brevity: "I never use an ornamental word, I use the shortest words I can and I tell a gag in the fewest words possible. If you can cut one word from any of my gags and not destroy it, I'll give you five dollars, and it'll be worth fifty to me to lose it."[100] The process of refining jokes essentially involved the extraction of humorous material and repackaging it in the smallest and most rigorously conceived packages possible.

Underlying the process of refining, then, was a notion of the joke as an already existing elemental form, containing only one "joke idea" and having the simplest structure possible. The emphasis on brevity and singularity was codified in the characteristic forms of joking in the twentieth-century monologue: the wisecrack, the one-liner or, more generally, the gag.[101] The primary feature of these forms, as Evan Esar noted, was that they involved no situation; their meaning was entirely dependent on the incongruity created within a given structure.[102] Whereas traditional theatrical comedy depended upon the representation of social situations involving various types of irony—mistaken identity, switching roles, deliberate deception—and the representation of comic character, the gag form was an attempt to separate the internal incongruity of what was said from both the situation in which it was said and the characters who said it. The commercial advantage of this strategy, of course, was that it allowed for the development of a body of distinct joke elements that could then be used in any number of different contexts. By removing the extraneous, the excess verbiage, and the possibility of multiple meanings, the gag-writer was able to make the joke into an entirely self-contained entity that could be incorporated into any situation; the gag itself was timeless, placeless, context-free. The practice of refining jokes, the hard work of removing words and discarding situation-related meanings, then, was intimately linked to the idea of the joke as a commodity.

Jokes, however, were rarely presented alone, as single entities. In the monologue form, they were grouped together and arranged into routines. The practice of routining jokes reaffirmed the notion of the individual joke as an independent entity while integrating it into a larger pattern. Brett Page's advice to the would-be vaudeville writer reveals how routines were constructed out of refined jokes. "Have as many cards or slips of paper as you have points or gags. Write only one point or gag on one slip of paper. On the first card write 'Introduction,' and always keep that card first in your hand." Page urged a systematic re-arrangement of the cards until "you eventually arrive at the ideal routine." [103] The principle by which jokes were ordered in the structure of the routine was not based on narrative unity, which would require an affirmation and development of situation, but on "rhythm" and timing; the monologue in this sense was more akin to musical composition than to storytelling. What counted in the structure of the routine was the pattern of laughs generated. An early theory held that, "like ocean waves, monologic laughs should come in threes and nines," moving from the grin to the chuckle to the belly laugh.[104] This idea remained influential throughout the period of radio comedy, providing the foundation for the standard routines of comedians like Bob Hope, whose quick-fire monologues often were structured as a repeated pattern of an initial joke quickly followed by two "toppers." [105] The relationship between jokes in the routine, then, was one of timing, pacing, and delivery, rather than content or narrative continuity. The content of the individual joke stood alone, isolated from the routine in which it was embedded.

The practices of refining and routining jokes, although dependent on an a priori concept of what a joke was as an ontological entity, also required an experimental method. For comedians and gag-writers, a joke or a routine was only as good as the laughs it was able to elicit from an audience. Gags had to be constantly refined as they were tested on audiences, and routines were subject to infinite revision, even as gag-writers insisted that every gag had its most perfect form and every routine its ideal structure. In late vaudeville, the monologist was able to experiment by adjusting his routines according to audience reaction night after night, but the introduction of radio as a national medium in which a performance was given only once required a different approach. If radio comedy aimed at an ideal rhythm of three solid laughs per minute, with the intervening time devoted to "feeding" and "setting up" gags, the comedy writer had to devise a method to guarantee the desired audience response. It was in the rehearsal for the live broadcast that the writer's most important work was done. The rehearsal often contained twice as much material as the live show. It was the writer's responsibility to re-routine the material into a shorter format in accordance with the laughs generated in the rehearsal audience, and with the idea that more than three laughs per minute threatened to overwhelm the audience and fewer than three to distract it. Every joke in the script was marked in terms of the kind and level of laugh it generated, and then the script was reworked into an "ideal form" in accordance with the experimental data.[106] This method reached its most developed expression in the radio shows of Bob Hope in the late 1930s and early 1940s. Hope would have two staffs of writers prepare material with a total running time of ninety minutes in order to produce a stripped-down, thirty-minute weekly show based on audience reaction to a live performance.[107] The stringing together of apparently unrelated gags, then, was in fact a rigorously constructed, empirically tested method.

The more sophisticated forms of routining jokes came to rely upon the development of the joke file as a tool of the professional gag-writer. A routine could be constructed out of the raw material of the joke file; because each joke was written independently on its own card, the joke file allowed the writer easy access to material that could be reordered and reshuffled at will. If a routine seemed to lack the requisite pacing or pattern of jokes, the writer could return to the joke file to fill the lacunae, experimenting with material until he found the proper or successful structure. The joke file was thus a kind of safety net for the writer pushing deadlines, an organized source of last resort, and an indispensable guide to structuring routines. The joke file and the practice of routining shared the conception of jokes as independent context-free units of humor that could be abstracted and reordered at will.

While the joke file was one of the dominant tools of professional comedy beginning in the late 1920s, not all radio comedians and gag-writers used files. Those who relied primarily on highly topical gags often found joke files to be less helpful than those who sought a more "generic" comedy based on stock ideas and typical representations. Fred

Allen and his cowriters, for instance, who developed the "Town Hall" format for his shows, rarely used joke files. But the emphasis on topical and up-to-the-moment gags exacted its own price and forced its own method. Here is Allen explaining his search for source material:

> I was reading nine newspapers a day looking for subject matter for jokes, topical ideas we could use for news vignettes. . . . Walking along the street, riding in cabs or in the subway, I always had my head in a newspaper or magazine. Every few minutes I was tearing some item out of something and stuffing it into a pocket.[108]

If the joke file forced the writer to live in an arid world of abstractions, stock gags, and recycled jokes, the writer of topical jokes seemed destined to swim in a mass-mediated sea of evanescent facts, available for the current week's show and just as quickly discarded. The hopeless impermanence of topical jokes in radio led Allen to conclude that "for the first time in history the comedian has been compelled to supply himself with jokes and comedy material to compete with the machine. Whether he knows it or not, the comedian is on a treadmill to oblivion."[109]

However, for others who specialized in topical gags, which increasingly were the order of the day, the situation was not so bleak. The use of the joke file in combination with the technology of "switching" allowed the gag-writers to create new topical jokes out of the universal, timeless jokes they had collected and catalogued. As Milton Wright put it, "The humor industry today is a manufacturing industry. The manufacturing process is switching. The raw material is old jokes. The finished product is new jokes."[110] According to Sidney Reznick, writing in 1941, switching was the process of extracting "the essence of humor" from an old setting and "fooling the audience into believing that they are listening to a brand-new joke."[111] Undergirding the notion of the switch, then, was the idea of all jokes as ancient universal things combined with the idea of the uniqueness of the specific topical expression; the joke switch relied on the idea that jokes were at once abstract types subject to analytical operations, and at the same time concrete expressions of the topical moment. Switching provided a method by which the universal joke could be remade for a specific audience. It allowed for a preservation of the idea of jokes as permanent given "things" in the face of the demand for production of ever-new jokes. As Joe Laurie, Jr., put it, while arguing that all jokes are old jokes, "You don't have to know too many jokes to get by. All you do is switch."[112]

The development of analytical formulas for switching jokes began in the 1930s and reached its peak in the 1940s. In 1948, the gag-writer Art Henley published a four-volume guide to writing radio comedy, subtitled *The Mathematics of Humor*, which sought a comprehensive and exhaustive set of "mathematical" rules for producing jokes. The absurd mathematical formulas by which Henley sought to legitimate a "scientific" approach to gag-writing functioned as a kind of gloss on the true principles of production. As Henley put it, after proclaiming comedy as a "humorous system of thought" that could be "clarified" by mathematics, "YOU NEED NOT KNOW MATH TO WRITE COMEDY. THE MATH HAS BEEN DONE FOR YOU. JUST FOLLOW THE PRINCIPLES AS OUTLINED AT LENGTH."[113] One of the keys to Henley's analysis was the principle of the switch. According to him, "To Switch a gag simply means to so reshuffle and transform its various ingredients that a new gag is produced." Using a given old gag as material, "the job is to *parallel* some element of the Original: the Formula, the Form, the Subject, the Straight-Line or Punch-Line."[114] By breaking the gag down into its constituent parts and seeing each as amenable to change through a process of parallel substitution, a system could be constructed by which a single gag could generate literally thousands of "new" gags. Henley's table of twelve basic switches that could be performed on any gag was in fact such a system.

Henley went well beyond other members of his professional cohort in advocating a thorough systematization of joke production. All gag-writers of his era relied to a greater or lesser extent on principles of refining, routining, and switching, but none tried to codify those principles as rigorously as he did. In addition to the twelve basic switches, Henley sought a reduction of all jokes to three basic gag formulas (misunderstanding, about-face, satire), three gag forms (grammatical form, speech form, relative form), a host of what he called "gag form-extensions," and a formalization of joke content as the three "keys" of comedy. These "keys" he defined as "by-products of our civilization" that "either have their own INNATE HUMOROUS CONNOTATION or else strike our ear as LUDICROUS EXAGGERATIONS OF WHAT IS COMMONLY ACCEPTED AND EXPECTED." The "pass key" was the "pat" gag, or standard joke, such as a reference to buying the Brooklyn Bridge. The "skeleton key" was the prefabricated structural line, such as "He's (lower? fatter?) than a (what?) with a (what defect?)." The "master key" was a list of names or expressions "funny in themselves": meatballs, egg foo young, diaper, Archibald, Ken-L-Ration, Pikes Peak, etc.[115] Through an understanding of the constitutive elements of the joke, Henley thought it possible to turn joke production into a thoroughly rationalized process accessible to all.

The gagmen of twentieth-century professional comedy were not theorists of humor; their task, as they saw it, was to produce humor, not to define what it was or how it worked. But built into the practice of production was a set of ideas about what constituted humor, what its ontological status was, what form it should take. The practice of switching in its most developed state in the 1930s and 1940s contained a notion of humor as embedded in an essentially objective, given form but also subject to endless manipulation and reconstruction. All jokes could be judged in terms of how "funny" they were in themselves, as if they "contained" humor, but at the same time they had to be judged in terms of their ability to generate laughs. Switching allowed the gag-writer to retain the objective, given element of humor in the joke form while gearing it toward an aesthetic of taste based upon the sense of humor found in a particular audience. The idea of the switch held that every joke was different from every other joke, determined by its specific meaning to a specific audience, while also affirming the universality of jokes; it held that every joke was both new and old at the same time. The gag-writers, with their joke files and systems of production, gave credence to the notion that the joke was, as Leacock had put it, "an item of humor reduced to a single point or particle," but they also saw it as composed of interchangeable parts that could be reorganized and reworked to new purposes.

The Joke and the Sense of Humor

What, then, is the historical relationship between the joke as the objective form of humor and the idea of the sense of humor? Professional comedy writers had little to say on this matter. They, of course, saw themselves as having senses of humor and their work as attempts to appeal to the sense of humor of their audiences, but they rarely sought a definition of the sense of humor in terms of their own practice. Others, as we have seen in the previous chapter, assumed that the sense of humor was an attribute far broader than the narrow ability to laugh at a joke, that it involved an orientation toward living, perceiving, toward the self and others, which was not captured by the sphere of professional comedy. The psychologist Gordon Allport, for one, clearly rejected the world of comic joking and laughing at "things" as a "lower" form, unworthy of being connected to the sense of humor; the latter required insight and self-objectification, accomplishments that could not be realized through the mere laughing at jokes. The joke was seen as narrow, parochial, specific, "cheap," while the sense of humor was cosmic, expansive, universal. But for many others, the sense of humor could be valued as a personality attribute, with many of those qualities Allport had associated with it, while at the same time being intimately connected with the world of joking. To have a sense of humor was to "get" the joke as much as it was to objectify the self.

Nowhere was the connection between the joke and the sense of humor drawn more clearly than in the empirically oriented psychology of the 1920s and 1930s. It would be a mistake to think that the burgeoning field of academic psychology, or even that subfield which concerned itself with the analysis of personality traits and attributes, put the question of the sense of humor at the center of its research agenda. There was, in fact, relatively little attention paid to defining and debating the sense of humor in a field that was largely devoted to the development of personality tests for industrial and other applied uses.[116] But the very marginality of the psychological research on the personality trait of the sense of humor, for the purposes of cultural history, is more revealing than if that research had been controversial or of central importance. The lack of debate and criticism reveals the extent to which that research embodied a set of unquestioned assumptions about humor and the sense of humor, assumptions common within the larger culture of which academic psychology was a part. There was little need to debate what was taken for granted. The empirical research on the sense of humor as a personality trait thus provides a window through which to see the relationship between the joke and the sense of humor in twentieth-century American culture.

Beginning in the mid-1920s and continuing through the 1940s, and to some extent echoing to the present day, a series of articles and monographs attempting to measure the sense of humor and correlate it with other personality traits—most frequently intelligence—appeared in psychology journals.[117] What virtually all these analyses had in common was an assumption that not only could the sense of humor be measured and typed, but the instrument for that measurement was the joke. Even if the sense of humor was recognized as a broad-based attribute involving self perception, the operational measure of the attribute was assumed to be jokes. In the psychological literature, as in so much of everyday life, the joke was imagined as the objective correlate to the sense of humor. The sense of humor was to be measured by the response of individuals to a test composed of jokes that had been previously defined as having objective humor-status by those administering the test. The sense-of-humor tests might vary in classing jokes into instances of different types of humor (e.g. humor of superiority, humor of incongruity, humor of the unexpected, etc.), so as to measure the differences between individuals' senses of humor, but they shared an assumption that the measurement could be made, that the "objective" humor of the joke could be correlated to the "subjective" sense of humor. Only rarely did this assumption come under question, as when N. Franklin Stump, in a 1939 article, noticed that "when college students adjudge themselves with respect to humor, aesthetic and social attitudes seem to be the traits considered, to a great degree, rather than the trait which is measured by the sense of humor test." For practical purposes, Stump seemed to conclude that the subjects of his test were simply using the term "sense of humor" to describe the wrong thing, since sense of humor was, by definition, what the test measured.[118]

The measurement of the sense of humor as it was performed in these tests would have been impossible without the mass production of jokes achieved in the later nineteenth and early twentieth centuries. The similarities between the psychologist's sense-of-humor test and the gagwriter's joke file are unmistakable. In all cases, the jokes compiled and organized for the sense-of-humor tests were drawn from newspaper and magazine columns and from contemporary joke books; most were structured as dialogue jokes in the two-act vaudeville form. John C. Almack, creator of the first and most frequently used test, appropriately titled the Almack Sense of Humor Test, collected 9,000 jokes published over the span of six years. He then categorized his collection by subject, just as the gag-writers did with their files. The inherent "funniness" of a subject, according to Almack's logic, was dependent upon the quantity of jokes in his collection that fell under that heading. From the 9,000, Almack randomly selected 200 jokes to construct two test forms of 100 jokes each. The test jokes were then rated for their humor value by "a small number of competent judges"; the tests were scored by the degree to which respondents agreed with each joke's "true" humor value, as defined by the experts. The answers that agreed with the judges' rating were deemed correct; those that disagreed, incorrect. If the gag-writers tested their routines on live audiences to see whether they "worked," and made adjustments accordingly, Almack preferred to trust the authority of his "competent judges" to define the humor value of his jokes, and to measure the sense of humor of his "audience" by the yardstick of a supposed "objective" value. The entire process of test construction and administration paralleled the processes of commercial comedy—from the collection of previously published jokes to the testing of audience reaction.[119]

The Almack Sense of Humor Test, and those tests that followed it, occupy a deservedly obscure corner in the history of psychological testing. Modeled on the intelligence tests and personality inventories that were so ubiquitous in twentieth-century applied psychology, they nevertheless failed to become widespread or employed in the standard situations of their more prominent relatives. That there were those who sought to measure the sense of humor by empirical means should not strike us as altogether absurd or strange; after all, there are many in the twentieth century who believe that all things can, and should, be measured. If we believe, as we commonly express in language, that some people have a sense of humor and others lack one, that some people have a "better" sense of humor than others, why should it appear odd that, in a scientistic culture, there would be those who would seek to quantify such differences? That the attempts to do so never achieved the wide-ranging success of intelligence testing speaks more of the lack of a perceived application of sense-of-humor tests to the corporate workplace than it does to the inherent inability of such tests to measure what they proclaimed to measure.

The two main assumptions underlying the sense-of-humor tests were that the sense of humor was a passive or consumer attribute, and that the "things" consumed by it were jokes. The notion of humor as a way of seeing, as a kind of perspective, manifested itself in the idea that the sense of humor was primarily a passive trait—although, as we have seen, passivity could be elevated to the level of activity, just as consuming could be viewed as a form of production. From the eighteenth century forward, with the construction of faculties of taste and sensibility as parts of the human makeup, the capacity for seeing, rather than doing, came to dominate the understanding of personhood. The sense-of-humor tests of Almack and his colleagues followed this underlying logic of personhood: what they sought to measure was a capacity for seeing humor, rather than a capacity for creating it. Their tests could be "objective" because they measured the individual sense of humor against a common set of consumer goods, rather than against the individual's ability to produce humor. Those "consumer goods" were, of course, the jokes that made up the substance of the tests. Instead of asking the test respondents to evaluate, for instance, the humor of social situations in which they found themselves, or the incongruity of the self in relation to others, the creators of the tests made the sense of humor into a capacity for seeing the point of jokes. The link between the joke and the sense of humor was so obvious and apparent to those who devised such tests that they never imagined an alternative way to measure the sense of humor. The joke was humor in its objective form; the sense of humor was the capacity of the individual to "get" the joke. The relationship between the two was thus the relationship between the consumer and the goods he or she consumes.

The development of the commodity form of the joke from the 1870s forward constituted a fundamental ambiguity in the relationship between the objective and subjective meanings of humor. The idea of the sense of humor had rooted humor in the ability of the subject to be objective, in the idea that the value of the self lay in its capacity to see from a perspective outside the self. The idea of the joke, conversely, lay in a notion that humor had a purely objective form, free from the particularity of the persons who created it, possessing a universal existence as an elemental structure. Jokes were subject to endless manipulation and reconstruction because they were objective "material" rather than the fanciful ephemera of minds bound by time and place. Yet the ultimate judge of the joke had to be the sense of humor; as "Senator" Ford, the radio comedian, said in 1944, "a joke is something that's laughed at. If nobody laughs, it's no joke." According to Ford, the problems of early radio comedy stemmed from the fact that "we worked only to a microphone, and no one has yet invented a microphone with a sense of humor."[120] In other words, as much as the professional comedy writers of the later nineteenth and twentieth centuries sought to free the joke from its multiple contexts and make it objective, in the final analysis it was not the sense of humor that was judged by how it aligned itself with the objectively funny joke, but the opposite. A joke was only as good as its capacity to appeal to the senses of humor of its audience members; it was an item of exchange that would succeed or fail in the marketplace.

Just as the sense of humor pushed the self into an "objective attitude," so the "objective" humor of the joke was pulled back into a standard defined by the subjective reaction of an audience.

This strange relationship between object and subject, product and consumer, joke and the sense of humor, was characteristic of the larger antinomies present in twentieth-century American culture. Perhaps the final word should be given to Art Henley, whose fervent belief in the objectivity of jokes led him to devise a system of mathematics for joke construction:

> Knowing the inner workings of a joke will in no way impair your sense of humor. On the contrary, your *perception* of the fun around you in everyday real-life situations will greatly increase. You will achieve an *awareness of humor* never known before and be able to make up your own gags, comedy situations and characters to financial and social advantage. *Your own personality* will dictate your own particular style of humor so that whether you are a man, or a woman, a youngster or an adult, well-schooled or untutored, you will find your place in the sun of comedy![121]

It is all here: the exploration and manipulation of the objective workings of the joke tied to the expansion of the sense of humor as a way of perceiving the world; the elevation of "everyday real-life situations" as a forum for the sense of humor; the linking of commercial benefits of joke production to social awareness; the idea of the sense of humor as both a component of the unique individual personality and an instrument of democracy shared by all. For Henley, to analyze the joke as an object is literally to increase the capacity of the sense of humor as a faculty of perception. By the time Henley wrote this passage in the late 1940s, almost all barriers to the valorization of the sense of humor in American institutional life had fallen, as we will see in the next chapter. The practice of joking and the idea of the joke, inseparable as they were, were part of the changes that helped make the sense of humor not only an attribute of the abstract individual, but also newly acceptable in spheres of American life as diverse as religion, politics, and education.

FIVE

The Humorous
and the Serious

In the late 1980s, an ambitious work in the sociology of humor suggested that everyday action in advanced industrial societies is divided into two related but opposed modes: the serious and the humorous. According to Michael Mulkay's *On Humor*, the serious mode is characterized by action —and, more specifically, language—meaning what it says; by accepting a set of commonly held conventions about the singular nature of the world, the social actor in the serious mode expects those conventions to render the intent and meaning of his actions transparent to others. We are serious when we mean what we say. The humorous mode, on the other hand, calls into question the assumptions of the social world as held in the serious mode; it allows the social actor to say and mean things that cannot be said in the serious mode. For instance, it allows for a kind of "plausible deniability," to borrow the language of the national security state, with regard to the intentions of the actor. The familiar phrases "I didn't mean anything by it," "I was only kidding," "Can't you take a joke?" and "Where's your sense of humor?" are statements in the serious mode referring to the different rules of interpretation characteristic of the humorous mode. The serious mode is characterized by singularity and consistency of meaning, by a unified view of the world free of ambiguity and contradiction. The humorous mode is its obverse, and necessary to sustain it; this is a world where meanings are multiple and incongruous—where the strictures of the serious no longer obtain—and by providing relief from those strictures, humor permits the fictive world of the serious to exist. Without humor, the ambiguity and multiplicity of existence would intrude upon and undermine any attempt at unitary action in the realm of the serious; without the serious mode, the world would be so fragmented and confused as to make meaningful action impossible. For Mulkay, then, the humorous and the serious are opposed realms of action, but absolutely necessary to each other.[1]

What is so compelling about Mulkay's analysis is that it partakes on an analytical level of an opposition that is widely recognized in everyday speech. We regularly say and hear that someone with a sense of humor doesn't take himself too seriously, that a joke is not to be taken seriously, that being humorous and being serious are two recognizably different things. The opposition between the humorous and the serious, then, is not simply the analytical tool of the sociologist, but one of the familiar ways in which our culture organizes meaning. Mulkay's analysis does not stand outside the social world, looking in—the preferred stance of the social scientist—but, in fact, reproduces the terms by which that social world organizes itself. And while Mulkay clearly limits his analysis to what he calls "advanced industrial societies," those of the United States and Britain during the past thirty years in particular, he gives no particular reason why such societies should be uniquely suited to the opposition of humorous and serious modes. Because his analysis of the two modes is based largely in a micro-sociological framework of interactionism, conversational analysis, and dramaturgy, with the focus on meaning and intent of social actors in circumscribed situations, the approach he adopts is largely silent about what distinguishes the situated action of advanced industrial societies from that of others. When Mulkay moves to a larger analysis of humor and social structure, his intent changes; following Mary Douglas, he seeks "a universal formulation of the connection between humor and social structure," not the role of humor in a specific kind of society.[2] The specificity of Mulkay's analysis to "advanced industrial societies," then, seems more a matter of convenience based on the source of his empirical materials than on any historical, theoretical, or comparative understanding. The de facto result of *On Humor* is a universalization of the opposition between the serious and the humorous to "society" in the abstract, hence to all particular societies.

What is necessary to counter that universalization is a historicization of the humorous/serious distinction as a pair of opposed categories within modern Anglo-American culture. Like the idea of the sense of humor, the modern opposition between the serious and the humorous was largely a creation of the nineteenth century; it was an attempt to preserve a "humor-free zone" of meaning and experience in the face of the localization of the sense of humor in the self. But it also represented a reproduction of other forms of nineteenth- and twentieth-century thought: the psychology and physiology of tension and release that envisioned the person as a relationship between a contractive and an expansive mode of being; the invidious distinction between a sacralized high culture of moral earnestness and gentility and the comic forms of a "popular" culture; the sharp division between work and leisure as separate spheres of activity in industrial society.

But like the work/leisure distinction, the humorous/serious opposition was unstable. Those spheres that the nineteenth century marked as "serious" were repeatedly subject to incursions by humor and laughter, even more so as the idea of humor absorbed the bourgeois values of sympathy, benevolence, and democratic universalism that made it less threatening. We still recognize the humorous/serious distinction as a normative guide in everyday life, holding that there are times, places, and situations in which humor and laughter are inappropriate. For contemporary Americans, however, this understanding is more a matter of tactful navigation between the serious and the humorous in terms of "situations" than it is the outright banishment of humor from spheres of social life deemed serious. For mid-Victorians, on the other hand, just as they valued the sense of humor as a necessary attribute of the individual, and saw benevolent humor as a welcome boon to sociality, they also attempted to carve out a sphere of social life marked "no joking." In this, as the history of the twentieth century reveals, they were largely unsuccessful: politics, religion, and education—the halls of state, the church, the classroom—all fell to the sense of humor. The "higher things" of the Victorian genteel imagination, it was discovered, could not be harmed by a sense of humor. In fact, humor served only to reinvigorate and reaffirm their essential seriousness. The history of the humorous/serious distinction, then, is the history of how the sense of humor became not only an acceptable personality trait in spheres where it was once barred but became indispensable to the very navigation between the humorous and the serious in *all* areas of social life.

Once again, the history of laughter is instructive as a guide to the shifting meaning of humor. Central to the modern distinction between the humorous and the serious was a new understanding of the meaning of laughter. The tension/release model of human energy expenditure that became widespread in the nineteenth century provided the basis for a new conception of laughter as a form of relief. The understanding of humor and seriousness as opposed but complementary modes or attitudes was supported by the notion that the laughter raised by humor could represent a form of release of the tension and stress produced by seriousness. The humorous/serious distinction was thus grounded not only in a new view of laughter but in a new view of the person as a kind of hydraulic machine capable of producing, storing, and releasing energy.

In an earlier chapter, I suggested a pattern for the historical understanding of laughter, a pattern characterized by a shift from an object-oriented conception of the risible to a conception of laughter centered on creative mental processes. The prevalence of incongruity in the modern conception of laughter represented an intellectualization of the source of laughter, a locating of laughter-inducing processes in the mind. At the same time, that intellectualization took place in a bourgeois culture of sense and sentiment where immediate intuitive judgment provided a new emotional depth for laughter. The emergence of the modern definition of humor hung on the relationship between the intellectual and the emotional; it involved a *sympathetic* appreciation of the incongruous. Humor, by the late nineteenth century, had given its meaning to the whole realm of laughter; it linked intellect to emotion, ideas to sentiment, in a new configuration of the relation between the interiority of the individual and the exterior social world. But this is not all there is to say about the modern history of laughter.

Contemporary philosophers, psychologists, and theorists of humor and laughter have divided "theories" of laughter into three groups: superiority, incongruity, and what they call "relief" theories.[3] Relief theories, however, are not historically separable from incongruity theories. In fact, the notion of laughter as based in relief is often coupled with a notion of incongruity in nineteenth-century discussions of laughter. The modern emergence of the idea of "comic relief" represents an extension of the principle of incongruity and its intellectualist foundation to the physical and emotional act of laughter. More important, by constructing laughter as an outcome of a process of tension and release—intellectual, emotional, and physical—the idea of comic relief provided a basis for the humorous/serious distinction. If tension was created in the realm of the serious, it could be released by laughter in the realm of the humorous; there could be no laughter without preceding tension, no punch line without a straight line, nothing humorous without the serious.

The connection between incongruity and relief as explanations of laughter can be seen as early as the eighteenth century, just as incongruity was becoming the generally accepted mode of understanding. Kant, for instance, is generally credited with the development of an incongruity theory of laughter, usually summarized in his pithy statement that "laughter is an affectation arising from the sudden transformation of a strained expectation into nothing." But already the notion of a "strained expectation" suggests the tension that is to be released with its transformation into "nothing." Further, Kant is concerned with the physical act of laughter and its relation to the mental process by which an idea that appears to represent *something* is suddenly transformed into its opposite —*nothing*. The "rapidly alternating tension and relaxation" of the mind, said Kant, corresponds to "an alternating tension and relaxation of the elastic portions of our intestines which communicates itself to the diaphragm."[4] The result is the physical act we describe as laughter. The attempt to provide an explanation that links incongruous mental representation to the natural physical act of laughter—that is, to answer the question why laughter, rather than any other physical action, should be the reaction to incongruity—leads to a notion of the release of tension as a parallel process of mind and body. In this, Kant would anticipate those whom the twentieth century has marked more properly as "relief theorists": Herbert Spencer, John Dewey, Sigmund Freud. Kant lacked a mechanism beyond a general notion of correspondence between bodily and mental states that would link the physical act of laughter to the perception of incongruity, but he clearly saw these mental and physical events as consequences of tension and relief, strain and relaxation.

Spencer, on the other hand, is generally credited with being one of the originators of the relief theory. And yet, like Kant, he offers a version of laughter based on incongruity. Unlike Kant, however, Spencer linked laughter to a mechanism by which that incongruity is translated into bodily action. Spencer's variation on incongruity theory is founded on a distinction between those incongruities that result in laughter and those that do not. The former he refers to as "descending incongruities"; that is to say, "laughter naturally results only when consciousness is unawares transferred from great things to small."[5] If Kant saw laughter arising from the transformation of something into nothing, for Spencer laughter was the transformation of something large, momentous, or important into something small, frivolous, or insignificant. For the absolute categories of "something" and "nothing," he substituted a relative scale of declining values. This notion of a shift from big to small, of course, is very much in line with the twentieth-century notion of the sense of humor as an alternately contractive and expansive personality trait. The intellectual shift in perception from large to small was akin to the "sense of proportion" that many in the twentieth century associated with humor.

What distinguishes Spencer's theory, and the relief theories that were to follow it, from the general understanding of laughter as rooted in incongruity is the idea that incongruity is an insufficient explanation. On the one hand, it does not cover all cases of laughter, excluding those such as nervous laughter and laughter provoked by tickling; on the other, it provides no reason why incongruity should produce the physical act of laughter. The idea of relief as fundamental to the process of laughter emerged, then, not so much in opposition to a static "incongruity theory," but as an elaboration of the conditions under which the perception of incongruity was translated into laughter. There was no doubt about the compatibility of "relief" and "incongruity" in Spencer's account of laughter. The principle of incongruity was integrated into an explanation of a different order, an order that sought a unified conception of body and mind.

While there had already been attempts in early modern Europe to describe the physiology of laughter, most notably by Laurent Joubert and René Descartes, it was not until the mid- to late nineteenth century that the idea of laughter as a physiological event was seen as organically tied to the mental and emotional "causes" of laughter.[6] Prior to that, it had appeared sufficient to describe the quality and character of the instances that provoked laughter without recourse to any organic mechanism that would account for the quality and character of laughter itself. The physical act of laughter was a kind of naturally accepted or given phenomenon, subject to explanation not in physiological terms, but in terms of the objects (and, later, the mental conceptions) that accompanied it. The translation of "incongruity" into "relief" occurred in a context in which the person was imagined as possessing a greater subjectivity or interiority, on the one hand, but was seen also as a unified psychological and physiological entity, on the other. In this context, any explanation of laughter would have to account for the physical act itself in terms of the mental processes and emotional states that gave rise to it. In the last decades of the nineteenth century, the James-Lange theory of emotions would reverse the process of explanation, attempting to account for the emotion of mirth by making it an awareness or consequence of the physical act of laughter.[7] It shared with other nineteenth-century explanations, such as Spencer's, however, the idea that any explanation of laughter would have to unify intellectual perception, emotional state, and physical action; no longer was it sufficient to describe the causes of laughter in purely perceptual terms.

What made integration of the intellectual, emotional, and physical aspects of laughter possible was the idea of psycho-physical energy. The body was imagined as a kind of industrial factory and storehouse of nervous energy, a site in which such energy was produced, contained, and released. Energy produced in the emotional realm, through a buildup of tension based upon perceptions that demanded an emotional readiness, could be released in the physical realm through bodily action. Energy could be expended in emotion as well as in physical action, or could be stored in preparation for situations that demanded its release. Once activated, however, stored energy demanded a pathway for its release; if not spent in emotional effort for which it had been prepared, energy found its outlet in physical action. The idea of energy thus provided for a commensurability of physical and emotional being, a common ground in which the physical and emotional could be translated into each other.

According to Spencer, what distinguished laughter from other forms of physical activity was the fact that it was activity with no purpose. The release of energy normally fulfilled some kind of biological function or purposeful end related to its cause; the energy produced by sexual arousal, for instance, was normally directed to its expenditure in sexual activity. For Spencer, "the movements of chest and limbs which we make when laughing have no object," but are the "results of an uncontrolled discharge of energy."[8] The reason that descending incongruity produced laughter was that the emotional energy produced by the perception of something invested with great significance was left with nowhere to go when that great thing was suddenly reduced to something smaller. Laughter was thus a spillway for energy no longer required for its original purpose. It was a mechanism for the release of tension, a kind of waste product of overproduction necessary to keep the nervous system functioning.

Although Spencer's theory of laughter has become fixed as one of the primary examples of a "relief theory," in some ways it is more appropriate to think of it as a "release theory" of laughter. Indeed, Spencer rejected the notion that "laughter is a result of the pleasure we take in escaping from the restraint of grave feelings" as an insufficient explanation, pointing to instances of laughter that arise in situations from which no relief could be desired.[9] While *relief*, as a conscious pleasurable feeling, was present in much laughter, it was so because it fell under the more general phenomenon of the *release* of energy common to all laughter. The line Spencer drew between release as a physiological event and the feeling of relief as a psychological event, based on the dispelling of specifically painful tensions, was blurred in the larger cultural appropriation of the idea of tension and discharged energy. Release and relief came to be understood as equivalents; both represented liberation from restraint, outlets for tension and stress that had become unbearable and needed to be defused.

For John Dewey, writing in 1895, the distinction between release and relief had disappeared. "The laugh," said Dewey, "is thus a phenomenon of the same general kind as the sigh of relief."[10] Dewey's understanding of laughter based on relief was also undergirded by the prevalence of the commodity form of the joke in the 1890s. If the sigh of relief "occurs when the interest is in the *process*," the laugh "occurs when the interest is all in the outcome, the result—the sudden abrupt appearance of the 'point.' "

> Now all expectancy, waiting, suspended effort, etc., is accompanied for obvious teleological reasons, with taking in and holding a full breath, and the maintenance of the whole muscular system in a state of considerable tension. . . . Now let the end suddenly "break," "dawn," let one see the "point" and this energy discharges—the getting the point is the unity, the discharge. This sudden relaxation of strain, so far as occurring through the medium of the breathing and vocal apparatus, is laughter.[11]

The "point," that fundamental element of the joke, was thus linked to the discharge of energy as not simply release, but as relief. One can see in Dewey's account the way in which the joke would become the foundation of "comic relief," both in dramatic representation and everyday life.

The notion of relief as the basis of the physiological act of laughter became standard in early twentieth-century explanations of laughter, just as the term "comic relief" became widespread in American culture. According to Boris Sidis's *Psychology of Laughter*, "any release of reserve energy is the source of all laughter."[12] *The Nature of Laughter*, by J. C. Gregory, found relief to be the "ground plan" of all laughter.[13] In 1915 Sylvia Bliss advocated a psychoanalytical theory, similar to Freud's, in which laughter is based on "suddenly released repression," and she saw such release as a specific form of "relief from strain."[14] G. Stanley Hall and Arthur Allin's 1897 survey of the symptomatology of laughter found respondents reporting laughter in terms of the need to expend energy and find relief from strain.[15] Even in accounts that were not specifically designed as "relief" theories of laughter, the understanding of laughter as an act of release and relief became common. A latter-day "superiority theory" such as Henri Bergson's, for instance, was preoccupied with notions of "tension," "rigidity," and their correction through the "elasticity" of relief as an adaptive mechanism.[16]

In fact, historically, the notion of relief from tension as a function of laughter in the broader culture preceded the elaboration of explicit "theories" of relief such as Spencer's and Dewey's. In the 1840s, just as the term "sense of humor" was being born, and as the concept of humor was becoming inextricably bound up with laughter, the idea of humor as a relief mechanism was articulated in popular discussions of laughter. According to H. T. Tuckerman, writing in *Godey's Lady's Book* in 1849, "Humor is doubtless intended as the safety-valve of concentrative minds," for "we need a sense of the ridiculous, a playful fancy, a capacity of abandon, to help us lighten the burden of care, to recreate the weary mind."[17] This notion of humor as a "safety-valve" was echoed through the nineteenth century down into our own day. William Mathews used the term "safety-valve" to refer to humor in the 1880s; the psychiatrist Milton Harrington called laughter and mirth "the safety valve of the nervous system" in 1938; C. H. Scherf, head of the social studies department at a high school in Montana, advised in 1948 that "humor is more than enjoyment; it is one of our best safety valves."[18] Dozens of instances of such usage could be cited. Like the notion of the sense of humor as a "balance wheel," the idea that humor and its accompaniment by laughter was a "safety valve" was based on a model of personhood in which compensation or correction was needed to right the disturbing effects of mental effort concentrated entirely in one direction. Relief, rest, recreation allowed the serious person to achieve an equilibrium through the venting of energy, thus preventing a dangerous concentration that would undermine the serious action and goals which produced that concentrated pressure.[19] The idea of humor as a safety valve shared with the relief theories of Spencer, Dewey, and Freud an opposition between the tension of serious action and the relief of humor and laughter, and saw the two realms as necessary to each other.

The relation between the pressures of serious action and the relief of humor was formulated in the context of a society in which work was increasingly organized along bureaucratic lines, and in which leisure was increasingly seen as a realm distinct from work, but necessary to it as a compensatory sphere of action. The reorganization of industrial work in the nineteenth century involved a new emphasis on time discipline and a destruction of traditional forms of integrated work and leisure activities under worker control. The usurpation of worker control by new strata of industrial management shifted leisure into distinct realms of time and space, apart from the hours of work and the shop floor in which such activity had previously taken place. The regimentation of work under industrial capitalism marked it as a sphere of tightly controlled, goal-oriented, and highly organized activity; the leisure of off-hours, the "eight hours for what we will" in the rallying cry of the eight-hour-day movement, was offered as an obverse image of such work, a world of organized play to compensate for the new industrial discipline. In leisure, the worker could find rest and relaxation, relief from the clock and the watchful eye of management, recreation so that he might return to work the next day, efficient, productive, and ready to submit to the industrial process.[20]

The general emergence of bureaucratic forms in nineteenth-century industrial society meant that the split between work and leisure was not limited to the lives of the industrial working class. Even if the work of the professionals and managers who composed the growing new middle class seemed to be justified as an end in itself, requiring no external compensation, the bureaucratic discipline of such work and its official "serious" nature demanded that leisure be abstracted from work. The work/leisure distinction was thus articulated throughout the social order as part of the general ideology of an emergent bureaucratic and corporate capitalism.[21]

The idea of humor and laughter as a form of relief related to amusement and play was part and parcel of this ideological articulation.[22] If the realm of work was construed as serious, it was also seen as a sphere in which tension and pressure were paramount; such tensions could be relieved through amusement and laughter. William Mathews, for one, gave clear voice to the idea that the relief of humor was intimately related to the conditions of work in late nineteenth-century society:

> In this closing quarter of the nineteenth century, pregnant with many cares, and heavy with questions that it cannot answer; when competition is keen, and men live and work at high pressure; when the stress and intensity of life age a man before his time; when so many of the noblest break down in harness hardly half way to the goal,—the beneficient agency of wit and humor is specially needed. . . . In such an age the need not only of bodily rest, but of recreation, of some amusement that shall divert and relieve the mind, is evident, and what better antidote to melancholy and 'low-thoughted care' can be provided than that which wit and humor—those safety-valves of concentrative minds—so happily supply?[23]

Similarly, Benjamin Franklin Clark, a New England Congregationalist, argued that the nature of specific kinds of work demanded a compensation in the relief of laughter. "While mirthfulness is part of our nature," said Clark in 1870, "its exercise is peculiarly profitable to persons heavily taxed with responsible cares and wearing labor." Among those whom Clark saw as benefiting from the relief offered by laughter were businessmen, legislators, lawyers, physicians, clergymen, and members of "the learned professions."[24] The nature of professional work, with its seriousness, its responsibilities, and its pressures, seemed to call for the relief of laughter, not as a way to undermine seriousness or responsibility, but as a way to restore them.

The connection of the tension/relief model of humor and laughter with the separation of work and leisure in modern industrial society was given additional importance in the twentieth century. J. C. Gregory, for instance, explicitly connected the growth of humor in modern societies to the emergence of a "civilization of leisure." Because humor was founded on relief, according to Gregory, it was most prominent in those societies in which the relief from work and necessity was widely diffused and institutionalized in leisure.[25] For Boris Sidis, it was the commercial forms of leisure—"the games, the theaters with their comic plays, places of amusement, clubs with their mirth, jokes, jest and anecdotes"—that provided momentary freedom and relief for "many a worker whose occupation is either monotonous or full of earnestness, of seriousness, effort and concentration of attention."[26] For G. T. W. Patrick, writing in 1916, laughter was "associated with our periods of relaxation, with our hours or moments of release from the burdens of daily life. It serves as a rest and a corrective. It is a relief from strain and tension. It is universally associated with play, and is the accompaniment of the relaxation of sports and pastimes, of feasting, drinking, and banqueting." In Patrick's view, laughter was a form of release from "the ever-present repressive forms of society," from "the constant galling grip of social claims."[27] The more "society" was imagined as a bureaucratic, regimented order external to the individual, the more laughter was seen as a functional mechanism of release from the strains created by that order.

Laughter and humor were thus not only associated with a generalized notion of "relief," but were linked to a host of terms used to characterize the sphere of leisure, terms such as those listed by H. A. Overstreet: "playfulness, freedom, creative spontaneity."[28] The idea of humor as a form of play, opposed to both work and seriousness, became common in the first half of the twentieth century. In 1936, Max Eastman constructed a theory based entirely on the notion that all laughter was a form of play, having no other ends than those of play itself. Recovering the "ludic" element in the ludicrous, a notion that shared much with Johan Huizinga's understanding of play as a discrete realm of activity opposed to seriousness, Eastman sought to dispense with all functionalist accounts of laughter. According to Eastman, the problem with all previous accounts of laughter was that "they take humor seriously. They try to explain it, I mean, and show what its value is, as a part of serious life. Humor is play. . . . It has no general value except the values possessed by play."[29] According to J. Y. T. Greig, "It is clear that the connection between laughter and play is very close." The proof, said Greig, lies in everyday language: "we all make use somewhat indiscriminately of words like 'amusement,' 'prank,' 'frolic,' 'fun,' 'sport,' 'joke,' and so on, leaving it to the context to determine whether they refer to play as such, or to the laughter that is supposed to accompany the play."[30]

Like the idea of laughter and humor as play, the notion of laughter as an act of freedom was closely bound up with the oppositions between work and leisure, tension and relief. For instance, L. W. Kline in 1907 noted that humor, if not identical with play, shared with play the sense of freedom. The relief that comes with humor represents a breaking through the "surface tension" of a "structure of consciousness become toughened, cramped and tense," into a realm of free and spontaneous action. Humor, said Kline,

> perverts and breaks up the mechanism and order about us. It appears as the only objective fact in our experience that dares to defy the world order with impunity, that can violate ruthlessly, without pain and without apology, the manifold human contrivances, social customs and relationships and thereby not only creates the sense of freedom, but also assures us that we may temporarily escape from the uniformities and mechanisms of life. . . . The humor stimulus gives glimpses of the world of uncertainties, of spontaneities and of life, and in so doing creates the sense of freedom of which the sense of humor is the obverse side.[31]

The connection between humor and freedom goes back to the later seventeenth century, when English liberty was offered as an explanation for the preponderance of the eccentric characters associated with the idea of humor. One of the major differences in the early twentieth-century configuration of humor and freedom was that freedom was now imagined not only as a state of political and economic being, but as a mode of psychological escape. The freedom of humor was opposed not simply to tyranny and despotism, but to the very mechanized rigidity of social life, from which it offered a temporary refuge. Society, all-external and coercive as it was imagined, created tensions by the demands it made on the natural psychological self; the self sought freedom from rigidity, and found it (if only as a brief respite) in play, in leisure, in humor.

This notion of laughter as an escape from restraint, as an act of freedom in the face of a constrictive social order, continues to our day, most prominently in the work of corporate humor consultants who advocate laughter as a means of reducing stress in the bureaucratic workplace.[32] But this idea, with its psychoanalytic overtones, infuses a much broader realm of discourse on laughter as well. A recent work of cultural history, for instance, reproduces the distinction between a coercive social order and the release of laughter, and applies that distinction to the Victorian society in which it was first created. According to the historian John Kasson, the etiquette books of the nineteenth century almost universally advocated restrictions on laughter. He concludes that this cultural "repression" of laughter and joking, by refusing any outward relaxation, "drove the tensions back within the individual self, providing ritual support for the psychological mechanisms of repression, displacement, and denial necessary to cope with the anxieties of the urban capitalist order."[33] In other words, laughter represents a release of tension, while the mannered "control" or "repression" of laughter represents an accommodation to a rigid social order. In interpreting the advice of Victorian writers through the lens of a tension/release model of laughter, Kasson reads Victorian culture as a repressive set of restrictions on the natural expression of the self. Just as in the popular understanding of Victorianism as "repressive" in regard to sexuality and sexual expression, the notion of Victorianism as a creed opposed to laughter partakes of a worldview that was constructed by the Victorians themselves. Michel Foucault has argued that "sexuality" was not so much repressed in Victorian society as it was constructed by discursive means;[34] in the same way, the notion of laughter as release from constrictive tensions is more a substantive part of late nineteenth-century culture than it is an adequate analytical explanation for the way laughter was regarded by those who would police manners in that society.

The dominant views of the nineteenth and early twentieth centuries were in no way opposed to humor and laughter. It is only the stereotypical image of the Victorian as a rigid, tightly controlled, pleasure-denying person, thoroughly imbued with the values of genteel earnestness, that would lead us to think that was the case, particularly if we share with Victorians the belief that laughter is antithetical to precisely those values invoked in the stereotype. But the Victorians who invented the sense of humor, who came to value it as a necessary personality attribute, who infused laughter and humor with the values of sympathetic benevolence and democratic universality, who believed that laughter could be "with" others and not just "at" them, can hardly be characterized as possessing antilaughter views.[35] To the extent that they saw laughter as a danger or a problem, their trepidation was far more limited than that of their seventeenth- and eighteenth-century predecessors, many of whom viewed laughter as a threat to the entire fabric of deference and authority, not to mention religious truth, upon which social order was founded. It was the medieval aristocratic ethos of antilaughter, the Puritan banishment of comedy, Hobbes's overwhelmingly negative view of laughter, and the eighteenth-century reaction to the notion of ridicule as the "test of truth" that were antipathetic to laughter, not the Victorian conversion of laughter into a benign realm of sympathy and sentiment, relief and release. As the eminently Victorian Caroline Kirkland wrote in 1853, "We have no patience with those who despise mirth as mirth."[36]

The etiquette books of the nineteenth century did indeed advocate restrictions on laughter, as Kasson has argued, but those restrictions were neither absolute nor tending toward a generalized conception of laughter as ill-mannered. Rather, they were based on a notion that laughter was inappropriate in specific realms of behavior and thoroughly appropriate in others, a view that lined up both with the tension/release model of laughter and with its articulation of the serious/humorous distinction. The one arena in which virtually all etiquette advisers forbade laughter was in public, on the street, among strangers. "Loud and boisterous conversation or laughter and all undue liveliness are improper in public" —so went the typical admonition.[37] But the problem of laughter in public was based more on a notion that it was improper to call attention to oneself among strangers, as loud laughter might do, than on any idea that what laughter expressed was in itself threatening or "vulgar"; above all, it was loud and indiscreet laughter at which the guardians of propriety looked askance, while they advocated a "refined" and inconspicuous laughter. Part of the intent in this advice was to provide a distinction between the laughter of the untutored "mob" and the behavior of the members of genteel society, but most nineteenth-century advisers sanctioned laughter, of the right kind and at the right time, for the latter class of persons. As one adviser wrote in 1882, "Broad laughter, welling up from a heart that is full of happiness, is as contagious as the sunshine and as refreshing; but this is heard more frequently in the home than in society, where stoicism is regarded as an essential of good-breeding."[38] Here we have both the high valuation of laughter as a form of expression and a recognition of the spheres in which such expression was deemed permissible and impermissible.

If laughter had its time and place, the dominant Victorian creed held that one place, above all others, must be held free from laughter. The sphere of religion, the sacred, and the space of the church, were all imbued with a seriousness that labeled laughter as an unacceptable intrusion. Laughter in church was considered not only a breach of etiquette but "highly improper."[39] Margaret Sangster, an early twentieth-century etiquette adviser, suggested that her readers avoid laughter not only while in church, but before and after the service so as "not to dissipate

the impression of the sacred service by silly laughter and jesting."[40]
Even as a prominent religious figure like Henry Ward Beecher was
introducing humor into the pulpit, and as liberal Protestantism was proclaiming Christianity a "happy religion," the pull of the sacred as an
ideal realm led many to conclude that laughter, whatever else its place,
did not belong in church. "We may thank God for humor," said one
author in 1867, but we must recognize that "there is a sphere into which
it may not intrude."[41] This view lingers into the present, although it is
no longer dominant as it once was. As late as the 1930s, Stephen Leacock
could proclaim that "if things are sacred we do not make fun of them. . . .
There is a province marked off as 'unjokeable': to intrude on it only
brings humor into disrepute, especially with people inclined in any case
to think it disreputable."[42] Under Victorianism, in the main, the distinction between laughter and solemnity, humor and seriousness, was given
additional dimension in the distinction between the profane and the
sacred.

What, then, does the idea of laughter as a form of release or relief,
formulated in the mid-nineteenth century and continuing to the present
day, have to do with the normative evaluation of laughter, the sense of its
propriety or impropriety, the restrictions placed upon it and the avenues
opened to it? Although the issue is complex, broadly we may say that it
was part of the redrawing of boundaries that allowed Victorians to value
humor and laughter in practice, while preventing the principle of incongruity associated with laughter from undermining the host of other values identified with Victorianism. The cluster of terms associated with the
distinction between the humorous and the serious in the late nineteenth
century reads as a kind of index to the concerns of the age. On the
one side: work, order, control, discipline, moral earnestness, stability,
gentility, a unified vision of the world. On the other: play, leisure, relaxation, freedom from restraint, recreation, perspective, the multiplicity of
an incongruous world. Instead of seeing the two sets of values historically
opposed in a transition from a nineteenth-century "culture of production" to a twentieth-century "culture of consumption," it makes sense to
see them as related values, given objective form, within Victorian culture
itself. The idea of the sense of humor as a "safety valve," and of laughter
as a form of relief from tension, allowed for a simultaneous valuation of
the serious world of work, order, and discipline and the humorous world
of play, freedom, and relaxation. Laughter could give vent to the supposed tensions accumulated in the sphere of the serious without un-

dermining those things that were to be regarded as serious; humor could occupy its own sphere, where it would do no harm to those matters that were not subject to laughter. The humorous and the serious could coexist, the one providing relief from the sometimes onerous and strenuous burdens of the other.

The Cult of the Sense of Humor and Its Critics

It is in the context of the distinction between the humorous and the serious that we must see the late Victorian critique of what Horace Kallen called "the cult of the sense of humor," or what Elizabeth Woodbridge referred to as "the humor-fetish."[43] Between 1890 and 1920, in the twilight of the genteel ethos of the nineteenth-century "cultivated classes," some observers targeted not the sense of humor itself, but what they saw as the inordinate importance attached to it. In fact, no one challenged the sense of humor as a valued personality attribute or advocated a world from which humor was to be banished; upon the existence and value of the sense of humor, there was a general consensus. What troubled a small band of critics was the elevation of the sense of humor to a value above all others. Such an elevation threatened the carefully constructed separation of spheres. The general valuation of the sense of humor, the ubiquity of laughter and joking in social life, even the use of humor as a means of relieving tension, seemed to undermine the sanctity of work, religion, marriage, high art, and other matters deemed serious. The sense of humor threatened to spill over the border separating the humorous from the serious, thereby casting important values and relationships in a light that was playful, incongruous, amusing. The critics sought to reaffirm the separation of the humorous and the serious, not by criticizing the sense of humor per se, but by holding it in a lower place on the scale of values. In proclaiming their commitment to an ethic of balance and proportion, however, they stressed the importance and value of the sense of humor as an attribute of the well-balanced, normal person.

The critics of the sense of humor, in fact, were at pains to show that they too appreciated humor and saw it as an invaluable and moderating aspect of social existence. "I beg my readers not to suppose that I would arraign humor or any element which gladdens and brightens existence," said the anonymous author of "A Plea for Seriousness." "Seriousness and light-heartedness are not at war; there is no merit in austerity; on the contrary, more harm can be done by solemn triviality and ascetic futility than by arrant tomfoolery."[44] For Katharine Roof, "True American humor, while it may deal lightly with some ceremony of grave superstition in which the question of real veneration is not involved, contains no real irreverence." Rather, it is "a thing that can play upon the surface of depths, that can assert itself in the face of disaster and apparent defeat. There is something fine and courageous in it aside from its charm as a mental quality."[45] Perhaps aware of the fact that to denounce humor in absolute terms was to open oneself to the unanswerable charge of lacking a sense of humor, these critics preferred to give humor its due by appealing to the cultural convention by which the sense of humor was an essential part of any life. More likely, however, their appeals were guided by a firm Victorian belief in the benevolent and recreative nature of humor within its proper sphere. In either case, their insistence on the value of humor, in the context of a critique of it, suggests something of the limits of criticism of humor and laughter within late nineteenth- and early twentieth-century culture.

What disturbed these critics, who perceived themselves as isolated and lonely voices in a culture surfeited with humor, was the intolerable elevation of the sense of humor above all other virtues. Looking around at the social landscape of "polite society" in 1917, Elizabeth Woodbridge saw the veneration of humor everywhere:

> A young man said gravely the other day, "One can't get to heaven without a sense of humor, you know." A gentleman writes from England to the editors of an American school paper to inquire into the status of the sense of humor among American boys, as compared with English. The word "humor" is on every one's lips. Humor is the one thing needful. We are warned against choosing friends who lack it; and as for marriage, if both parties do not possess it, the altar is but a prelude to the divorce court, if not to suicide. If any man fail of success in any way, we are told that it is because he lacks humor; if he is dissatisfied with existing conditions, this accounts for it. Nearly every human vaguery, from eccentricities in dress to curious tastes in the naming of children, is ascribed to the absence or inadequacy of this one virtue. Everything, from dinner-parties to matrimony, must be ordered with a view to this test.[46]

Woodbridge was not alone in seeing evidence of the ranking of humor above all other virtues as a fact of social life. "There is such a thing as an over-developed sense of humor," said the poet Eunice Tietjens, "and surely our country is suffering from it."[47] The "over-development" of the sense of humor, Tietjens and others were sure, was attributable to the dominant voices everywhere that saw in the sense of humor only good.

The problem with this "over-development," with the making of humor a primary and absolute value, was that "no longer do we hold our humor within bounds, but like a spoiled, over-grown child it gambols over the pastures of our life laying smutty fingers on what is deepest and truest there, on religion, on sentiment, on love."[48] Humor had become boundless, free-floating, able to override the serious concerns that once called for reverence and respect. "We seem to have acquired a class of individuals," said Katharine Roof, "whose so-called sense of humor takes the form of an uncouth flippancy . . . and laughs noisily at the things that should command respect."[49] The denunciation of "the common disposition to take a humorous view" was grounded on the idea that the elevation of humor left "nothing to appeal to. Virtue, honor, public fidelity and purity, commercial probity, the dignity of office, the sanctity of home, have become subjects of jest; men and women who uphold them are called fogies, or, by a favorite locution of the day, are said to take themselves too seriously."[50] The careful balance in which humor brought joy, relieved the tensions of the workaday world, and provided respite from melancholy and care now threatened to break down, as humor spilled over and seemed, in the words of one author, to be "turning everything serious into fun."[51]

The invidious distinction between the serious and the humorous, whereby the latter was imagined as a necessary but secondary virtue, was shot through with a fear of the values of the "lower classes" and a deep antipathy toward the popular forms of a commercial culture. Those who were troubled by the excessive importance that seemed to be attached to the sense of humor in turn-of-the-century America were very much "cultural custodians" in a sense quite beyond what Henry May meant by the term: these were late Victorian protectors of an Arnoldian creed that seemed threatened by the breakdown of "standards" and the rise of the untutored "mob."[52] Arnold himself noted in 1888 that the American "addiction to the funny man" was a sign of the absence of "the discipline of awe and respect," and one of the reasons Americans lacked "distinction."[53] The complaint of "A Plea for Seriousness" was, very much in the same vein, that "our standards have lowered, our principles have slackened," and the incessant laughter of the public was, if not to blame, at least a sign of such declension.[54] And, like Arnold, the American protectors of "standards," "distinction," and "reverence" saw as their main problems the challenge of "alien" values, associated with a new and vocal lower class, and the commercial forms that threatened to swamp all higher things.

In the United States, however, this genteel fear of lower-class dominance and its elevation of laughter above the "traditional" concerns of reverence, respect, and serious moral authority was given an added ethnic dimension. In effect, the cult of Anglo-Saxonism was arrayed against the cult of the sense of humor: the excessive value attached to humor and laughter was seen as a foreign import, and the challenge of the working-class "mob" was remade as the challenge of the un-American "rabble." Nowhere was this clearer than in Katharine Roof's 1910 denunciation of the new flippancy observable everywhere in America. Roof, of course, had no problem with "true" American humor, which knew its place, never offended, and never challenged the verities of late Victorianism. However, the new emphasis on humor, she was certain, was attributable to elements that had no respect for Anglo-Saxon institutions and morality:

> The tremendous influx of Continental foreigners—the raw and often the waste material of the countries they come from—into a democracy, English-speaking and founded upon Anglo-Saxon morality, is a powerful factor in the creation of a new type. The second-generation product, evolved from our polyglot population, is actually a very different being mentally from the native American. . . . And among other changes a perversion of the idea of humor occurs when the American mental habit is grafted upon minds of a different color. Yet these second-generation citizens (a weed-like growth essentially un-American) . . . assist to support public amusements . . . and so have come to affect the character of popular entertainments of the kind where supply and demand were formerly regulated by a more enlightened class.[55]

The attempt to uphold the humorous/serious distinction as a matter of separate and inviolable spheres, then, was articulated by Roof and others in terms of both class and ethnicity. The challenge of a humor and laughter that respected no bounds was associated with various other corruptions that the genteel Protestant elite attributed to the mass of new immigrants. It was not humor per se, but a new kind of humor which refused deference, welling up from below, imported from foreign lands, failing to accept its subordinate place in the order of virtues, that troubled Roof and those of like mind.

But the threat to gentility and to preservation of a sphere of the serious apart from the world of laughter came, in the minds of those who perceived such a threat, not only from without but more especially from within. The expansion of commercial forms incorporating humor in the late nineteenth and early twentieth centuries, the development of a nascent mass culture of comic forms, and the infusion of those forms into everyday life seemed to make the practice of laughter ubiquitous. Eunice Tietjens identified the newspapers, periodicals, theaters, public amusements, and popular songs of the early twentieth century as the main source of overdeveloped humor. In the daily press "the pale cast of would-be humor, cynical, ironical or coarse, according to the 'policy of the paper,' is over it all, tinging the political reports, creeping into the editorials and dictating to the critics, who must write 'readable' stuff often at the cost of justice." The vaudeville house and the musical comedy, heavily favored over the legitimate theater by the public, "have avowedly no other object than to cater to the abnormally developed craving of the average American for 'something funny.' " [56] The daily papers and the theater could be held responsible, said Roof, for creating among "the uncultured and unthinking classes who are influenced by them," what she called "a flippant attitude toward the real issues of life." [57] The joke, that quintessentially modern commercial form of humor, spread from its base in vaudeville and periodicals to all spheres of social life. According to one critic, writing in 1903, "the joke is fast becoming mightier than the pen. The orator has learned its value, and even the clergyman resorts to it when he desires to stir the flagging interest of his flock. It furnishes sufficient excuse for the impertinence of children, and in its name the daily papers deride the highest national dignitaries." [58] Everywhere the critics looked, they saw the destructive effects of a market-driven emphasis on humor, an emphasis that respected no limits and was accountable only to the demands of its uncultivated audiences.

The consequence of this expansion of commercial humor was not only that it destroyed reverence, respect, and seriousness, but that, ironically, it destroyed humor as well. Agnes Repplier, a Philadelphia critic and essayist who wrote widely on humor and laughter for nearly half a century, was certainly no enemy to humor. Yet, she grew increasingly wary of commercial humor because, by breaking the Victorian relationship of the humorous and the serious, it devalued humor itself. Repplier began her half-century of writing on humor with an 1889 essay entitled "A Plea for Humor," in which she advocated humor as a form of relief from the overwhelming seriousness of modern life. "We are called on repeatedly to face problems which we would rather let alone," she wrote, "to dive dismally into motives, to trace subtle connections, to analyze uncomfortable sensations, and to exercise in all cases a discreet and conscientious severity, when what we really want and need is half an hour's amusement."[59] In many ways, this view was characteristic of the late Victorian ethos. Humor was needed to balance an overwhelming orientation toward earnestness—to provide relief without shirking the duties and obligations to God, family, work, and nation.

More than two decades later, she cast her eye on the ubiquitous professional humorist, who was undermining both humor and seriousness:

> The truth is that humour as a lucrative profession is a purely modern device, and one which is much to be deplored. . . . The essence of humour is that it should be unexpected, that it should embody an element of surprise, that it should startle us out of that reasonable gravity which, after all, must be our habitual frame of mind. But the professional humourist cannot afford to be unexpected. The exigencies of his profession compel him to be relentlessly droll.[60]

For Repplier, the value of humor was dependent upon the "reasonable gravity" to which it was counterposed. When seriousness ceased to be a "habitual frame of mind," humor could no longer provide the sudden relief, the shift in perspective, the sense of proportion that would mitigate the cares and concerns of serious living. Humor existed only in relationship to "nonhumor"; when, under the pressure of commercial production, it became an end in itself, its purpose and value were lost. Commercial humor threatened not only the value of seriousness and moral earnestness, but the value of humor.

Repplier's concern with the dangers of a modern American orientation toward humor went deeper than that of most of her contemporaries. Unlike most critics of the cult of the sense of humor, Repplier was a strong advocate for the value of laughter and humor throughout her career, even as she remained Anglocentric, culturally conservative and, indeed, strongly antimodernist in her orientation. In fact, it was the laughter of medieval England, as she imagined it, that provided the standard against which to judge the diminished laughter of the modern age. In terms similar to Bahktin's, her 1936 text *In Pursuit of Laughter* contrasted the "scant pretence of cheerfulness" of the twentieth-century American with "the echo of laughter ringing from every side" which she saw as characteristic of the Middle Ages. The loss of that laughter under the shadow of modern self-consciousness, and the attempt to recover it, was her theme. "No man," she said, "recognizes the need of pursuit until that which he desires has escaped him." The result of the waning of laughter was the modern form of its "ill-organized pursuit." Instead of the laughter of the Middle Ages, said Repplier, "Americans have a sense of humour. Such a sense does not mean the possession of humour but the appreciation of it. We want to laugh, even if we have little to laugh at." [61] The desire for humor, endless and ungratified, seemed to coalesce with the relentless production of humor in the commercial marketplace to devalue laughter; everywhere there was humor, but it provided little relief and was in danger of losing its necessary connection with the world of serious concerns. Repplier looked back to a medieval Europe in which a hearty, unself-conscious laughter was part of a worldview that was deeply reverential, infused with awe and respect for God, profound in its simplicity. Whether such a world ever existed is less important than the fact that she imagined it as an alternative to a modern world in which both the joy of laughter and the reverence of God were always just out of reach. The preponderance of commercial humor, the ever-present desire for laughter, the excessive valorization of the sense of humor: all were signs of a world lost, a world in which "true" laughter and reverence were not at odds but were one.

Despite her unconventional linking of robust and ubiquitous laughter to a worldview in which mystery, fear, and awe were primary elements, when it came to dealing with the problem of humor in modern life, Repplier shared many of the conventional views of other genteel critics. Her appreciation of humor and laughter was mitigated by a fear that the values associated with humor would spill over the boundaries erected by Victorianism and do irreparable moral harm. The valuable features of humor—its provision of relief from strain, its relaxing and recreative powers, its enlarged perspective—were also the elements that might undermine morality, seriousness, and the sacred. If in 1889 Repplier had been an enthusiastic advocate for the need of humor in a culture that she perceived as deadened by its narrow earnestness, by the late 1910s and 1920s, in the wake of World War I, she had become more wary of the dangers of humor and laughter:

> We hear so much about the sanitary qualities of laughter, we have been taught so seriously the gospel of amusement, that any writer, preacher, or lecturer, whose smile is broad enough to be infectious, finds himself a prophet in the market-place. Laughter, we are told, freshens our exhausted spirits and disposes us to good-will—which is true. It is also true that laughter quiets our uneasy scruples and disposes us to simple savagery. Whatever we laugh at, we condone.[62]

Once a promoter of the "gospel of amusement" herself, Repplier had grown ambivalent about the moral consequences of the cult of the sense of humor. If laughter was a universal promoter of "good-will," might it be possible that laughter would create a sympathetic and understanding perspective toward behavior and persons that morality justly sought to censure? Might it not condone cruelty, the shirking of obligation, blasphemy, and other moral evils? How was a serious sense of moral obligation to be a check on the sense of humor, how could humor be kept in its appropriate place, when it was promoted as an unalloyed good?

The heart of the problem, for Repplier, was that the tolerance that came with the widened perspective of the sense of humor could easily shade into indifference. In her 1924 essay "The American Laughs," she took as her text a photograph of two young American women laughing at Verdun, the site of one of the most destructive battles of World War I. Here, certainly, on the bloody ground where thousands lost their lives, a certain respect and solemnity were due. Laughter at Verdun was not simply an easing of tension or a recognition of a broader perspective in which the devastation of war was minor in the context of the great benefits of civilization; no, laughter here was a violation, a refusal to solemnly respect the dead, their sacrifices, and the utter horror of modern warfare. To laugh in such situations was to diminish their importance, to condone and tolerate what ought never to be condoned or tolerated, to lose any scale of moral significance by casting grave events at the same level as minor personal problems and vaudeville jokes. The ultimate sympathetic tolerance of all things could lead only to an absolute moral indifference.[63]

As a student of abnormal psychology would say later in the twentieth century, the overdevelopment of the sense of humor created a specific maladjustment in which an attitude of "What's the difference anyway?" prevailed. The social result of such maladjustment: gruesome murders, moral nihilism, a rise in the divorce rate.[64] Having too great a sense of humor, it turned out, was as bad as having none at all. If humor and laughter were associated with what Gordon Allport would come to call the "syndrome of tolerance," it was also true that they represented the dark shadow of tolerance: the detached and bemused indifference of the cosmopolitan. The moral problem of excessive tolerance was summed up by William Lyon Phelps: "For while the sense of humour is a health-ful check on egotism, and enables one to derive vast enjoyment out of watching the human comedy, it may destroy the soul."[65] Repplier, like other critics of her era, sought to preserve both the value of humor and the sphere of the serious, but found humor constantly leaking into and staining the higher values of late Victorianism.

Those who saw only good in the sense of humor in effect agreed with Repplier: humor *was* a mode of perceiving and regarding the world in such a way that the subject was released from the respectable standards of society and granted freedom to see those standards in a diminished light. The difference was that the promoters of humor could see no harm in a capacity for belittling social standards, while they saw a great deal of harm resulting from the failure to take a humorous view. "The man with a sense of humor," said Katharine Wilson, "would be society's darling if it were not that he hurts the solemn by laughing at things they rever-ence." But the shock caused by such a man is not his fault, but rather the fault of "those who cannot turn this uncharitable, this unsocial, this absurd thing into their mental rag-bag." Lacking a sense of humor, "the solemn man keeps his shocking experiences and unsocial impulses bot-tled up within his own personality, where they remain dangerous."[66] It is precisely the verities and respectabilities that must be laughed at if the tension of living in society is to find release. H. A. Overstreet concurred:

It would almost seem as if the willingness and the wish to be some-what flippant toward the solemn respectabilities—of state and church and sex and family—were a prerequisite for a sense of humor. For apparently the person who submits himself utterly to the social and moralistic compulsions can hardly possess that gay freedom which delights in building a world for itself; which delights, therefore, every now and then, in knocking the long-faced respectabilities endwise.[67]

The "solemn respectabilities," in this view, were not founded on absolute moral principles but were "merely" social conventions, standing in the way of a free, broad, and tolerant perspective.

Here lay the difference between those late Victorians who were troubled by the importance attached to the sense of humor and those harbingers of the twentieth-century view of the sense of humor as an unconditional good. The genteel Victorian critics had insisted that there were spheres of life that must remain fundamentally serious, into which laughter could not intrude. Twentieth-century thinkers rejected this view. Their perspective was neatly summed up by Leo Markun, who simply asserted that "nothing is too sacred, nothing is too gross, to be laughed at. As soon as we start to outline proper fields for the sense of humor, we take it away from its necessary companion, freedom."[68] Because humor had come to be associated with such values as freedom, tolerance, sympathy, and perspective, any attempt to limit humor would seem to represent an attack on those values.

As much as the critics of the cult of the sense of humor attempted to find a place in social life for a humor that would provide relief and recreation without challenging the fundamental seriousness of truth, beauty, and morality, the notion of laughter as a form of relief undermined this doctrine of separate spheres. It was precisely those areas of social life that were most serious and solemn that seemed to provoke laughter. If laughter was a release of tension, where else but in response to the earnestness of work, religion, and politics would one expect it to break forth? Indeed, in the years surrounding the turn of the century, psychologists began to note the phenomenon of "laughing in church" or "laughing in the schoolroom" as a result of the demand for seriousness in those situations.[69] The more the situation required seriousness, it seemed, the more participants felt the need of release through laughter. As Repplier observed, "Just as we are often moved to merriment for no other reason than that the occasion calls for seriousness, so we are correspondingly serious when invited too freely to be amused."[70] The relief from seriousness provided by humor could not be isolated, as if in some adjacent building, from the seriousness itself; by marking a host of objects and values with the No Joking sign, the critics of the cult of the sense of humor were in effect saying that it was precisely these objects and values that were the greatest stimulus to laughter.

By the late 1920s, the moderate critique of the sense of humor as a central value had receded, along with the late Victorian ethos of which it was a part. The humorous/serious distinction was to remain, but in a much attenuated form; instead of referring primarily to spheres of objects and values that were to be taken one way or the other, it came increasingly to refer to the mode of perception of the social actor, a mode that could switch from the serious to the humorous at any given instant. The distinction became less a matter of distinguishing those things that could be joked about from those that could not, than one of distinguishing whether a person was being serious or being humorous. All areas opened themselves to humor; it became a matter of tact and social sensitivity to know when it was appropriate to "use" humor, rather than a matter of judging the object as something serious or humorous in itself. Politics, religion, and education could all be joking matters or spheres in which joking could take place. The triumph of a subjectivist notion of humor as a mode of perception associated with benevolence, sympathy, tolerance, and democracy meant that humor could be everywhere and of no danger to anyone. This was not so much a case of the genteel ethos being overwhelmed by an insurgent mass culture bursting from below, as these critics had feared, as it was a case of the internal logic of the humorous/serious distinction undermining that which it had been constructed to preserve.

Politics and the Democracy of Humor

One of the main areas of social life that the Victorian creed, dominant from the mid-nineteenth century until World War I, declared as a sphere of serious action, was politics. This did not mean that political life was not a subject of jest and laughter; indeed, there is a rich tradition of nineteenth-century political humor, from Major Jack Downing to the "phunny phellows" of the Civil War period to Thomas Nast's political cartoons and Mr. Dooley's Progressive Era columns. And one might safely assume that such humor was not limited to well-known published forms, but was also present in the public meeting places and private parlors of the nineteenth century. Nor did the casting of politics as a sphere of seriousness mean that humor was never used by politicians and political leaders; a few elected leaders, such as Ben Hardin, Tom Corwin, and J. Proctor Knott, not to mention Lincoln himself, even developed reputations for humor. What it did mean was that political action and issues were conceived of as fundamentally serious, requiring dignity and solemnity of judgment, and that strong strictures were raised against the use of humor by political leaders. The overwhelming gravity of nineteenth-century political oratory; the serious stature of public figures from Webster and Calhoun, to Sumner and Stevens, to Bryan and Wilson; the vehemence with which Americans identified themselves with the symbols and organizations of political parties: all were signs of a regard for political life as an arena of profound and solemn import. Nineteenth-century Americans took their politics seriously in a way that it is difficult for the detached twentieth-century observer to appreciate. In this context, for a political leader to shift or expand perspective by being humorous was to court disaster.

We may contrast that situation with the place of humor in politics today. Not only is a sense of humor an acceptable attribute of political leaders, it is often deemed a necessity. Political campaigns hire professional joke writers and humorists such as Robert Orben, who became head of Gerald Ford's speechwriting staff, and Don Penny, who has written jokes for at least three presidents, thirty-two senators, fifty congressional representatives, and numerous other members of the federal government.[71] The joke, in today's media-driven campaigns, furnishes the perfect "sound bite" for the evening news. Every president since Franklin Roosevelt has had his collection of humorous anecdotes and pithy sayings published as an illustration of his genial sense of humor.[72] Even Richard Nixon, the president least likely to be identified as possessing a sense of humor, made it a point to appear on television's *Laugh-In* as if to prove that he could laugh at himself. Ronald Reagan's reputation as "the great communicator" was undergirded by a use of self-deprecating humor, particularly in regard to his age. Morris Udall has been eulogized for the great sense of humor he brought to national politics. Telling the wrong sort of joke, of course, can be politically damaging, as Earl Butz discovered, but in the main, humor is viewed as an essential part of political campaigning and political life.[73] In today's environment, it is the political leader who refuses humor and laughter that runs the risk of damaging his credibility. No politician wishes to be accused of lacking a sense of humor. The demagogue and the fanatic, the autocrat and the dogmatist, it is widely believed, are without a sense of humor. Humor is a sign of political flexibility, moderation, willingness to see both sides of a question, capacity for compromise. It is a feature of a liberal-pluralist model of politics.

It was not always so. As early as the 1870s, as the sense of humor began to be promoted as a positive and necessary good, commentators such as Samuel Cox sought to challenge the view that statesmanship was incompatible with humor. They were fighting a lonely uphill battle, and no matter how many instances of congressional humor they cited to show the relief laughter furnished in the solemn world of politics, the dominant view remained opposed to it.[74] This remained the case even into the 1920s. It became something of a convention to note that a reputation for a sense of humor was a death warrant for a politician's career. In 1906, *The Nation* opined that to "confess to being a humorist . . . would be almost suicidal for a Congressman."[75] In 1912, H. B. Fuller claimed that "a law of public life . . . forbids any dalliance with the gentle art of humor. The penalty for infractions is political oblivion."[76] "It is a long tradition in this country," said the *New York Times* in 1922, "that it is fatal for a public man to display a marked sense of humor in his speeches." Those who break that rule, even once, are "never able afterward to get themselves taken seriously by the public."[77] Albert J. Beveridge concurred, noting that even some of the most able of men "have ruined their reputations for statesmanship by thus acquiring reputations as wits and humorists."[78] The message for anyone aspiring to political office was to conceal the sense of humor, to keep it out of the public forum in which issues of great seriousness and import were to be debated.

What was it about a sense of humor, in the older ideal of statesmanship, that made it so damaging to the political leader who would display it? A sense of humor, it was believed, involved an attitude of taking life lightly, a tolerance of incompatible views, and such an attitude seemed to threaten the conception of politics and public life as an arena of serious action and responsible leadership. How could the politician with a sense of humor be counted on to defend principles, to take responsibility, to define and achieve political ends with a singularity of vision, when he was willing to see the incongruity of his own actions or to sympathize with his opponent's point of view? As one analysis of character had it, the true political leader could not, by definition, have a sense of humor: "The person with a sense of humor does not put himself in too serious a light, and does not desire to be taken seriously. He avoids the responsibility of exercising power. People with humor are not directly leaders in the world's affairs."[79] Politics was an arena of moral earnestness that could brook no levity, and was generally regarded as such through the Progressive Era and even beyond. The rule that "public men do well to tickle every instinct and prejudice of the people except their sense of humor," wrote one editorialist in 1925, was in fact a tribute to the democratic masses, for it revealed how seriously they regarded their government.[80]

Although the nineteenth-century view of humor as a political liability would wither under the new political conditions of the twentieth century, it was deep-rooted and had staying power well into the twentieth century. Perhaps the last gasp took place in the 1952 presidential election when Dwight Eisenhower and the Republican Party attempted to turn Adlai Stevenson's sense of humor into a campaign issue. Eisenhower presented himself as the "serious" candidate—principled, firm, capable of dealing with the grave problems faced by the nation—and Stevenson as the joker—flippant, unconcerned, lacking in leadership qualities. Stevenson, according to the Republicans, was unqualified for the presidency because he had a habit of making light of serious issues. Countering the attack, Stevenson claimed the legacy of Lincoln's humor, and his supporters rallied by seeing his humor as a sign of his political fitness: "a Woodrow Wilson with a sense of humor" is how the *New Republic* described him.[81] Although Stevenson lost the election, his humor won the larger political battle. Six years later, Eisenhower could be found lecturing the graduating class of the U.S. Naval Academy on the benefits of a sense of humor:

> One of the characteristics of a free people is their ceaseless search for knowledge and truth, and highest standards of excellency. Their capacity to accept their mistakes in good humor—to experience setbacks without fear or resentment—adds vitality to their searching. A sense of humor goes hand in hand with independence of thought and an eternally questioning mind.
>
> A communist is not permitted the adventure of this kind of searching. To him there is only one truth—that ordained by the party and that truth must be grimly and subserviently followed. Communists would find no meaning in the old saying "always take your work seriously, never yourself."

The antihumor tradition of American political leadership that Eisenhower had tried to marshall in the election of 1952 had succumbed to the twentieth-century mainstream values by which "a healthy and lively sense of humor" fitted men "for the difficult and important posts."[82]

The rise of the sense of humor as a political value in twentieth-century life occurred against the backdrop of a fundamental reorganization of national politics: the relative detachment of the citizen from the political process, and from loyalties to party and region, and his reinvention as an observer or consumer of political action; the transformation of political oratory from the lengthy eloquence of serious speech to the media- and advertising-dominated sound bite; the rise of a managerial model of politics as a domain of expertise, compromise, and consensus, as opposed to a nineteenth-century arena of popular conflict; the development of an internationalist orientation and its expression in the form of a national security state; the widening of the suffrage coupled with the withdrawal of the public from politics and a reorientation toward private life. The increasing complexity of politics, its bureaucratization and control by professionals, went hand in hand with a notion of mass democracy. The more that political decisionmaking was figured as a domain of expertise, the more it was seen as an expression of democratic will. In this context, the idea of humor fit perfectly; the sense of humor was the ideal personality trait for dealing with the tensions, complexities, and demands of the bureaucracy, while also being the valued attribute of the universal "Everyman" upon which the mass democracy was founded.[83]

The notion that politics, as a realm of complexity and compromise, required a sense of humor was articulated as early as 1914, although it would not become the dominant view until the 1930s. Henry S. Pritchett accepted the conventional view of the Progressive Era that "a man must have two qualities if the people are to trust him as a political leader—he must have moral purpose and he must be able to think straight." But to these, he added a third—the sense of humor. For Pritchett, the failings of those leaders guided solely by moral principle and clear thinking arose from the fact that the sphere of politics created pressures that made the leader lose his perspective on himself. What made the sense of humor indispensable for the political leader was not simply that it was "the best lubricator for the machinery of civilized society," or that it removed "the friction of his many-sided human contact," although these things it surely did. Rather, because the sense of humor was "that faculty of imagination so humane and sympathetic in its nature that it can perceive at the same time serious and jocose things," it also allowed the statesman to see outside the narrow parameters of his own principles without losing his moral bearings. Humor was not, from this perspective, opposed to seriousness. Instead, it integrated seriousness into a wider perspective, allowing those who possessed the sense of humor to hold incompatible conceptions in balance. The politician with a sense of humor did not run the risk of undermining cherished principles that were deemed serious, but was saved from taking himself so seriously as to allow egotism to undermine those principles. The world of politics was simply too complex to let moral purpose and clear thinking, unmoderated by a sense of humor, be the sole guides to leadership.[84]

The sense of humor was valued by Pritchett not only because it allowed the statesman to function in the complex and pressure-filled world of modern politics, but more especially because it was a quality associated with democracy and universal humanity. As we have seen, the wit/humor distinction in the nineteenth century arrayed a set of values linked to aristocracy—intellect, artifice, elitism—against a set of values linked to democracy—emotion, nature, universalism. The twentieth century inherited those associations, and remade them in terms of political leadership. The sense of humor could now mark the political leader as a "man of the people." No better example existed for the early twentieth century than the image of Lincoln as both humorist and natural untutored democrat. "Above every other political leader of his time," said Pritchett, Lincoln "had the saving grace of a humane imagination, a true sense of humor. . . . And this endowment comes rarely except to him who rises directly out of the common people." The quality that was most valuable for providing a sense of perspective in the elite world of politics thus turned out to be the most democratic of qualities, so democratic as to be inaccessible to those who were not themselves "of the people." "One cannot imagine," Pritchett concluded, "Lincoln born to the purple."[85]

Despite Pritchett's Progressive Era linkage, it was not until the 1930s that the equation of humor with democracy would become the dominant view, making a sense of humor among statesmen a check against all forms of tyranny and authoritarianism. If in 1917 Stephen Leacock could claim that Germany had no humor because it was not a democracy, as opposed to both the United States and Canada, where humor flourished, there were still many who saw humor as threatening to the serious business of politics, particularly in wartime.[86] Christine Ladd Franklin of Columbia University, for instance, was disturbed by the "light-heartedness" of Americans in time of war. "Continued serious talk is almost an impossibility," she said. "Someone is sure to break in with the

light-minded aspect of any subject, with the perennial American joke."
Even granting that humor might represent a "nervous let-down of
strain" among overworked businessmen, she found it "inexcusable" that
humor intruded into matters of grave import facing the nation.[87] By the
time of World War II, the residue of the Victorian view exemplified by
Christine Franklin had been wiped out by the advocates of the sense of
humor as an antiauthoritarian preservative of democracy and common
sense. The more war produced strain and tension, the more humor was
needed as a form of relief and a safety valve; the more single-minded the
enemy appeared, the more humor was necessary to put the international
situation in perspective.

By the 1930s, the perceived threat of humor and laughter undermining
serious political discourse and action had all but disappeared. Far more
threatening in the imagination of contemporaries were the political dangers of a world without humor, a world that was by definition antidemo-
cratic. Orlo J. Price of Pittsford, New York, for instance, saw a grave
threat to democracy in the tone of the 1936 presidential campaign. According to Price, the recent death of Will Rogers and the lack of tolerance and a sense of humor in politics boded ill for the nation. "A nation
or group that is not amused at its own antics, and cannot lose or be
laughed at without losing its temper, is good soil for disease, if it is not
already sick." Price concluded that "a sense of humor is not incompatible
with seriousness; it serves as a cathartic."[88] Here the relief model of
laughter and the humorous/serious distinction were harnessed to a view
that brought laughter into political life, rather than a Victorian view of
politics as falling solely on the serious side of the divide. Price's concerns
were echoed throughout the 1930s and 1940s. In 1940, Edward G. Lindeman of the New York School of Social Work made almost exactly the
same analysis of the presidential campaign of that year. The lack of
humor was "ominous," said Lindeman, and symptomatic of "the development of the state of mind in which fascism finds its breeding place."[89]
James L. McConaughy, president of Wesleyan University, argued in
1938 that "Franklin Roosevelt's sense of humor is one of the best curbs
on his dictatorship tendencies."[90] Others were also quick to note Roosevelt's sense of humor as a great benefit in relieving the stress of the
awesome responsibilities of governing, in providing a tolerant outlook,
and in fostering a democratic connection between the people and their
government.[91] In fact, Roosevelt himself made the connection between
the sense of humor and American democracy. "I sometimes think that

the saving grace of America," said Roosevelt in 1933, "lies in the fact that the overwhelming majority of Americans are possessed of two great qualities—a sense of humor and a sense of proportion."[92] Humor had ceased to be a danger to reverence; the political danger of a lack of humor seemed far more real in the world of the twentieth century.

In the period of Roosevelt's rule, the image of the man without a sense of humor came to possess a new political content. If in the later nineteenth century the man without a sense of humor was envisioned as a crank, a fanatic, an overardent reformer, a one-dimensional egoist, in the 1930s and 1940s his image was codified as the dictator. Hitler, Stalin, Mussolini: these were the highest examples of men who lacked the fundamental and necessary attribute of the sense of humor. And it was against these figures and the nations they represented that the American sense of humor as a bolster of democratic government was counterposed. "If [Hitler and Mussolini] had a sense of humor," wrote a *New York Times* editorialist in 1941, "they could not tolerate their own company." No great dictator has ever had a sense of humor, declared McConaughy at matriculation services at Wesleyan in 1938. According to F. E. Lumley, "tyrants have no sense of humor." "Dictators Don't Laugh" was the title of a speech given by Stewart McClelland. This theme was returned to again and again in the 1930s and 1940s.[93]

If the dictator was a figure who took himself too seriously, who lacked perspective and tolerance, he gave his character to the society over which he ruled. Many Americans saw in Germany, Italy, Japan, and the Soviet Union not simply nations headed by dictators who lacked humor, but societies that, because they were not democracies, could not possess humor. After the Nazi-Soviet Pact was revealed in 1939, for instance, the *New York Times* editorialized: "How long is it since a laugh has been heard on a public platform in Germany or Soviet Russia? . . . The totalitarian climate simply does not favor risibility."[94] The connection between humor and democracy in the United States was reaffirmed by the lack of humor in totalitarian societies. "We have always had that balance which comes from seeing all sides of a question," said Stewart McClelland, "and as a nation we have practiced the tolerance of understanding. Only a democracy can have a sense of humor."[95] The American sense of humor could even be exported to countries suffering under the yoke of dictatorship, thus preparing the way for democratization. Bob Hope saw the U.S. military as advance forces for humorizing the world in the American model. "As our armed forces flow in to stop the earth's decay," wrote Hope in 1944, "where Hitlerism and fascism and Tojoism have set in, they take with them . . . their sense of humor, and its ready infection is being spread through the countries and people they visit."[96] The sense of humor had its small role to play in a Pax Americana, bringing democracy to countries that had suffered under the grim purposefulness of totalitarian rule, countries that had, perhaps, taken themselves "too seriously."

Given all the evils that the totalitarian states of the 1930s and 1940s could have been accused of, why would anyone single out the lack of a sense of humor as worthy of attention? The fact that such a claim was repeatedly made suggests two things: first, the values that the sense of humor had come to signify—tolerance, sympathy, perspective, balance, freedom—were so closely allied with the meaning of liberal democracy that the idea of humor served as a kind of easily understood shorthand or signpost for democracy itself; second, the American propaganda effort marshalled every available resource to picture the totalitarian enemy as unalterably "other," a threat to all American values. No value was insignificant or politically irrelevant in the ideological climate of the era, least of all the sense of humor. The harnessing of the sense of humor to this propaganda effort was a way of saying that not only were fascists and Nazis opposed to liberalism and democracy, but they also were not personable or friendly people; that they were un-American not only in the values they held, but in their very character attributes.

In the Cold War world that emerged out of the postwar peace, the sense of humor was associated even more deeply with liberal democracy, and was juxtaposed to the grim determinism of international communism. Eisenhower's claim that a communist could not have a sense of humor was, not surprisingly, an unoriginal observation. According to one Cold War sociology textbook, for instance, "appeal to the sense of humor" was "an effective anti-Communist propaganda device" because "Communists take themselves so seriously." The American sense of humor helped "to relieve the tension and to help keep a sense of balance concerning the true nature of the Red threat."[97] And in the era of the national security state, humor could help ward off internal threats as well. As Joost Meerloo wrote in his 1956 volume on the social psychology of "brainwashing" and propaganda, *Mental Seduction and Menticide*, "We must learn to treat the demagogue and aspirant dictator in our midst just as we treat our external enemies in a cold war." He continued:

The demagogue himself is almost incapable of humour of any sort, and if we treat him with humour, he will begin to collapse. Humour is, after all, related to a sense of perspective. . . . Put the demagogue's statements in perspective, and you will see how utterly distorted they are. How can we possibly take them seriously or answer them seriously?[98]

In an era that saw prominent intellectuals declare an "end of ideology" in politics as an affirmation of the pragmatic nature of Western liberal democracies against the ideologically driven politics of communism, humor was an element that aided pragmatism by putting the rigidity of ideologies "in perspective."[99] In the words of one sociologist, humor and laughter "render all our legitimating ideologies and hopeful utopias powerless and helpless. This may be humor's most important function: it often works as a de-ideologizing and disillusioning force."[100]

In the Cold War imagination, then, the relationship of humor to American politics had come to be the reverse of that constructed by mid-Victorians. For the nineteenth century, humor had appeared as a threat to political principle and the integrity of statesmanship. By the 1950s, humor was a valuable asset in politics precisely because it guarded against an undue attachment to rigid moral principle, now defined as "ideology." In a statement that would have been impossible fifty years, or even twenty-five years, earlier, Leon Ormond commented in 1941 about "what excellent use our political leaders make of humor. More than one man has joked and clowned himself into Congress." For Ormond, "the man with a sense of humor is a protector of liberty and someone to be prized in a democratic society."[101] In a world where political action was defined as "pragmatic" rather than "ideological," where consensus and compromise fended off the dangers of totalitarian rule, where balance and tolerance were the norms, the sense of humor was a welcome, indeed necessary, trait of the political leader.

It was not only in the mainstream world of electoral politics that the sense of humor came to be a value. The American left in the twentieth century has been pilloried as lacking in humor and thus is regarded by many as politically dangerous. Despite this sometimes justified charge, from the Progressive Era to the present many on the left have shared the notion of the sense of humor as an enemy to rigidity, but they have seen that rigidity as characteristic of the institutions of capitalist power in America. *The Masses*, under the editorship of Max Eastman, carried on its masthead, from February 1913 forward, a declaration that it was "a Revolutionary and not a Reform Magazine; a Magazine with a Sense of Humor and no Respect for the Respectable; Frank; Arrogant; Impertinent: Searching for True Causes; a Magazine Directed against Rigidity and Dogma wherever it is found." [102] The sense of humor, as the Yippie activists Jerry Rubin and Abbie Hoffman discovered in the 1960s, could provide a means to challenge the official pronouncements of the political establishment. "MAINTAIN A SENSE OF HUMOR," advised Hoffman in his "Messages to the Brothers": "People who take themselves too seriously are power-crazy. If they win it will be haircuts for all." [103] Was this vision of the sense of humor as a guarantor of freedom and a challenge to authority so different from that which was embraced by the Cold War establishment? The American left, insofar as it advocated humor as a political value, shared with mainstream politics the notion that rigidity, one-dimensionality, and fanaticism needed to be challenged; that a shift in perspective was necessary in order to see the meaning of political action. The difference was that mainstream politicians saw rigidity and fanaticism in the enemies of the American state, while those on the left tended to see those qualities in American corporate, political, and military institutions. That groups so opposed to each other shared the same values suggests the degree to which the sense of humor as a political value, like the idea of freedom, had become part of a twentieth-century ideological consensus.

The Sense of Humor Educated

As in politics, so too in the sphere of education; laughter, once barred from a realm conceived of as essentially serious, in the twentieth century became an acceptable and desirable element of that realm. Under the aegis of the progressive education movement, and gaining particular force in the 1930s and 1940s, humor was invented as a pedagogical tool in the grade school and as a substantive object of study in higher education. Not only were the senses of humor of both teacher and student brought into play in the educational process but, for many advocates of laughter in the classroom, the sense of humor itself was envisioned as an attribute of the "whole person" to be educated and developed. The new emphasis on bringing humor into the classroom differed in one fundamental way, however, from the parallel revolution in political life.

In politics, a long-standing tradition of explicitly rejecting humor from the public role of statesmen is part of the historical record of the nineteenth and early twentieth centuries; in education and pedagogical thought, no such explicit refusal of laughter can be found. The historical record provides only silence.

In nineteenth-century thought on education, laughter is, in effect, nonexistent. Those who advocated a new place for humor in the classroom had to invent a prevailing tradition of stern-faced pedagogy and somber, rote education to which they could juxtapose their progressive agenda. This "tradition" was a fixed rhetorical type, rather than what was bound to be a more diverse historical "reality" of many pedagogical assumptions and approaches, but it captures the novelty of the ethic of laughter. The stern disciplinary classroom of nineteenth-century education was to give way, in the minds of reformers, to the progressive classroom of experimentation, joy, and creative laughter.

The stock images of teacher and classroom as dry, dull, and rigid were used as a backdrop against which to promote laughter in education. "The value of humor in the schoolroom is great," said William Burnham in 1924, even as he recited the cultural truisms that "there seems to be something about the dust of the schoolroom that dulls the sense of humor," and "a teacher, from the very fact of his profession cannot have a sense of humor." [104] For those educators who tried to use humor as a pedagogical tool, their failure to get students to relax and "use" humor could be attributed to the long-standing view of the schoolroom as a laughter-free zone. Florence Brumbaugh, acting principal of the Model School at Hunter College in New York, and one of the primary advocates for humor and laughter in grade-school education in the late 1930s and 1940s, conducted a number of experiments with laughter and schoolchildren. "It must be admitted that the students did not rock with laughter" when one sustained attempt to use humor was made, said Brumbaugh, "but three months were not long enough to counteract the effect of years of the repression of laughter in the classroom." [105] Or, as James E. Warren, Jr., wrote in 1949, "Humor has for so long been omitted from educational procedure that many students are unable at first to think of it as other than opposed to classroom accomplishment." [106] When humor did not seem to provide the magical benefits its promoters were sure it offered, it was easy to blame the failure on prevailing and ingrained restrictions. The advocates of laughter in the school constructed a past of harsh restrictions against laughter—of formality, rigidity, and discipline—in order to offer the relief of laughter as a sign of a new style of education.

One of the reasons put forward for the rejection of laughter in education was that it seemed to be a potential threat to order in the classroom, to teacher control and discipline. Yet for those who saw humor and laughter as benign forces to be harnessed for personal growth, laughter was no threat to discipline; rather, it was a way of solidifying teacher control. It was true, as Leon Ormond said, that "laughter and formality are poor bedfellows," and that classroom discipline based on "fear, resentment and boredom," was antithetical to the hearty laughter of "a free and easy classroom atmosphere." [107] But by removing fear and dread as the basis of discipline, and replacing them with the sympathy and playfulness of humor, the teacher was actually able to be more effective in directing students' intellectual and emotional behavior. According to Brumbaugh, "those teachers who permitted or encouraged the laughter of their pupils had fewer problems of control than did the stern pedagogues."

> Hilarity was not difficult to handle if the teacher herself appreciated the humor in the situation which had stirred the class or individuals to mirth. She who could laugh with and not at the children was a good disciplinarian, whether judged by old or new standards of what constitutes good behavior on the part of children.[108]

Brumbaugh was equally quick to criticize teachers who used mocking and derisive remarks toward their students as taking laughter down the wrong pedagogical path by retreating to fear and resentment as the basis of control. True discipline could be achieved only through sympathetic, not derisive, laughter.

The educational reformers who clamored to introduce laughter into the classroom had two goals: to utilize humor as a pedagogical tool that would contribute to educational goals, on the one hand, and to educate and develop the student's sense of humor, on the other. The difference between the two, of course, was a difference between *humor* as method or instrument and *sense of humor* as object or goal. But in the minds of those educational progressives, the two ends were often conflated, particularly since the development of the child's sense of humor was seen as indicative of the personal growth that progressive educators desired. Developing the student's sense of humor could become a method for further education, rather than simply an end in itself. Conversely, the use of humor as a pedagogical tool could contribute to the growth of the sense of humor itself. Leon Ormond, one of the most fervent promoters of laughter in the 1940s, reveals the way in which humor as an educational instrument could easily be refigured as an element of the student's personality to be developed:

> Laughter has a direct, considerable and wholesome influence on the growth of the whole personality. Because of its objective nature humor in practice sharpens the wits and provides for intellectual development. It is a marvelously effective means of social growth in that it makes for self-confidence, poise and adequate adjustment. It is an instrument of moral maturation. It smooths the way for the acquisition of occupational and avocational skills. In short, a lively sense of humor is necessary to the emergence of the complete man.[109]

Humor, in Ormond's discussion, is an "effective means," an "instrument," a tool for personal development. But the sense of humor, precisely because it is such an effective instrument in so many realms of social life, is also a substantive element of "the complete man," a sign that personal growth has been achieved. Humor could be grafted onto the traditional educational goals of teaching substantive material, and made a subordinate tool to be judged by its effectiveness. "When laughter is involved in the learning process," said Ormond, "students will retain the same material about thirty percent better."[110] Alternatively, it could become one of the ends of education itself.

The latter was particularly the case in that vein of progressive educational thought which aimed to educate the child as a thoroughly social being, possessing social "skills." The focus on the "whole personality" often tended to elevate social abilities and attributes above academic skills and knowledge; the sense of humor, of course, was one of those traditionally nonacademic attributes that could be cultivated by the new approach to education. Winifred Nash, writing in 1938, made the distinction between the important elements of "social education" and those traditional elements of rote academic learning that had relatively little "social value."

> What is more important in the social education of the individual, correct sentence structure or a sense of humor? The answer is obvious.

Yet, in the ordinary modern curriculum, educating the pupil's sense of humor is not among the objectives of the teacher of English, nor is there any hint to be found that laughter may be a civilizing and educative force.[111]

The answer may well have been obvious to Nash, if not to all her contemporaries, many of whom continued to believe in the value of teaching grammar. However, by the late 1930s, humor, and the whole idea of "social education" of which it was a part, had indeed made serious inroads into the classroom, even if the grade school was never to assume the dimensions of a comedy training ground. Because the sense of humor was figured as an attribute of sympathy, perspective, growth, mental health, even of "civilization"—all requirements of social life in the twentieth century—its development was a goal congenial to the orientation of many progressive educators.

One may, in fact, see the progressive school as the training site for what I have referred to as the "bureaucratic individual," an individual who possessed important traits such as the sense of humor. The attempt to instill a sense of humor in the child was guided not solely by a desire for the student to learn an appreciation for humor, but by a model of personhood to which the student might conform. "Because humor is essentially an objective thing," said Ormond, "it is the easy, ideal first step in yanking a person out of an exclusive preoccupation with Self and leaving his mind receptive to external impressions." [112] This wrenching of the subject into an objective stance, in order to make him a willing template for "external impressions," could be seen as the very definition of the educational process. The growth of the complex individual, the nurturing of his subjective faculties and attributes, was predicated on his subordination of those faculties to the objective attitude; developing the student's sense of humor was a way to enrich his inner life and at the same time make him more adaptable to the rigid demands of a bureaucratic society. The paradox of the simultaneous valuation of a free and open creativity, on the one hand, and a conformity to objective social requirements, on the other, found its key in the term "adaptability." In bringing the sense of humor into the educational process, reformers sought—above all else—to encourage adaptability and, in doing so, to make the child into what might be called a "creative conformist."

If the 1930s were the years in which humor made its way into mainstream politics and progressive educational reform, that decade also saw humor introduced into the university curriculum. College humor, as a distinct subgenre, had been present since the Gilded Age, but it was not until the 1920s that anyone saw a need to instruct students in humor, and not until the following decade that courses in humor became institutionalized. In fact, when Meredith Nicholson of Indianapolis originally proposed instruction in humor as a mandatory element of the university curriculum in 1923, he was ridiculed. "Before it is too late," said the *New York Times* in mock horror, "let somebody endow a Graduate School in the Sense of Humor at some good Fundamentalist university."[113] When William McAndrews, former superintendent of schools in Chicago, made a similar proposal a decade later, it found its supporters as well as the ever-present nay-sayers. For McAndrews, the absence of formal instruction in humor was "one of the great tragedies of education." Humor should be studied in the university, said McAndrews, because "it gives more tolerance and understanding of human nature than almost anything else."[114] The *Times* once again saw the teaching of humor as bringing "coals to Newcastle," and *The Nation* wondered "if the jocular future of the nation can safely be left in the hands of persons who believe that the appreciation of jokes has to be taught."[115] But the Mark Twain Association created a fund to endow a chair in humor to move from university to university, and supporters saw a definite role for humor in higher education. Ida Benfey Judd, for instance, agreed with detractors that humor could not be taught, but argued that an appreciation of humor could be gained by studying Aristophanes, Rabelais, Cervantes, and Molière. "A student of architecture feels that he must know what the giants in his world have done in Europe," she said. "One interested in humor should also know what the four giants of his world have done."[116] Humor in higher education could thus be harnessed to the notion of European culture and great books.

The decade of the 1930s saw not simply the promotion of humor in higher education, but the establishment of courses in humor. Dana K. Merrill, for instance, taught a course in American humor in the English Department of the Pennsylvania State College, and W. E. Moore's course, "Types of Humorous Literature," at the University of Florida, claimed to be "the first course ever offered in an American college with the avowed purpose of developing the student's sense of humor." Moore even developed a sense-of-humor test to be given to students at both the beginning and the end of the course.[117] And just as humor began to be taught in English departments, scholars such as Constance Rourke and

Walter Blair were discovering humor as a legitimate area of study. By the end of the decade, humor had found an institutional home in the American university, apart from the extracurricular place it had occupied in the college humor magazines. Humor, thankfully, never became a required part of the curriculum at any college, nor did it even become a prominent field of study; the number of schools without courses in humor surely outweighed those that provided such offerings, even with the boom in humor studies that came in the 1980s. What is important to note is that the introduction of humor as an object of study broke with a long-standing, if silent, tradition. Prior to the twentieth century, nobody would have even conceived of the purpose of teaching humor in the university; such a notion ran contrary to the sobriety and seriousness with which education and "culture" were endowed. That humor could be regarded as an area of study, with its own peculiar benefits, speaks of the inroads laughter had made within the realm of serious education.

Faith and Humor

For late Victorians, as I have indicated, religion was the one sphere above all others upon which laughter was forbidden to intrude. But with the twentieth-century transformation of mainline Protestantism into an ever "softer," more flexible, even therapeutic creed, humor and laughter with their restorative effects came to seem less disrespectful of religious faith and more a benign accompaniment to it.[118] At the same time, the intellectual reaction to religious modernism and its willingness to make faith easy—a reaction usually referred to as "neo-orthodoxy"—found the intense contradictions of a serious faith in a fallen world to have much in common with the sense of humor as it had come to be understood. Religious modernists and conservatives alike agreed not only that humor and laughter were not inherently opposed to religious belief, but that they had a good deal in common with it. The relief of laughter, the expansive sympathy of humor, the sense of proportion and perspective that came with the recognition of incongruity; these, it turned out, were very much like what religion had to offer in the twentieth century. No wonder that the sense of humor was so frequently referred to as "the saving sense."

"Does not Jesus promise us exactly what Charlie Chaplin promises us, rest and restoration?" So wrote Dudley Zuver, an Episcopalian minister

and Harvard-trained theologian, in his 1933 work *Salvation by Laughter*.[119] Here was the "soft" element of twentieth-century Protestant modernism, a willingness to turn religion into a form of leisure or escape, to make it popular by accommodating it to the terms of mass culture. The psychology of the church was to be remade as the psychology of the movie house. The appeal of laughter, envisioned as a form of relief from the stresses and burdens of work in industrial society, could be harnessed to the worship of God. The work of providing relief made the mass culture of comic forms and the liberal church both competitors and partners in the institutionalization of a therapeutic ethos. The Victorian sanctions against laughter in the realm of the sacred seemed to melt away when the values associated with laughter and Christianity came to parallel one another: gentle, benign, sympathetic relief from the burdens of everyday life, a willingness to accept rather than challenge the incongruities of life, salvation through the achievement of "perspective." Christ, remade as Chaplin's sympathetic Little Tramp, made the leisure of laughter an integral part of his offering.

The reinvention of the image of Christ was in fact central to the cultural reinvigoration of Protestantism in the twentieth century. One of the most popular and influential new images of Christ was that to be found in the advertising man Bruce Barton's 1925 best-seller, *The Man Nobody Knows*. Barton's remaking of Christ, not as sympathetic comic figure but as genial business executive, rejected one of the prevailing Victorian views of Christ: that he never laughed. Barton's Jesus was a jokester, a humorist, a guy whose idea of amusement was turning water into wine. In his sequel, *The Book Nobody Knows*, Barton claimed that a sense of humor was "a quality not too common in the Bible"; Jesus was different from the Old Testament prophets and figures, all of whom were deficient in humor. Christ's humor, like Lincoln's, was a sign of his leadership qualities, of his ability to handle tensions and manage crisis. Jesus's power and appeal was to be located not in some somber or serious message but in his good-natured fun and humor.[120]

The general turn toward an acceptance of laughter and humor in mainline Protestantism by the 1930s was spearheaded by this rejection of the prevailing view of religion as somber, harsh, and melancholy. The most prominent purveyors of the new view of Christianity, beginning around the turn of the century, were those associated with mind-cure, whom Donald Meyer has called the "Positive Thinkers."[121] Orison Swett Marden, who wrote book after book on the themes of self, success,

leisure, abundance, and mental power, was an ardent advocate of a new Christian spirituality based on happiness and laughter. In *Peace, Power, and Plenty*, for instance, he argued that "melancholy, solemnity used to be regarded as a sign of spirituality, but it is now looked upon as the imprint of a morbid mind. There is no religion in it." Instead of accepting this dated view of Christianity, said Marden, we need to return to the original offering of Christ. "The religion Christ taught was bright and beautiful. . . . There was no cold, dry theology in it. It was just happy Christianity." [122] As an advocate of humor, Marden saw it as opposed to cold and dry theology, as well as to melancholy, thus rearranging the terms of an older humoral inheritance. The new religion was to be one that was happy rather than somber, that welcomed laughter and humor as signs of mental power and spirituality, rather than rejecting them. Although not all of those who introduced laughter into the previously forbidden realm of the sacred went as far as Marden and some of his mind-cure colleagues in making Christianity into a bright, bubbling, "fun" religion, the general orientation of twentieth-century thought pointed in the direction staked out by the mind-curists. Laughter was not a challenge to faith, but a partner with it.

The reaction against Protestant modernism in its mainline embodiment took two forms—fundamentalism and neo-orthodoxy. [123] The former had little to say on the issue of laughter. The neo-orthodox school of thought, on the other hand, with its restoration of the Calvinist sense of man as a fallen creature, the world as a place of evil, and the difficulties of faith, found room for laughter and humor in the life of the faithful. As Reinhold Niebuhr, the most prominent of the neo-orthodox theologians, put it, "The intimate relation between humor and faith is derived from the fact that both deal with the incongruities of our existence." The notion that humor was based on incongruity, and particularly the achievement of a perspective that held opposites intact, put it very much in line with the "ironic" vision of moral order based on the coupling of sin and faith that was characteristic of Niebuhr's thought. Humor, like faith, sought a detachment from the world and the particular place of the person within it, in order to see more "objectively." "Both humor and faith," said Niebuhr, "are expressions of the freedom of the human spirit, of its capacity to stand outside of life, and itself, and view the whole scene." If the modernist orientation in American Protestantism offered humor as a form of relief and relaxation that made religion more accommodating to the world, neo-orthodoxy latched onto the no-

tion of humor as cosmic incongruity that allowed for a detachment, if only temporarily, from the world.[124]

By offering perspective on the self, humor was envisioned by Niebuhr not as a way of freeing the self from sin, but as a means of developing a *greater sense* of sin. Humor did not represent a flight from religion and its demands, but an affirmation and identification of the sinfulness of the individual. Sin, rooted in the preoccupation with self, could be exposed by laughter and the sense of humor:

> The sense of humour is even more important provisionally in dealing with our own sins than in dealing with the sins of others. Humour is a proof of the capacity of the self to gain a vantage point from which it is able to look at itself. The sense of humour is thus a by-product of self-transcendence. People with a sense of humour do not take themselves too seriously. They are able to "stand off" from themselves, see themselves in perspective, and recognize the ludicrous and absurd aspects of their pretensions. All of us ought to be ready to laugh at ourselves because all of us are a little funny in our foibles, conceits and pretensions. What is funny about us is precisely that we take ourselves too seriously.[125]

Niebuhr's vision of the sense of humor as a "by-product of self-transcendence," of course, shared much with the notion of "self-objectification" that had come to be associated with humor in the twentieth century. Rabbi Joshua Liebman, for instance, in his contemporary best-selling *Peace of Mind,* advocated a kind of self-detachment by which he meant "the ability to look at ourselves with a kind of laughing humor, a nodding acquaintance with our fragilities, a tipping of the hat, as it were, to the petulant angers which vanish as we recognize them." [126] Liebman's integration of Freudian psychology and religious faith, as much as it inspired a spate of postwar works in the mind-cure school, also shared with Niebuhr a sense of religion as a struggle for faith, one in which humor could be a self-objectifying aid to the individual.

The sense of humor, for Niebuhr, was very much like the ironic vision he advocated as the basis for international relations in the Cold War world. In *The Irony of American History,* he warned against the humorless view of the world in which self-avowed "innocent" Americans proclaimed a righteous battle against the sins of communism. At the height of the Red Scare of the early 1950s, Niebuhr criticized the failures of the nation: "Collective man always tends to be morally complacent, self-righteous and lacking in a sense of humor. This tendency is accentuated in our own day by the humorless idealism of our culture with its simple moral distinctions between good and bad nations, the good nations being those which are devoted to 'liberty.' " Hardly an apologist for Soviet communism, Niebuhr went on to embrace the view of communists as lacking a sense of humor: "No laughter from heaven could possibly penetrate through the liturgy of moral self-appreciation in which the religion of communism abounds." [127] An ironic stance, a sense of humor, was what was required to deal with the complex problems raised by international relations after World War II, but such a stance was rooted in a religious and ethical view of the world. The sense of humor was a political value, for Niebuhr, because it was first a religious value, an aid and accomplice to faith. Seriousness was self-righteousness, pride, arrogance; humor was consciousness of sin.

As much as he embraced the sense of humor, however, there remained an ultimate sphere of faith into which humor and laughter could not enter—"the holy of holies." Compared to the Victorian prohibition against laughter in church and at matters religious, it appears initially as if Niebuhr had ceded a great deal to laughter, keeping only the inner sanctum uncontaminated. But his concerns were very much the same concerns that troubled some late Victorian critics of the cult of the sense of humor. Like Agnes Repplier, the Catholic antimodernist, Niebuhr valued the detachment and perspective offered by humor, but saw the troubling moral and religious implications of a detachment with no ultimate end or loyalty, a detachment that could easily slide into indifference. "Laughter," he said, is "the no-man's land between cynicism and contrition. Laughter may express a mood which takes neither the self nor life seriously." Humor, then, could be only a "prelude to faith," a "vestibule to the temple of confession," rather than an element of faith within the "holy of holies." What separated faith from humor was that the form of self-transcendence offered by the former was ultimate, while that offered by the latter was only immediate. Humor was a boon to preparing the self for faith; it was in no way an enemy to faith, but by itself it was "not able to deal with the problem of the sins of the self in any ultimate way." Laughter was a means of preparation, but ultimately, said Niebuhr, there is "no laughter in the holy of holies." Humor could be harnessed to religion, made compatible with it, offered as a perspective of self-transcendence, but faith still marked off a realm, however circumscribed, in which the injunction against laughter was to be enforced.[128]

In Niebuhr's post-World War II acceptance of humor as a component of an ironic vision informed by religious faith, there is a willingness to embrace humor as an aid to religion, rather than its enemy or, at best, an irrelevancy. The greatest threat to faith was now seen to be orthodoxy, absolutism, dogmatism; the sense of humor was the ideal weapon for fighting the unified and singular view of the world that orthodoxy demanded. Political freedom, psychological freedom, and religious freedom were yoked together in a rejection of the threat posed by any and all forms of absolutism. The recent view of Conrad Hyers is representative of the modern embrace of humor as a rejection of orthodoxy:

> There is a marked affinity between religious absolutism, ideological dogmatism, and political tyranny. All share in the attempted abolition of humor in relation to themselves. A common trait of dictators, revolutionaries, and ecclesiastical authoritarians alike is the refusal both to laugh at themselves and to permit others to laugh at them.[129]

The equation of religious orthodoxy with political tyranny reveals that the foundation for faith had moved away from a commitment to doctrine and the objective forms of religious expression. Humor was a sign of freedom of conscience, individual perspective, the living faith of the self; seriousness was, in this view, dead religion. And if religion, the realm of the sacred, now requires the sense of humor, what spheres of cultural life might reasonably still demand restrictions against humor's presumed benefits?

Whatever restrictions against laughter still exist are rapidly disappearing, and the role they have played in defining cultural boundaries is waning. We still have before us the serious and the humorous, but American culture has discovered that the serious is not a fixed category. At any moment it can be transformed into the humorous. The story of the distinction between the serious and the humorous in the twentieth century has been the story of humor penetrating ever deeper into the realm fenced off as being *in essence* serious. That sense of an essential seriousness has now virtually disappeared; one can *be* serious, as a kind of stance, as an attitude, but that stance can easily be transformed into the detached perspective offered by humor. There seems to be very little left to support a notion of "the serious" as an objective entity. The sense of humor is no longer simply the partner and complement to seriousness; it is the defining attribute by which the apparently serious is rendered humorous. The credo of the twentieth-century American bourgeois could well be: "Have a sense of humor—don't take yourself so seriously."

Conclusion

The past two decades have seen a rebirth of interest in humor and laughter in several important cultural venues: the expansion of stand-up comedy and the clubs and cable television outlets that support it; the affirmation of medical and health benefits to be derived from laughter in the wake of Norman Cousins's self-medication with Marx Brothers movies; the rise of humor consultants flogging their message of increased productivity and well being within corporations and other large, bureaucratic institutions through development of the sense of humor; the increasing use of humor as a sales technique, particularly in television advertising. Within the academic world, specialists in psychology, sociology, linguistics, literary criticism, anthropology, biology, philosophy, and related disciplines have been responsible for an enormous quantity of research; interdisciplinary forums and journals specializing in humor studies are the most visible evidence of a shared set of interests that transcend disciplinary boundaries. Those in cultural studies tell us that popular humor is a "transgressive" or "subversive" expression of "resistance" to oppression; those in gerontology, that humor and laughter have therapeutic benefits for the aging; those in communications, that humor aids effective speaking. Encompassing the fields of academic research and the popular renewal of interest in humor is what some have dubbed the "world humor movement," an umbrella term used to designate those groups interested in researching and promoting the uses and benefits of humor.[1]

The present book was written in the context of this cultural "rediscovery" of humor—perhaps, in fact, inspired by it. Yet it is not of it. My concern has not been with the great benefits to be wrought by teaching what Agnes Repplier called "the gospel of amusement," nor with mobilizing the study of humor as a substantive object, or set of practices, that would lead to an understanding of either the universal nature of laughter or the great cultural diversity in the forms of humor. It is not the uses of humor, not even the uses of the *idea* of humor, that have prompted my concern. Rather, I was inspired by the promotion of the value of humor everywhere around me to ask: What kind of sensibility, what kind of way of knowing and being, was it that could celebrate the sense of humor in such overwhelmingly positive terms? Instead of asking questions about the utility of humor, I looked to the larger cultural values that were associated with, and gave shape and meaning to, something that came to be called "the sense of humor"; instead of asking what humor was good for, I asked what people understood it to mean. My concern has always been with sensibility, the constitution of the culturally defined relationship between intellect, emotion, and object, between the internal and the external world, and never with humor in and of itself. The consequence of the turn my eye has taken is that the various contemporary attempts by the world humor movement to come to terms with humor and laughter are, I think, more understandable. The cultural assumptions, the philosophical underpinnings, the ontological foundations of contemporary views of humor and laughter are illuminated by the light of historical understanding.

Take the promotion of humor as an advertising device, for instance. A half-century ago it would have been unthinkable to advertising executives, copywriters, and their clients that they could mobilize an attitude of comic detachment for the purpose of selling products. The classic analysis of early twentieth-century advertising held strict warnings against the use of humor in advertising. Humor was thought to cast the product in an unfavorable light, to undermine the direct message of the advertiser, possibly to lower the tone associated with the product. Claude Hopkins, one of the founders of modern American advertising, put it bluntly:

> Frivolity has no place in advertising. Nor has humor. Spending money is usually serious business. . . . Money represents life and work. It is highly respected. To most people, spending money in one direction

means skimping in another. So money-spending usually has a serious purpose. People want full value. They want something worth more to them than the same amount spent in other ways would buy. . . . People do not buy from clowns.[2]

Similarly, Gerald Wadsworth warned advertisers away from the use of humor: "Humor is the result of man created stimuli which lacks the elements of naturalness or logicalness to permit of its being definately [sic] imaged. . . . Therefore, it should be resorted to only with the greatest care."[3]

In the late 1950s and early 1960s, a revolution in the use of humor in advertising began. Young admen like Stan Freberg and Ed Graham became advocates for the centrality of humor in advertising. Don Herold, writing in 1963, provided the legitimation. "Humor," he said, "provides amiable acceptance. Isn't that the number one thing we are seeking in advertising?" According to Herold, "Humor in advertising is so effective that it makes most other techniques in advertising look extravagant."[4] By the 1970s, marketing researchers had begun to do empirical studies of the effectiveness of humor in advertising; they had thoroughly instrumentalized humor in terms of its use value. Their conclusions about effectiveness have been ambiguous at best, but a majority of advertising executives now believe that humor is better than nonhumor for many kinds of advertising.[5] The practice of television advertising has followed this belief; indeed, the past twenty years have seen a saturation of television advertising with humor.

This sea change has been replicated in various other realms of contemporary cultural life. What are we to make of this phenomenon? The sense of humor, as its history warrants, has meant a capacity for shifting perspective, for engaging with multiplicity, for relief from stress. How has it been possible to harness this sensibility to the instrumental rationality of selling products, of communicating information, or of increasing productivity? If the reengagement with humor and laughter in recent decades has meant anything, after all, it has meant a subordination of humor to use value. Advertisers do not value the sense of humor in and of itself, but for its ability to aid them in achieving specifically defined goals, just as corporate humor consultants sell the uses of humor for achieving corporate goals, or as health-care professionals stress the physical and psychological benefits of using humor. The punch line, it is said, bolsters the bottom line. For those who see the sense of humor as that personal attribute which allows for freedom from restraint, as that which rejects the unity of linear rationality by recognizing the cosmic incongruity of existence, it might seem strange to think of humor as an instrument for achieving specific goals.

Yet that contradiction lies at the heart of the idea of the sense of humor, just as it lies at the heart of the modern American configuration of the relationship between self as subject and self as object. Because the sense of humor means a deep-seated perceptual ability to take the self unseriously, to stand as a detached observer of the self, to find relief or release in self-abnegation, it is figured as an instrumental value; it transcends a narrow rationality of circumscribed self-interest by favoring a thorough instrumentalization of the self. In the value of self-objectification, which Gordon Allport associated with the sense of humor, lies the capacity for treating the self as an instrument to achieve goals. What is new about the use of humor in advertising, about the corporate consultants selling humor, or about the generalized promotion of the sense of humor in contemporary America is just how bald and explicit their advocates are in stressing self-objectification as a tool to be used in achieving the goals of a corporate order. I have said that these advocates do not value the sense of humor in and of itself—but in a sense they do, for they have only made explicit the instrumental values that are embodied in the history of the idea of the sense of humor.

What is left to say? Cultural historians at this point in the narrative regularly trot out some heroic figure who is said both to be subject to the terms of a culture but also, in some sense, to transcend them. This is itself a genre convention. At the risk of violating an established practice, I confess that there is no such figure here; Norman Cousins will not do, nor will Lenny Bruce, nor the latter-day stand-up comedians of Comic Relief who have committed their profession to raising funds for the homeless. There are no candidates that could possibly qualify. This history has never been about individuals, or particular figures or groups of people; it has been about an idea, a cultural sensibility, a powerful way of thinking. To the extent that this history of the sense of humor has served to illuminate our understanding of modern American culture, it has accomplished what I set out to do. And if the reader now feels the need of some relief from a work that seems to take itself too seriously, there are plenty of places in the world outside this book to find it.

Notes

Introduction

1. Clifford Geertz, "Blurred Genres: The Refiguration of Social Thought," in *Local Knowledge: Further Essays in Interpretive Anthropology* (New York: Basic Books, 1983), 19–35.

2. R. G. Collingwood, *The Idea of History* (London: Oxford University Press, 1956). The first edition was published in 1946, three years after Collingwood's death. Most of the text was composed between 1936 and 1940.

3. For an overview of the field, although now slightly dated, see Walter Blair and Hamlin Hill, *America's Humor: From Poor Richard to Doonesbury* (New York: Oxford University Press, 1978).

4. Arthur O. Lovejoy, "The Historiography of Ideas" (1938), in *Essays in the History of Ideas* (New York: Capricorn Books, 1960), 1–13; idem, *The Great Chain of Being: A Study in the History of an Idea* (Cambridge: Harvard University Press, 1936). For an influential statement arguing that Foucault marks a fundamental break with the Lovejoy understanding of the history of ideas, see Mark Poster, "The Future according to Foucault: *The Archaeology of Knowledge* and Intellectual History," in *Modern European Intellectual History: Reappraisals and New Perspectives*, ed. Dominick LaCapra and Steven L. Kaplan (Ithaca: Cornell University Press, 1982), 137–52.

5. On objectivity in journalism, see Dan Schiller, *Objectivity and the News: The Public and the Rise of Commercial Journalism* (Philadelphia: University of Pennsylvania Press, 1981); Michael Schudson, *Discovering the News: A Social History of American Newspapers* (New York: Basic Books, 1978). On the idea of objectivity (and the varieties of objectivities) in science, see Lorraine Daston and Peter Galison, "The Image of Objectivity," *Representations* 40 (Fall 1992): 81–128; Lorraine Daston, "Objectivity and the Escape from Perspective," *Social Studies of Science* 22 (November 1992): 597–618; Theodore Porter, *Trust in Numbers: The Pursuit of Objectivity in Science and Public Life* (Princeton: Princeton University Press, 1995). See also the essays collected in Allan Megill, ed., *Rethinking Objectivity* (Durham: Duke University Press, 1994). On objectivity in history and the social sciences, see Peter

Novick, *That Noble Dream: The "Objectivity Question" and the American Historical Profession* (Cambridge: Cambridge University Press, 1988); Robert C. Bannister, *Sociology and Scientism: The American Quest for Objectivity, 1880–1940* (Chapel Hill: University of North Carolina Press, 1987); Mark C. Smith, *Social Science in the Crucible: The American Debate over Objectivity and Purpose, 1918–1941* (Durham: Duke University Press, 1994); Stephen Linstead, "Objectivity, Reflexivity, and Fiction: Humanity, Inhumanity, and the Science of the Social," *Human Relations* 47 (November 1994): 1321–46. For an account of sociological objectivity in terms of gender and masculinity, see Barbara Laslett, "Unfeeling Knowledge: Emotion and Objectivity in the History of Sociology," *Sociological Forum* 5 (September 1990): 413–34.

6. See, for instance, Charles Taylor, *Sources of the Self: The Making of Modern Identity* (Cambridge: Harvard University Press, 1989); Louis P. Masur, " 'Age of the First Person Singular': The Vocabulary of the Self in New England, 1780–1850," *Journal of American Studies* 25 (1991): 189–211.

7. Lovejoy, "The Historiography of Ideas," 3.

8. Warren I. Susman, " 'Personality' and the Making of Twentieth-Century Culture," in *Culture as History: The Transformation of American Society in the Twentieth Century* (New York: Pantheon, 1984), 271–85.

9. M. M. Bakhtin, *The Dialogic Imagination: Four Essays*, ed. Michael Holquist, trans. Caryl Emerson and Michael Holquist (Austin: University of Texas Press, 1981); Ian Watt, *The Rise of the Novel: Studies in Defoe, Richardson and Fielding* (London: Chatto and Windus, 1957).

10. Susan Sontag, "Notes on 'Camp,' " in *"Against Interpretation" and Other Essays* (New York: Farrar, Straus, and Giroux, 1966), 275–92; Andrew Ross, "Uses of Camp," in *No Respect: Intellectuals and Popular Culture* (New York: Routledge, 1989), 135–70; Jacob Brackman, *The Put-on: Modern Fooling and Modern Mistrust* (Chicago: Henry Regnery, 1971).

1. The Idea of Humor

1. The literature on individualism is voluminous. For the diversity of meanings of individualism, see Steven Lukes, *Individualism* (New York: Harper and Row, 1973). For an older style of intellectual history that sees individualism as an explicit ideology rooted in political theory, see C. B. Macpherson, *The Political Theory of Possessive Individualism: Hobbes to Locke* (New York: Oxford University Press, 1962); for individualism premised on tacit assumptions, still in the realm of political theory, see Louis Dumont, *From Mandeville to Marx: The Genesis and Triumph of Economic Ideology* (Chicago: University of Chicago Press, 1977). For the general history of the word "individualism," particularly the distinction between individualism and individuality, see Raymond Williams, *Keywords: A Vocabulary of Culture and Society*, rev. ed. (New York: Oxford University Press, 1983), 161–65. For individualism in its American context, as a general social ethic opposed to external controls, particularly from the state and the corporation, see Richard Weiss, *The American Myth of Success: From Horatio Alger to Norman Vincent Peale* (New York: Basic Books, 1969). Weiss, like many American historians, sees individualism as a once accurate description of social reality which, in the later nineteenth and early twentieth centuries, became a "myth" that no longer corresponded to "reality." See, for instance, pp. 9–14. For two recent analyses of individualism in American history, see Wilfred M. McClay, *The Masterless: Self and Society in Modern America* (Chapel Hill: University of North Carolina Press, 1994), and Christopher Newfield, *The Emerson Effect: Individualism and Submission in America* (Chicago: University of Chicago Press, 1996). On the notion of individualism as not simply a

set of attitudes toward the individual but a "constitution of the subject," the authority is Michel Foucault. See, for example, "What Is an Author?" in *Textual Strategies: Perspectives in Post-Structural Criticism*, ed. Josué V. Harari (Ithaca: Cornell University Press, 1979), 141–60. Although individualism is usually seen as a purely modern phenomenon, often originating in the Renaissance, cf. Alan MacFarlane, *The Origins of English Individualism: The Family, Property, and Social Transition* (Oxford: Basil Blackwell, 1978), who sees it as a social ethic among medieval English peasants.

2. Thomas C. Heller, Morton Sosna, and David E. Wellbery, eds., *Reconstructing Individualism: Autonomy, Individuality, and the Self in Western Thought* (Stanford: Stanford University Press, 1986); Michael Carrithers, Steven Collins, and Steven Lukes, eds., *The Category of the Person: Anthropology, Philosophy, History* (Cambridge: Cambridge University Press, 1985); Clifford Geertz, "Person, Time, and Conduct in Bali," in *The Interpretation of Cultures* (New York: Basic Books, 1973). For a valuable discussion of why anthropology in particular has turned to the category of the person, see George E. Marcus and Michael M. J. Fisher, *Anthropology as Cultural Critique: An Experimental Moment in the Human Sciences* (Chicago: University of Chicago Press, 1986), 45–76. On the notion of the self as the center of individualism, see Charles Taylor, *Sources of the Self: The Making of Modern Identity* (Cambridge: Harvard University Press, 1989); Louis P. Masur, " 'Age of the First Person Singular': The Vocabulary of the Self in New England, 1780–1850," *Journal of American Studies* 25 (1991): 189–211.

3. Dumont, *From Mandeville to Marx*; idem, *Essays on Individualism: Modern Ideology in Anthropological Perspective* (Chicago: University of Chicago Press, 1986).

4. On internalization as a historical process in Western societies, see Norbert Elias, *The History of Manners*, trans. Edmund Jephcott (New York: Pantheon, 1978); on the penetration of market relations into all spheres and its consequences for representations of persons, see Jean-Christophe Agnew, *Worlds Apart: The Market and the Theater in Anglo-American Thought, 1550–1750* (Cambridge: Cambridge University Press, 1986).

5. Taylor, *Sources of the Self*, 177. On the reflexivity of the self, see also Anthony Giddens, *Modernity and Self-Identity: Self and Society in the Late Modern Age* (Stanford: Stanford University Press, 1991).

6. Dumont, *From Mandeville to Marx*.

7. Christopher Shannon, "A World Made Safe for Differences: Ruth Benedict's *The Chrysanthemum and the Sword*," *American Quarterly* 47 (December 1995): 659–80.

8. Taylor, *Sources of the Self*, 211–302; on the valorization or foregrounding of "everyday life," see Henri Lefebvre, *Critique de la vie quotidienne*, 3 vols. (Paris: L'Arche, 1958–1981).

9. Ian Watt, *The Rise of the Novel: Studies in Defoe, Richardson and Fielding* (London: Chatto and Windus, 1957), 9–34, 60–62, on "formal realism" as a foregrounding of "ordinary life" and the rise of individualism in eighteenth-century Britain as related to the emergence of a new middle-class reading public.

10. Taylor, *Sources of the Self*. The interpretations of the moral sense in key thinkers such as Shaftesbury and Hutcheson differ on the extent to which the concept is seen as "subjectivist," but all interpretations suggest a new relationship between objective and subjective morality based on the idea of a moral sense. See, for instance, T. A. Roberts, *The Concept of Benevolence: Aspects of Eighteenth-Century Moral Philosophy* (London: Macmillan, 1973), 2–26; and Ernest Tuveson, "Shaftesbury and the Age of Sensibility," in *Studies in Criticism and Aesthetics, 1660–1800*, ed. Howard Anderson and John S. Shea (Minneapolis: University of Minnesota Press, 1967), 73–93.

11. David Summers, *The Judgment of Sense: Renaissance Naturalism and the Rise of Aesthetics* (Cambridge: Cambridge University Press, 1987), 327–28.

12. For general background on the "cult of sensibility" and the philosophy and literature of sense and sentiment, see Janet Todd, *Sensibility: An Introduction* (London: Methuen,

1986). See also John Mullan, *Sentiment and Sociability: The Language of Feeling in the Eighteenth Century* (New York: Oxford University Press, 1988); G. J. Barker-Benfield, *The Culture of Sensibility: Sex and Society in Eighteenth-Century Britain* (Chicago: University of Chicago Press, 1992).

13. Hooker's reading of the early eighteenth century as "the era of rugged individualism" suggests a fairly heavy dose of presentism. Edward N. Hooker, "Humour in the Age of Pope," *Huntington Library Quarterly* 11 (1947–48): 361–85; Charles Read Baskervill, *English Elements in Jonson's Early Comedy* (Austin: University of Texas, 1911), 40.

14. Louis Cazamian, *The Development of English Humor* (Durham: Duke University Press, 1952), 310. Much of my discussion of the changing object-subject relations in the meaning of the word "humor" is indebted to Cazamian's initial formulation of the historical process. For the etymology of humor, see Ernest Weekley, *An Etymological Dictionary of Modern English* (New York: Dover, 1967), 735.

15. Taylor, *Sources of the Self*, 188–89.

16. *OED*, 2d ed., s.v. "humor."

17. Ibid.; Baskervill, *English Elements in Jonson's Early Comedy*, 38.

18. Baskervill, *English Elements in Jonson's Early Comedy*, 39. The didactic literature referred to by Baskervill includes writers such as John Lyly, Robert Greene, Thomas Nashe, and Thomas Lodge.

19. Henry L. Snuggs, "The Comic Humors: A New Interpretation," *PMLA* 62 (March 1947): 114–22.

20. Stephen Greenblatt, *Renaissance Self-Fashioning: From More to Shakespeare* (Chicago: University of Chicago Press, 1980).

21. Watt, *Rise of the Novel*.

22. Baskervill, *English Elements in Jonson's Early Comedy*, 40.

23. This disagreement began as early as the seventeenth century in the dispute between Shadwell and Dryden over the proper form of comedy. See Thomas Shadwell, "Preface to *The Humorists, A Comedy*," in *Critical Essays of the Seventeenth Century*, ed. J. E. Spingarn (Oxford: Oxford University Press, Clarendon Press, 1908), 2:152–62. For the full dispute, see Richard L. Oden, ed., *Dryden and Shadwell: The Literary Controversy and "Mac Flecknoe" (1668–1679)* (Delmar, N.Y.: Scholars' Facsimiles and Reprints, 1977).

24. G. Gregory Smith, ed., *Elizabethan Critical Essays* (Oxford: Oxford University Press, Clarendon Press, 1904), 2:390.

25. There is, of course, no way of knowing directly the usages and meanings of a word among the illiterate members of a now-vanished society, and the vast majority of sixteenth-and seventeenth century Englishmen were illiterate. In addition, it was not until the eighteenth-century development of the dictionary that the systematic definition of terms became a priority. It would probably be fair to assume that most of the people of England never thought twice about the meaning of the word "humor," and simply used it as they saw fit. This does not mean, however, that one cannot infer meanings within a broad cultural sphere from literary writings alone. One may, for instance, consider the social range of Jonson's audience and the implied meanings he is clearly responding to in his definition of humor. One such inference is that the repeated efforts to explicitly define humor indicate a perception of diverse and contradictory meanings among the population as a whole, and that such concerns were not merely literary. On the social composition of Jonson's audiences and his rhetoric in relation to that audience, see L. A. Beaurline, *Jonson and Elizabethan Comedy: Essays in Dramatic Rhetoric* (San Marino, Calif.: Huntington Library, 1978), 1–34.

26. Smith, ed. *Elizabethan Critical Essays*, 390–91.

27. Cazamian, *Development of English Humor*, 320.

28. Smith, ed., *Elizabethan Critical Essays*, 392.

29. George H. McKnight, *English Words and Their Background* (New York: D. Appleton, 1923), 420.

30. Owen Barfield, *History in English Words* (New York: George H. Doran., n.d.), 127.

31. Spingarn, ed. *Critical Essays of the Seventeenth Century*, 1:lxii-lxiii.

32. One of the main reasons Shadwell tended to be explicit about his definitions and purposes was that they were fundamental to his literary debate with John Dryden over the purposes of comedy. For the full debate, and an analysis of the points of contention, see Oden ed., *Dryden and Shadwell: The Literary Controversy and "Mac Flecknoe" (1668–1679)*.

33. Shadwell, "Preface to *The Humorists, A Comedy*," in *Critical Essays of the Seventeenth Century*, ed. Spingarn, 2:162.

34. Ibid., 2:157.

35. H. D. Traill, "The Analysis of Humor," *Living Age* 155 (1882): 112.

36. Cazamian, *Development of English Humor*, 230, 393.

37. Samuel S. Cox, *Why We Laugh* (New York: Harper and Bros., 1876), 102.

38. Corbyn Morris, *An Essay toward Fixing the True Standard of Wit, Humour, Raillery, Satire, and Ridicule* (London: J. Roberts, 1744), xxvii-xxviii.

39. Ibid., 15.

40. Henry Home, Lord Kames, *Elements of Criticism* (Edinburgh, 1762), 4th American ed. (New York: S. Campbell and Son et al., 1823), 1:291.

41. [James] Burnet, Lord Monboddo, *Of the Origin and Progress of Language* (Edinburgh: J. Balfour, 1776), 3:343.

42. Stuart Tave, *The Amiable Humorist: A Study in the Comic Theory and Criticism of the Eighteenth and Early Nineteenth Centuries* (Chicago: University of Chicago Press, 1960), 167.

43. W. Alfred Jones, *Characters and Criticism* (New York: I. Y. Westervelt, 1857), 2:146. See also Edwin P. Whipple, *Lectures on Subjects Concerned with Literature and Life*, 2d ed. (Boston: Ticknor, Reed, and Fields, 1850), 49.

44. Herman Melville, *Moby Dick*, quoted in David S. Reynolds, *Beneath the American Renaissance* (New York: Knopf, 1988), 544. Reynolds thoroughly misunderstands the nineteenth-century use of the terms "humor" and "humorist" because he wishes to root the work of what he calls "the major writers" in the "popular humor" of the antebellum period, rather than look to the British literary roots of the terms. For instance, he recognizes no distinction between wit and humor, although that distinction was central to nineteenth-century understandings of the ludicrous. Similarly, he fails to recognize that Thoreau's notion of humor derives almost entirely from Carlyle rather than from the grotesque humor of the Southwest or the urban underworld. While there may be something to the notion that Emerson's image of himself as a transparent eyeball owes something to the eye-gouging narratives of southwestern humor, the view of one of his contemporaries that Emerson was "an inveterate humorist," who "writes as if he was half quizzing and half in earnest," has more do with the perception of Emerson as a peculiar character than with any conscious attempt on his part to be amusing. Reynolds's entire chapter on popular humor is riddled with similar misinterpretations. See pp. 439–560.

45. "The Humourists," *Philadelphia Minerva* 1 (17 October 1795): 2.

46. Bernard quoted in Joseph Boskin, *Sambo: The Rise and Demise of an American Jester* (New York: Oxford University Press, 1986), 60–62. On blackface minstrelsy, see also Robert Toll, *Blacking Up: The Minstrel Show in Nineteenth Century America* (New York: Oxford University Press, 1974); Alexander Saxton, "Blackface Minstrelsy and Jacksonian Ideology," *American Quarterly* 27 (Summer 1975): 3–28; idem, *The Rise and Fall of the White Republic: Class Politics and Mass Culture in Nineteenth-Century America* (London: Verso, 1990), 165–82; Eric Lott, *Love and Theft: Blackface Minstrelsy and the American Working*

Class (New York: Oxford University Press, 1993). The whole issue of blacks as humorists goes right to the heart of the object-subject dialectic of slavery. The classic analysis is Eugene Genevese, *Roll, Jordan, Roll: The World the Slaves Made* (New York: Pantheon, 1974). On the humor of blacks, see Lawrence Levine, *Black Culture and Black Consciousness: Afro-American Folk Thought from Slavery to Freedom* (New York: Oxford University Press, 1977), 298–366; Mel Watkins, *On the Real Side: Laughing, Lying, and Signifying—The Underground Tradition of African-American Humor That Transformed American Culture, from Slavery to Richard Pryor* (New York: Simon and Schuster, 1994).

47. This mitigation of guilt is particularly evident in the case of white views toward blacks as humorists. The vision of blacks as happy objects of amusement can be seen in the context of the antebellum cultural movement to alleviate the guilt arising from the contradiction between slavery and racism, on the one hand, and the egalitarian principles underlying republican institutions on the other. As Jean Baker argues, "the vision of blacks as contented with their lot in both North and South relieved guilt about their condition and dispelled what other popular sources had created—anxiety about organized interracial conflict." See Baker, *Affairs of Party: The Political Culture of Northern Democrats in the Mid-Nineteenth Century* (Ithaca: Cornell University Press, 1983), 242. For the broader context of white racial views, see George M. Fredrickson, *The Black Image in the White Mind: The Debate on Afro-American Character and Destiny, 1817–1914* (Hanover, N.H.: Wesleyan University Press, 1987) and, more recently, especially for the psychological underpinnings of these views, David Roediger, *The Wages of Whiteness: Race and the Making of the American Working Class* (London: Verso, 1991).

48. This is the main thesis of Stuart Tave's *The Amiable Humorist*, and my understanding of the transformation occurring in the eighteenth century is heavily indebted to that work. On the relation of sympathy and sentiment to the characterological notion of the humorist, see John K. Sheriff, *The Good-Natured Man: The Evolution of a Moral Ideal, 1660–1800* (University: University of Alabama Press, 1982), 38–58.

49. Roger B. Henkle, *Comedy and Culture: England 1820–1900* (Princeton: Princeton University Press, 1980), 226–27.

50. Jonathan Swift, "To Mr. Delany," quoted in Raymond Anselment, *Betwixt Jest and Earnest: Marprelate, Milton, Marvell, Swift and the Decorum of Religious Ridicule* (Toronto: University of Toronto Press, 1979), 134–35.

51. On Witherspoon, see Donald H. Meyer, *The Democratic Enlightenment* (New York: G. P. Putnam's Sons, 1976), 182–98; Terence Martin, *The Instructed Vision: Scottish Common Sense Philosophy and the Origins of American Fiction* (Bloomington: Indiana University Press, 1961); Agnew, *Worlds Apart*, 192. For a challenge to the notion that Witherspoon was primarily a proponent of Common Sense philosophy, see Peter J. Diamond, "Witherspoon, William Smith and the Scottish Philosophy in Revolutionary America," in Richard B. Sher and Jeffrey R. Smitten, eds. *Scotland and America in the Age of the Enlightenment* (Edinburgh: Edinburgh University Press, 1990), 130. Diamond's aim is to distinguish more sharply between modes of Scottish thought instead of accepting the general term "Common Sense" as a catch-all for eighteenth-century Scottish thought. He sees Witherspoon as influenced by Francis Hutcheson and his moral concerns rather than by the philosophical concerns of Thomas Reid, James Beattie, Dugald Stewart, and others more properly associated with "Common Sense." This stress on the importance of Hutcheson's thought in America accords well with the general argument being advanced here.

52. John Witherspoon, "Lectures on Eloquence," in *Works* (Philadelphia: William W. Woodward, 1802), 3:463.

53. *OED*, 2d ed., s.v. "talent."

54. George Campbell, *The Philosophy of Rhetoric* (Carbondale: Southern Illinois Univer-

sity Press, 1963), 15–16. The first American edition of Campbell's work was published circa 1818, and it was widely reprinted throughout the nineteenth century.

55. Kames, *Elements of Criticism*, 1:291.

56. Monboddo, *Of the Origin and Progress of Language*, 3:345.

57. "An Essay on Humour," *The Columbian Magazine, or Monthly Miscellany* 4 (January 1790): 31.

58. Sydney Smith, "On Wit and Humour," in *Selections from Sydney Smith*, ed. Ernest Rhys (London: Walter Scott, n.d.), 19. The first American edition was published in Smith's *Elementary Sketches of Moral Philosophy* (New York: Harper and Bros., 1850), 112–46. Although the lectures were given in the first decade of the nineteenth century, they did not become widely known until published at midcentury.

59. Leigh Hunt, *Wit and Humour Selected from the English Poets*, 2d ed. (London: Smith, Elder, 1846), 11–12. Emphasis in the original.

60. Sir William Temple, "Of Poetry" (1690), in *Works* (London: printed for J. Clarke, 1757), 3:424–25.

61. William Congreve, *"An Essay concerning Humour in Comedy* to Mr. Dennis," in Morris, *An Essay toward Fixing . . . Wit, Humour . . . [etc.]*, 75. Congreve's essay was originally published in 1695.

62. J. E. Spingarn, for instance, claimed that the original derivation of humor as "the keen perception, or the unconscious expression, of the odd and incongruous" was not of English origin at all, but was made in France. See Spingarn, ed. *Critical Essays of the Seventeenth Century*, 1:lxii. Others have claimed an early derivation in Italian: see Cazamian, *Development of English Humor*, 325. But even Spingarn admits that the French usage quickly disappeared after its initial derivation, and the term rapidly became distinctively English in the later seventeenth century. Further credence to the claims of Anglo distinctiveness is given by Owen Barfield's recognition of "humor" as one of the words borrowed by other languages in the post-seventeenth-century period. According to Barfield, words are usually borrowed for one of two reasons: because no word exists in the borrowing language to describe a particular object, or because the object itself has no prior existence in the culture and is borrowed along with the word. In the case of "humor," the latter reason applies. See Barfield, *History in English Words*, 66. Whether or not "humor" was originally derived in England, by the mid-seventeenth century it was largely recognized as a distinctively English term and borrowed in other languages as such.

63. Max Eastman, *The Sense of Humor* (New York: Charles Scribner's Sons, 1921), 166–67; Samuel McChord Crothers, "The Mission of Humor," in *The Gentle Reader* (Boston: Houghton Mifflin, 1903), 88.

64. Morris, *An Essay toward Fixing . . . Wit, Humour . . . [etc.]*, 20–21.

65. Hugh Blair, *Lectures in Rhetoric and Belles Lettres*, 8th ed. (London: T. Cadell Jun. and W. Davies, 1801), 3:348.

66. George Farquhar, "A Discourse upon Comedy in Reference to the English Stage," in *The Complete Works of George Farquhar*, ed. Charles Stonehill (Bloomsbury: Nonesuch Press, 1930), 2:337.

67. [William A. Jones], "American Humor," *Democratic Review* 17 (September 1845): 215.

68. Cox, *Why We Laugh*, 37, 162.

69. Ibid., 162, 38.

70. See, for instance, Alan Dundes, "Laughter behind the Iron Curtain: A Sample of Rumanian Political Jokes," in *Cracking Jokes: Studies of Sick Humor Cycles and Stereotypes* (Berkeley: Ten Speed Press, 1987), 159–68.

71. Professor John Millar, *Works*, 4 vols. (1812), quoted in "On Wit and Humour," *Blackwood's Magazine* 6 (March 1820): 641–42.

1. Mikhail Bakhtin, *Rabelais and His World*, trans. Helene Iswolsky (Bloomington: Indiana University Press, 1984), 59–144. The interpretation of the history of laughter offered here is very different from that suggested by Bakhtin.

2. See, for instance, John Morreall, ed., *The Philosophy of Laughter and Humor* (Albany: State University of New York Press, 1987); idem, *Taking Laughter Seriously* (Albany: State University of New York Press, 1983), 1–37.

3. On Madius and the early modern adaptation of the theory of the risible, see Marvin T. Herrick, *Comic Theory in the Sixteenth Century* (Urbana: University of Illinois Press, 1950), 37–56; Vincenzo Maggi (Madius), from *On the Ridiculous* (1550), in *Theories of Comedy*, ed. Paul Lauter (New York: Doubleday, 1964), 64–73.

4. Thomas Hobbes, *Leviathan; or, The Matter, Forms and Power of a Commonwealth Ecclesiasticall and Civil*, ed. Michael Oakshot (New York: Collier Books, 1962), 52.

5. Joan Wildeblood and Peter Brinson, *The Polite World: A Guide to English Manners from the Thirteenth to the Nineteenth Century* (London: Oxford University Press, 1965), 8–9, 125, 216.

6. On laughter as a threat to the social order and established institutions of the eighteenth century, see John Redwood, *Reason, Ridicule and Religion: The Age of Enlightenment in England 1650–1750* (Cambridge: Harvard University Press, 1976), 183. For a different view, one that sees eighteenth-century discussions of laughter as based in social stability and consensus, as opposed to the threat of laughter in the sixteenth and seventeenth centuries, cf. Raymond Anselment, *Betwixt Jest and Earnest: Marprelate, Milton, Marvell, Swift and the Decorum of Religious Ridicule* (Toronto: University of Toronto Press, 1979), 3.

7. *OED*, 2d ed., s.v. "ridicule" and "ridiculous."

8. Redwood, *Reason, Ridicule and Religion*, 196.

9. The argument for what came to be called, "ridicule as the test of truth" was most widely known in Anthony Ashley Cooper, Earl of Shaftesbury, "A Letter concerning Enthusiasm" (1708) and "*Sensus Communis*; An Essay on the Freedom of Wit and Humour" (1709). Both essays were published and circulated in the author's *Characteristicks of Men, Manners, Opinions, Times*, vol. 1. I used the fifth edition (Birmingham: J. Baskerville, 1773). According to Alfred O. Aldridge, Shaftesbury himself never made the argument for ridicule as the test of truth—it was his contemporaries and followers who constructed a debate over this issue. See Aldridge, "Shaftesbury and the Test of Truth," *PMLA* 60 (1945): 129–56. On "the doctrine of ridicule," see R. L. Brett, *The Third Earl of Shaftesbury: A Study in Eighteenth Century Literary Theory* (London: Hutchinson House, 1951), 165–86. My understanding of Shaftesbury and the eighteenth-century conflicts over ridicule is indebted to Ernest Tuveson, "Shaftesbury and the Age of Sensibility," in *Studies in Criticism and Aesthetics, 1660–1800*, ed. Howard Anderson and John S. Shea (Minneapolis: University of Minnesota Press, 1967), 73–93; and to Redwood, *Reason, Ridicule and Religion*.

10. Francis Hutcheson, *Reflections upon Laughter*, in *Francis Hutcheson: An Inquiry concerning Beauty, Order, Harmony, Design*, ed. Peter Kivy (The Hague: Martinus Nijhoff, 1973), 106. Hutcheson's criticism of Hobbes is misdirected, for although Hobbes's theory of laughter as sudden glory lent itself well to the concept of ridicule, Hobbes himself did not use the word "ridicule." It is symptomatic of the extent to which ridicule was omnipresent in the eighteenth century that Hutcheson would find it in Hobbes, where it did not exist. Hutcheson's essays on laughter were originally published in the *Dublin Journal* in 1725.

11. On the ludicrous and the risible, and their relation to each other, see, for instance, Henry Home, Lord Kames, *Elements of Criticism* (Edinburgh, 1762), 4th American ed.

(New York, 1823) 1:220; William Hazlitt, *Lectures on the English Comic Writers*, 3d ed. (London: John Templeman, 1841), 7. Hazlitt's lectures were originally published in 1811.

12. Stuart Tave, *The Amiable Humorist: A Study in the Comic Theory and Criticism of the Eighteenth and Early Nineteenth Centuries* (Chicago: University of Chicago Press, 1960), 27. My quarrel with Tave here is that ridicule was never consistently regarded as either ill-natured (as distinguished from good-natured) or as wit. While it is necessary to use contemporary terms such as "wit" to define terms of laughter in comprehensible ways, ridicule was not limited to wit in either the eighteenth- or the twentieth-century meanings of the latter. Equally, ridicule could be good-natured as well as ill-natured, even though it retained its association with scorn and contempt. "Ridicule" was used in so many ways that it seems limiting and arbitrary to fix its eighteenth-century meaning as the category of ill-natured wit.

13. Anselment, *Betwixt Jest and Earnest*, 17; *OED*, 2d ed., s.v. "raillery."

14. Sir William Temple, "Of Poetry" (1690), in *Works* (London: printed for J. Clarke, 1757), 3:421–22.

15. George Campbell, *The Philosophy of Rhetoric* (Carbondale: Southern Illinois University Press, 1963), 8.

16. On the rise of conversation as an arena of instruction in eighteenth-century Britain, see Peter Burke, *The Art of Conversation* (Ithaca: Cornell University Press, 1993), 108–12. On the relation of conversation to the emergence of a bourgeois ethic of gentility, see Richard L. Bushman, *The Refinement of America: Persons, Houses, Cities* (New York: Alfred A. Knopf, 1992), 83–89.

17. On raillery and its relation to ridicule, and particularly on its lack of an object, see Norman Knox, *The Word Irony and Its Context, 1500–1755* (Durham: Duke University Press, 1961), 187–221.

18. Ibid., 208–10.

19. Campbell, *The Philosophy of Rhetoric*, 26.

20. Anthony Ashley Cooper, Earl of Shaftesbury, *Sensus Communis: An Essay on the Freedom of Wit and Humour* (reprint, New York: Garland Publishing, 1971), 72.

21. The classic statement for the position that, by the later eighteenth century, laughter had come to seem less scornful and dangerous, remains Tave, *The Amiable Humorist*. My own thoughts owe much to this work, although they differ with it in some ways. An argument that eighteenth-century thought on laughter was characterized by "unease," rather than a thorough rejection of the Hobbesian paradigm, is made in Allan Ingram, *Intricate Laughter in the Satire of Swift and Pope* (London: Macmillan, 1986), 1–39. Because scholarly study has focused on the relative evaluation of laughter as beneficial or malevolent in the eighteenth century, it has tended to overlook the underlying shift in the understanding of the relationship between the causes of laughter and the status of laughter-producing objects.

22. John M. Bullitt, "Swift's 'Rules of Raillery,' " in *Veins of Humor*, ed. Harry Levin (Cambridge: Harvard University Press, 1972), 93–108.

23. Sydney Smith, "On Wit and Humour," in *Selections from Sydney Smith*, ed. Ernest Rhys (London: Walter Scott, n.d.), 14–15.

24. Hutcheson, *Reflections upon Laughter*, 109.

25. See Alexander Gerard, *An Essay on Taste*, 3d ed. (Edinburgh: J. Bell and W. Greech, 1780), 62–68; James Beattie, "On Laughter and Ludicrous Composition," in *Essays* (Edinburgh: William Greech, 1776), 583–706; Mark Akenside, "The Pleasures of Imagination," in *The Poetical Works of Mark Akenside* (Edinburgh: James Nicol, 1857), 74.

26. Hazlitt, *Lectures on the English Comic Writers*, 7; see also, for instance, Leigh Hunt, *Wit and Humour Selected from the English Poets* (London: Smith, Elder, 1890), 6–7.

27. On changes in attitude toward rudeness in general see Elias, *The History of Manners*, trans. Edmund Jephcott (New York: Pantheon, 1978).

28. On the latter point, see Robert Bernard Martin, *The Triumph of Wit: A Study in Victorian Comic Theory* (Oxford: Oxford University Press, Clarendon Press, 1974). I find Martin's argument unpersuasive and limited to the discussion of a very few texts.

29. For an analysis of older meanings of wit and their relation to humor, see Daniel Wickberg, "The Sense of Humor in American Culture, 1850–1960" (Ph.D. diss., Yale University, 1993), 104–9. Changes in the meaning of wit are discussed in J. E. Spingarn, ed., *Critical Essays of the Seventeenth Century* (Oxford: Oxford University Press, Clarendon Press, 1908), 1:xxviii–xxxi; Judson Milburne, *The Age of Wit: 1650–1750* (New York: Macmillan, 1966). On the history of the word "wit," see C. S. Lewis, *Studies in Words* (Cambridge: Cambridge University Press, 1960), 86–110.

30. For the difficulty in drawing a distinction between wit and humor in eighteenth-century practice, see Knox, *The Word Irony and Its Context*, 189. For examples of a variety of wit/humor distinctions and the confusing and contradictory uses of the terms, see Corbyn Morris, *An Essay toward Fixing the True Standard of Wit, Humour, Raillery, Satire, and Ridicule* (London: J. Roberts, 1744), 13; William Congreve, *"An Essay concerning Humour in Comedy* to Mr. Dennis," in Morris, *An Essay toward Fixing. . . . Wit, Humour. . . .* [etc.], 67–68; Beattie, "On Laughter and Ludicrous Composition," 586; [James] Burnet, Lord Monboddo, *Of the Origin and Progress of Language* (Edinburgh: J. Balfour, 1776), 3:315–16, 342; Kames, *Elements of Criticism*, 1:299; Campbell, *The Philosophy of Rhetoric*, 19–20.

31. John Dryden, "Preface: An Evening's Love," in *Dryden and Shadwell: The Literary Controversy and "Mac Flecknoe" (1668–1679)* ed. Richard L. Oden (Delmar, N.Y.: Scholars' Facsimiles and Reprints, 1977), 60.

32. Morris, *An Essay toward Fixing . . . Wit, Humour . . .* [etc.], 23–25.

33. Edwin P. Whipple, "Wit and Humour," *Hogg's Instructor*, n.s., 5 (1850): 167, 181. This is the text of a lecture given before the Boston Mercantile Library Association in December 1845. It was reprinted in idem, *Lectures on Subjects Concerned with Literature and Life* (Boston: Ticknor, Reed, and Fields, 1850), 84–121.

34. Historians are just beginning to recognize the relationship between the sympathetic imagination and the detailed representation of empirical reality in bourgeois culture. See, for instance, Karen Halttunen, "Humanitarianism and the Pornography of Pain in Anglo-American Culture," *American Historical Review* 100 (April 1995): 303–34. On the significance of realism in nineteenth-century culture, see David E. Shi, *Facing Facts: Realism in American Thought and Culture, 1850–1920* (New York: Oxford University Press, 1995). On realism in the twentieth century, see Miles Orvell, *The Real Thing: Imitation and Authenticity in American Culture, 1880–1940* (Chapel Hill: University of North Carolina Press, 1989); T. J. Jackson Lears, *Fables of Abundance: A Cultural History of Advertising in America* (New York: Basic Books, 1994), 345–78.

35. Hazlitt, *Lectures on the English Comic Writers*, 23–24.

36. "American Humour," *North British Review* 33 (November 1860): 463; "Wit and Humour," *Littel's Living Age* 114 (24 August 1872): 479; Richard Haywarde, "On Wit and Humor," *The Knickerbocker* 36 (December 1850): 197. See also W. Alfred Jones, *Characters and Criticisms* (New York: I. Y. Westervelt, 1857), 2:145–47.

37. On the use of "culture" as a class identity in a new hierarchy, see Lawrence Levine, *Highbrow/Lowbrow: The Emergence of Cultural Hierarchy in America* (Cambridge: Harvard University Press, 1988).

38. Whipple, "Wit and Humour," *Hogg's Instructor*, 167; "American Humour," *North British Review*, 464. See also, for instance, Horace Bushnell quoted in Hamilton Wright Mabie, "A Word about Humor," in *Essays in Literary Interpretation* (Toronto: Morang, 1905), 209.

39. Samuel S. Cox, *Why We Laugh* (New York: Harper and Bros., 1876), 30–31.

40. "Some Doubts on the Popular Supposed Distinction between Wit and Humor," *The Nation* 2 (18 January 1866): 73.

41. "Wit and Humor," *Atlantic Monthly* 100 (September 1907): 427.

42. X., "Wit and Humor," *The Nation* 2 (1 February 1866): 144.

43. Robert Kiely, "Victorian Harlequin: The Function of Humor in Thackeray's Critical and Miscellaneous Prose," in *Veins of Humor*, ed. Harry Levin (Cambridge: Harvard University Press, 1972), 149.

44. Melville D. Landon, *Comical Hits by Famous Wits: Comprising Wit, Humor, Pathos, Ridicule, Satire* (Chicago: Thompson and Thomas, 1900), 9–13.

45. Ibid., 80.

46. Tave, *The Amiable Humorist*, 202–26. On the importance of the modern concept of sympathy, and its prevalence in America, see John Stafford, "Sympathy Comes to America," in *Themes and Directions in American Literature*, ed. Ray B. Browne and Donald Pizer (Lafayette, Ind.: Purdue University Studies, 1969), 24–37. The continuing relationship between humor and this culture of sympathy and benevolence is often overlooked by those who consciously identify modernity with a specific reading of Freud and who believe that modern interpretations of humor and laughter stress its antipathetic and aggressive elements. See, for instance, Peter Gay's misinterpretation of Victorian bourgeois laughter in *The Bourgeois Experience: Victoria to Freud*, 4 vols. (New York: W. W. Norton, 1984–1995), vol. 3: *The Cultivation of Hatred* (New York: Norton, 1993), 368–423. An even more peculiar misreading of the relationship between humor and sentimentality in twentieth-century America can be found in Elliott Oring, "Humor and the Suppression of Sentiment," *Humor* 7 (1994): 7–26. Oring locates the culture of sentiment and sensibility in the eighteenth and nineteenth centuries, and then insists that sentiment has become unacceptable in the culture of the twentieth century. In his view, humor in the twentieth century has become an acceptable way to express, in hidden form, the unacceptable: sentimentality. This view, of course, overlooks the central facts that the concept of humor itself became acceptable precisely because it was linked to sympathy and sentiment, that humor is part and parcel of the culture of sentiment, and that sentimentality is ubiquitous in twentieth-century culture, even if some intellectuals find it disagreeable.

47. Thomas Carlyle, "Jean Paul Friedrich Richter," *Edinburgh Review* 91 (1827), in *Critical and Miscellaneous Essays* (Chicago and New York: Bedford, Clarke [1890]), vol. 3, sec. 3, pp. 20, 19. For an analysis of Carlyle's views on humor, see Richard J. Dunn, " 'Inverse Sublimity': Carlyle's Theory of Humour," *University of Toronto Quarterly* 40 (Fall 1970): 41–57.

48. Henry David Thoreau, "Thomas Carlyle and His Works," *Graham's American Monthly Magazine* 30 (April 1847): 242; reprinted in *Early Essays and Miscellanies*, ed. Joseph J. Moldenhauer and Edwin Moser, with Alexander C. Kern (Princeton: Princeton University Press, 1975). This essay was originally given as a lecture at the Concord Lyceum, 4 February 1846.

49. "Wit and Humour," *Westminster Review* 80 (October 1863): 450.

50. Whipple, "Wit and Humour," *Hogg's Instructor*, 167.

51. "Wit and Humour," *Westminster Review* 48 (October 1847): 47; Haywarde, "On Wit and Humor," 493.

52. "Traits of American Humour," *Irish Quarterly Review* 2 (1852): 177. For a classic statement of the Victorian view of kindly, genial, sympathetic humor, see the address given by William Makepeace Thackeray in New York City in 1852: "Charity and Humor," in *Works* (New York: Charles Scribner's Sons, 1904), 26:399–421.

53. "Wit and Humor," *Atlantic Monthly*, 428.

54. Disney and Loos quoted in Max Eastman, *Enjoyment of Laughter* (New York: Hal-

cyon House, 1939), 341, 332. Many other prominent humorists from the turn of the century through the 1930s are quoted by Eastman in his supplementary appendix. The idea of humor and laughter as sympathetic is maintained by a majority of them.

55. Boris Sidis, *The Psychology of Laughter* (New York: D. Appleton, 1919), 64, 145; J. C. Gregory, *The Nature of Laughter* (New York: Harcourt, Brace, 1924), esp. 9–19.

56. Max Eastman, *The Sense of Humor* (New York: Charles Scribner's Sons, 1921); idem, *Enjoyment of Laughter*; J. Y. T. Grieg, *The Psychology of Laughter and Comedy* (London: George Allen and Unwin, 1923).

57. Bruce Mazlish, *A New Science: The Breakdown of Connections and the Birth of Sociology* (University Park: Pennsylvania State University Press, 1993).

58. On Adam Smith, see Tave, *The Amiable Humorist,* 204. For a similar view, see "Reflections on Humour," *Massachusetts Magazine* 5 (1793): 422.

59. Alexander Bain, *English Composition and Rhetoric* (New York: D. Appleton, 1888), 2:239–42; see also idem, *The Emotions and the Will,* 4th ed. (London: Longmans, Green, 1899), 259–61. Bain's tactics for "softening" and "redeeming" laughter include stressing "the slighter form of pain," mixing "tender and kind feeling" with a ludicrous effect, and turning degradation into a compliment.

60. William McDougall, *Outline of Psychology* (New York: Charles Scribner's Sons, 1923), 165–70.

61. While there are clearly differences between sentiment, sensibility, and the humanitarian sensibility—and I do not wish to conflate the three terms—there are also some common bonds that seem to make them a coherent set of values. For a general overview of the eighteenth-century English culture of sensibility, see Janet Todd, *Sensibility: An Introduction* (New York: Methuen, 1986). Also see Louis I. Bredvold, *The Natural History of Sensibility* (Detroit: Wayne State University Press, 1962) and Paul Langford, *A Polite and Commercial People: England 1727–1783* (New York: Oxford University Press, 1989), 461–518. On sentimentalism, see Erik Erämetsä, "A Study of the Word 'Sentimental' and of Other Linguistic Characteristics of Eighteenth-Century Sentimentalism in England," *Annales Academiae Scientiarum Fennicae,* ser. B (Helsinki, 1951); John Mullan, *Sentiment and Sociability: The Language of Feeling in the Eighteenth Century* (New York: Oxford University Press, 1988). On nineteenth-century American sentimentalism, see Ann Douglas, *The Feminization of American Culture* (New York: Knopf, 1977); Shirley Samuels, ed., *The Culture of Sentiment: Race, Gender, and Sentimentality in Nineteenth-Century America* (New York: Oxford University Press, 1992). The critical historical importance of the culture of sensibility is stressed in two recent works: Colin Campbell, *The Romantic Ethic and the Spirit of Modern Consumerism* (New York: Basil Blackwell, 1987); G. J. Barker-Benfield, *The Culture of Sensibility: Sex and Society in Eighteenth-Century Britain* (Chicago: University of Chicago Press, 1992). On the humanitarian sensibility, see Thomas Bender, ed. *The Antislavery Debate: Capitalism and Abolitionism as a Problem in Historical Interpretation* (Berkeley: University of California Press, 1992); Keith Thomas, *Man and the Natural World: A History of the Modern Sensibility* (New York: Pantheon, 1983), 143–91; A. R. Humphrey, " 'The Friend of Mankind,' 1700–1760—An Aspect of Eighteenth-Century Sensibility," *Review of English Studies* 24 (July 1948): 203–18; Maurice Parmalee, "The Rise of Modern Humanitarianism," *American Journal of Sociology* 21 (November 1915): 345–59; Norman S. Fiering, "Irresistible Compassion: An Aspect of Eighteenth-Century Sympathy and Humanitarianism," in *Race, Gender, and Rank: Early Modern Ideas of Humanity,* ed. Maryanne Cline Horowitz (Rochester: University of Rochester Press, 1992), 378–401; Karen Halttunen, "Humanitarianism and the Pornography of Pain in Anglo-American Culture," *American Historical Review* 100 (April 1995): 303–34; Elizabeth B. Clark, " 'The Sacred Rights of the Weak': Pain, Sympathy, and the Culture of Individual Rights in Antebellum America," *Journal of American History* 82 (September 1995), 463–93.

62. Lewis, *Studies in Words*, 133–64. It is also interesting to note that before the five senses—sight, hearing, touch, taste, and smell—had the word "sense" applied to them in English, they were referred to as "the five wits," suggesting another, deeper connection between intellect, judgment, and perception. See pp. 87–88.

63. David Summers, *The Judgment of Sense: Renaissance Naturalism and the Rise of Aesthetics* (Cambridge: Cambridge University Press, 1987), 204–11.

64. Ibid., 78–89. The quote is from p. 131.

65. Lewis, *Studies in Words*, 142. The idea of sense as "unspecified awareness," according to Lewis, "now exists in an almost fossilised condition in 'sense of humour.' " The fact of this "fossilization" should suggest that the term meant much more than an awareness of humor.

66. Ernest Tuveson, "Shaftesbury and the Age of Sensibility," in *Studies in Criticism and Aesthetics 1660–1800*, ed. Howard Anderson and John S. Shea (Minneapolis: University of Minnesota Press, 1967), 80–81. My understanding of Shaftesbury's notion of the moral sense is based on Tuveson as well as on Brett, *The Third Earl of Shaftesbury*, 81, and Bredvold, *The Natural History of Sensibility*, 3–26. See also T. A. Roberts, *The Concept of Benevolence: Aspects of Eighteenth-Century Moral Philosophy* (London: Macmillan, 1973), esp. 2–26; D. Daiches Raphael, *The Moral Sense* (London: Oxford University Press, 1947), 15–46, on Hutcheson's use of the concept after Shaftesbury.

67. My reading of Hutcheson concerning the sense of beauty is based largely on Peter Kivy, *The Seventh Sense: A Study of Francis Hutcheson's Aesthetics and Its Influence in Eighteenth-Century Britain* (New York: Burt Franklin, 1976), 1–9, 27. On the emergence of aesthetics, in particular the category of the sublime, see Peter de Bolla, *The Discourse of the Sublime: Readings in History, Aesthetics, and the Subject* (New York: Basil Blackwell, 1989).

68. Hutcheson, *Reflections upon Laughter*, 113, 116; Kivy, *The Seventh Sense*, 55.

69. Akenside, *Poetical Works*, 74–75.

70. Kames, *Elements of Criticism*, 1:298.

71. Gerard, *Essay on Taste*, 62.

72. [Eliza Ware Rotch {Mrs. John} Farrar], *The Young Lady's Friend* (Boston: American Stationers' Co., 1836), 375–76.

73. Oliver Wendell Holmes, *The Autocrat of the Breakfast Table* (Boston: James R. Osgood, 1872), 101.

74. Dickens quoted in James R. Kincaid, *Dickens and the Rhetoric of Laughter* (Oxford: Oxford University Press, Clarendon Press, 1971), 17.

3. Bureaucratic Individualism and the Sense of Humor

1. The term "bureaucratic individualism" is my own coinage, but I later came across Alasdair MacIntyre's use of the term to mean something related but quite different; the use of the term in this book should not be confused with MacIntyre's meaning. MacIntyre is concerned with some of the same issues I am, however: e.g., how modern ideology tries to reconcile the insistence on individual freedom and self-creation with the equally insistent commitment to the priority of bureaucratic institutions. See MacIntyre, *After Virtue: A Study in Moral Theory* (Notre Dame: University of Notre Dame Press, 1981) and, in Wilfred M. McClay, *The Masterless: Self and Society in Modern America* (Chapel Hill: University of North Carolina Press, 1994), 269–95, the discussion of "The Hipster and the Organization Man." My thanks to Chris Shannon for pointing out MacIntyre's use of the term.

2. On Tönnies and German sociology of the later nineteenth and early twentieth centu-

ries, see Arthur Mitzman, *Sociology and Estrangement: Three Sociologists of Imperial Germany* (New York: Knopf, 1973), 39–134. The fear of mass society as the extension of individualism to all persons is best expressed by José Ortega y Gasset, *The Revolt of the Masses* (New York: W. W. Norton, 1932). The Spanish original was published in 1930.

3. Robert H. Wiebe, *The Search for Order, 1877–1920* (New York: Hill and Wang, 1967). Wiebe's account remains the standard interpretive synthesis of the period, even as it embraces the dichotomies it explores.

4. Ibid., 133ff. This theme, in one way or another, seems to make its way into almost all accounts of the cultural and intellectual history of the period between the Civil War and World War I.

5. See Dorothy Ross, *The Origins of American Social Science* (Cambridge: Cambridge University Press, 1991); Jean B. Quandt, *From the Small Town to the Great Community: Social Thought of Progressive Intellectuals* (New Brunswick: Rutgers University Press, 1970). For a different view, which sees progressive intellectuals primarily as critics of individualism, see R. Jackson Wilson, *In Quest of Community: Social Philosophy in the United States, 1860–1920* (New York: John Wiley and Sons, 1968), esp. 87–113 on Edward Ross. For the larger intellectual and cultural dimensions of the Progressive Era view of the past as a solution to the destructive elements of an urban industrial order, see T. J. Jackson Lears, *No Place of Grace: Antimodernism and the Transformation of American Culture 1880–1920* (New York: Pantheon, 1981). For a general overview of the crisis of the 1890s and the elements of progressive thought, see David W. Noble, *The Progressive Mind, 1890–1917* (Chicago: Rand McNally, 1970).

6. The Lynds, of course, inaugurated the community study as a form of cultural analysis, and gave it a central role in American social thought. See Robert Lynd and Helen Merrel Lynd, *Middletown: A Study of American Culture* (New York: Harcourt Brace Jovanovich, 1929). For a synthetic overview of the community study in American sociology, see Maurice R. Stein, *The Eclipse of Community: An Interpretation of American Studies* (New York: Harper and Row, 1960).

7. On the place of the lament for the lost order in American culture, see Perry Miller, *Errand into the Wilderness* (Cambridge: Harvard University Press, Belknap, 1956), 1–15; Sacvan Bercovitch, *The American Jeremiad* (Madison: University of Wisconsin Press, 1978). For the role of the concern with decline as a republican value, see J. G. A. Pocock, *The Machiavellian Moment: Florentine Political Thought and the Atlantic Republican Tradition* (Princeton: Princeton University Press, 1975); Gordon F. Wood, *Creation of the American Republic, 1776–1787* (Chapel Hill: University of North Carolina Press, 1969); Daniel T. Rodgers, "Republicanism: The Career of a Concept," *Journal of American History* 79 (June 1992): 11–39.

8. David Riesman, Nathan Glazer, and Reuel Denney, *The Lonely Crowd: A Study of the Changing American Character* (New Haven: Yale University Press, 1950).

9. On American social thought in the 1950s, see Richard H. Pells, *The Liberal Mind in a Conservative Age: American Intellectuals in the 1940's and 1950's* (New York: Harper and Row, 1985), 183–261; John Patrick Diggins, *The Proud Decades: America in War and Peace 1941–1960* (New York: W. W. Norton, 1988), 207–11; McClay, *The Masterless*, 226–68; Stephen J. Whitfield, *The Culture of the Cold War* (Baltimore: Johns Hopkins University Press, 1991); Terence Ball, "The Politics of Social Science in Postwar America," in *Recasting America: Culture and Politics in the Age of Cold War*, ed. Lary May (Chicago: University of Chicago Press, 1989), 76–92.

10. The distinction between "character" and "personality" as representative modes of the self commensurate, respectively, with nineteenth- and twentieth-century social forms is made by Warren I. Susman, " 'Personality' and the Making of Twentieth-Century Culture," in *Culture as History: The Transformation of American Society in the Twentieth Century*

(New York: Pantheon, 1984), 271–85. Susman's essay originally appeared in John Higham and Paul K. Conkin, eds., *New Directions in American Intellectual History* (Baltimore: Johns Hopkins University Press, 1979), 212–26. For a critical reinterpretation of this shift in modes of the self, a reinterpretation that reverses the trajectory from one of declension to one of liberation, see James Livingston, *Pragmatism and the Political Economy of Cultural Revolution, 1850–1940* (Chapel Hill: University of North Carolina Press, 1994). On "the emergence of psychological man" in the wake of the reign of economic man, see Philip Rieff, *Freud: The Mind of the Moralist* (New York: Viking, 1959), 329–57. For another, if somewhat different, attempt to make a historical generalization about the values associated with two modes of selfhood, see Lionel Trilling, *Sincerity and Authenticity* (Cambridge: Harvard University Press, 1972).

11. On the expansion of bureaucratic and corporate forms and their cultural representations, see Wiebe, *The Search for Order*; Livingston, *Pragmatism and the Political Economy of Cultural Revolution*; Alan Trachtenberg, *The Incorporation of America: Culture and Society in the Gilded Age* (New York: Hill and Wang, 1982); John Higham, "The Re-orientation of American Culture in the 1890s," in *Writing American History* (Bloomington: Indiana University Press, 1973), 73–102; Burton Bledstein, *The Culture of Professionalism: The Middle Class and the Development of Higher Education in America* (New York: W. W. Norton, 1976); George M. Fredrickson, *The Inner Civil War: Northern Intellectuals and the Crisis of the Union* (New York: Harper and Row, 1965); Richard D. Brown, "Modernization: A Victorian Climax," in *Victorian America*, ed. Daniel Walker Howe (Philadelphia: University of Pennsylvania Press, 1976); Martha Banta, *Taylored Lives: Narrative Production in the Age of Taylor, Veblen, and Ford* (Chicago: University of Chicago Press, 1993); Cindy Sondick Aron, *Ladies and Gentlemen of the Civil Service: Middle-Class Workers in Victorian America* (New York: Oxford University Press, 1987); Olivier Zunz, *Making America Corporate 1880–1920* (Chicago: University of Chicago Press, 1990); Walter Benn Michaels, *The Gold Standard and the Logic of Naturalism: American Literature at the Turn of the Century* (Berkeley: University of California Press, 1987); Henry Steele Commager, *The American Mind: An Interpretation of American Thought and Culture since the 1890's* (New Haven: Yale University Press, 1950); Donald J. Mrozek, *Sport and American Mentality, 1880–1910* (Knoxville: University of Tennessee Press, 1983).

12. Edwin Whipple, "Wit and Humour" (1845), in *Lectures Concerned with Literature and Life* (Boston: Ticknor, Reed, and Fields, 1850), 84–85.

13. Edwin Whipple, *Success and Its Conditions* (Boston: James R. Osgood, 1871), 204.

14. Leigh Hunt, *Wit and Humour Selected from the English Poets*, 2d ed. (London: Smith, Elder, 1846), 38.

15. I am indebted to Anne Denise Brennan, "From Medicine to Mirth: Humor, Sense of Humor and Characterization in 'Tom Jones,' 'Tristram Shandy' and 'Vanity Fair' " (Ph.D. diss., St. Louis University, 1986), for pointing out the early appearance of the term "sense of humor" in *Vanity Fair*. Her work and the present book share a number of concerns, and her research and thought have contributed to my own conceptualizations of the historical problem examined here. Her concerns, however, are largely confined to the use of terms in literary representation as a reflection of forms of characterization; I am making somewhat broader cultural and historical claims.

16. Nathaniel Hawthorne, *"The Scarlet Letter" and Other Tales of the Puritans* (Boston: Houghton Mifflin, Riverside Press, 1960), 18.

17. Harold Frederic, *The Damnation of Theron Ware* (Cambridge: Harvard University Press, Belknap, 1960), 19; Edith Wharton, *The Age of Innocence*, in *Novels* (New York: Viking, 1985), 1051; Tom Robbins, *Skinny Legs and All* (New York: Bantam, 1990), 43, 372.

18. O. S. Fowler, *Human Science or Phrenology, Its Principles, Proofs, Faculties, Organs, Temperament, Combinations, Conditions, Teachings, Philosophies, etc., etc.* (New York: Fowler

and Welles [1850?]), 967–74, 942; [James S. Grimes], *Grimes' Improved Phrenology and Chart* (n.p., [19——?]), 63–65. For an overview of phrenology, see David De Giustino, *Conquest of Mind: Phrenology and Victorian Social Thought* (London: Rowman and Littlefield, 1975). In many ways—e.g., in its focus on type, rather than individual, or its attempt to give character traits a physiological, objective status—phrenology can be seen as closer to medieval humoral thought than to modern psychology. Phrenology shares some of these orientations with twentieth-century sociobiology and genetics as well, however, so it should not be seen as a throwback to earlier forms of characterology.

19. "American Humour," *North British Review* 33 (November 1860): 470.

20. X., "Wit and Humor," *The Nation* 2 (1 February 1866): 144.

21. Review of *Artemus Ward: His Travels*, in *North American Review* 102 (April 1866): 589; *New York Times*, 24 June 1877, p. 6; the latter is quoted in Neil Harris, *Cultural Excursions: Marketing Appetites and Tastes in Modern America* (Chicago: University of Chicago Press, 1990), 36.

22. See Raymond Williams, *Keywords: A Vocabulary of Culture and Society*, rev. ed. (New York: Oxford University Press, 1985); Daniel T. Rodgers, *Contested Truths: Keywords in American Politics since Independence* (New York: Basic Books, 1987); Philip Gleason, *Speaking of Diversity: Language and Ethnicity in Twentieth-Century America* (Baltimore: Johns Hopkins University Press, 1992). For examples of non-keywords see Donald Fleming, "Attitude: The History of a Concept," *Perspectives in American History* 1 (1967): 287–365, esp. 287–90; Patricia Meyer Spacks, *Boredom: The Literary History of a State of Mind* (Chicago: University of Chicago Press, 1995); Susie I. Tucker, *Enthusiasm: A Study of Semantic Change* (Cambridge: Cambridge University Press, 1972).

23. Clifford Geertz, "Ethos, World View and the Analysis of Sacred Symbols," in *The Interpretation of Cultures: Selected Essays* (New York: Basic Books, 1973), 126–41.

24. [Leslie Stephen], "Humour," *Cornhill Magazine* 33 (March 1876): 318; reprinted in *Littell's Living Age* 129 (22 April 1876): 234.

25. Max Beerbohm, "The Laughter of the Public," *Littell's Living Age* 233 (5 April 1902): 52.

26. H. A. Overstreet, *Influencing Human Behavior* (New York: W. W. Norton, 1925), 257.

27. Riesman, Glazer and Denney, *The Lonely Crowd*, 278.

28. On the end of the "invisible hand" as the basis for economic activity, and on the emergence of managerial organization in the twentieth century, see Alfred D. Chandler, *The Visible Hand: The Managerial Revolution in American Business* (Cambridge: Harvard University Press, 1977).

29. Douglas Malloch quoted in J. E. Wallace Wallin, *Personality Maladjustments and Mental Hygiene*, 2d ed. (New York: McGraw-Hill, 1949), 313.

30. Richard Armour quoted in Harvey Mindess et al., *The Antioch Humor Test: Making Sense of Humor* (New York: Avon, 1985), 6.

31. Leon Ormond, *Laugh and Learn: The Art of Teaching with Humor* (New York: Greenberg, 1941), 7.

32. Samuel McChord Crothers, "The Mission of Humor," *Atlantic Monthly* 84 (September 1899): 372; reprinted in idem, *The Gentle Reader* (Boston: Houghton Mifflin, 1903), 64–100.

33. See, for example, H. A. Overstreet, *About Ourselves: Psychology for Normal People* (New York: W. W. Norton, 1927), 261.

34. Burges Johnson, "The Right Not to Laugh," *Harper's* 132 (April 1916): 785.

35. G. P., "On a Sense of Humor," *Living Age* 305 (5 June 1920): 605.

36. Leo Markun, *How to Develop Your Sense of Humor* (Girard, Kans.: Haldeman-Julius [1928]), 38.

37. James Russell Lowell, "Democracy," in *The Works of James Russell Lowell* (Boston: Houghton Mifflin, 1890), 6:7.

38. Agnes Repplier, "The Mission of Humor," *Americans and Others* (Boston: Houghton Mifflin, 1912), 56–57.

39. W. Béran Wolfe, *How to be Happy though Human* (New York: Farrar and Rinehart, 1931), 160–61, 192.

40. H. L. Hollingworth, *The Psychology of Functional Neuroses* (New York: D. Appleton., 1920), 64–65.

41. Donald A. Laird, assisted by Eleanor C. Laird, *The Technique of Personal Analysis* (New York: McGraw-Hill, 1945), 402; see also Raymond A. Moody, Jr., *Laugh after Laugh: The Healing Power of Humor* (Jacksonville, Fla.: Headwaters Press, 1978), 66.

42. Overstreet, *About Ourselves*, 253.

43. William McDougall, *Outline of Abnormal Psychology* (New York: Charles Scribner's Sons, 1926), 391.

44. Lowell, "Democracy," 7.

45. S. H. Butcher, "Evolution of Humor," *Harper's* 80 (May 1890): 907.

46. Johnson, "The Right Not to Laugh," 785.

47. Nancy A. Walker, *A Very Serious Thing: Women's Humor and American Culture* (Minneapolis: University of Minnesota Press, 1988). See also Alfred Habegger, *Gender, Fantasy and Realism in American Literature* (New York: Columbia University Press, 1982), 158–59; Zita Z. Dresner, "Sentiment and Humor: A Double-Pronged Attack on Women's Place in Nineteenth-Century America," *Studies in American Humor* 4 (Spring-Summer 1985): 18–29; Frances Gray, *Women and Laughter* (Charlottesville: University of Virginia Press, 1994). The field of feminist humor-criticism has been growing rapidly over the past several years. See June Sochen, ed., *Women's Comic Visions* (Detroit: Wayne State University Press, 1991) and Regina Barreca, ed., *Last Laughs: Perspectives on Women and Comedy* (New York: Gordon and Breach, 1988).

48. Without wading into the muddy waters of contemporary debate about the "use" of culture to achieve ends defined independently of culture, I want to stress that, in my reading, an emphasis on the uses of culture tends to ignore the content of culture and its capacity to signify, emphasizing instead its capacity to do a job; meaning is reduced to practical consequences. I am well aware that critics will insist that the specific meaning and content of concepts cannot be separated from their "uses." If the alternative to making a distinction between content and use is to subordinate meaning to use value, I defend such a separation on epistemological and ontological (if not political) grounds.

49. Walker, *A Very Serious Thing*, 73–99; see also Nancy A. Walker, "Wit, Sentimentality, and the Image of Women in the Nineteenth Century," *American Studies* 22 (Fall 1981): 5–22.

50. Robert J. Burdette, "Have Women a Sense of Humor?" *Harper's Bazaar* 36 (July 1902): 598.

51. Elizabeth Stanley Trotter, "Humor with a Gender," *Atlantic Monthly* 130 (December 1922): 785, 786.

52. Mary Austin, "The Sense of Humor in Women," *New Republic* 41 (26 November 1924): 13.

53. F. P. Robertson, letter, *New York Times Saturday Review* (27 January 1900): 53.

54. On woman's sphere and domesticity as related to women's nature, see Nancy F. Cott, *The Bonds of Womanhood: "Woman's Sphere" in New England, 1780–1835* (New Haven: Yale University Press, 1977); Barbara Welter, "The Cult of True Womanhood: 1820–1860," *American Quarterly* 18 (1966): 151–74.

55. X., "Wit and Humor," 144.

56. Appleton Moran, letter, *New York Times Saturday Review* (10 February 1900): 92–93.

57. My characterization of this debate is drawn from the following sources, as well as those cited in the relevant notes above: Adair Welker, *For People Who Laugh: Showing How, through Woman, Came Laughter into the World* (San Francisco: Adair Welker, 1904); Martha Bensely Bruere and Mary Ritter Beard, *Laughing Their Way: Women's Humor in America* (New York: Macmillan, 1934); Kate Sanborn, *The Wit of Women* (New York: Funk and Wagnalls, 1885); Margaretta Newell, "Are Women Humorous?" *Outlook and Independent* 14 (October 1931): 206–7; Alice Wellington Rollins, "Woman's Sense of Humor," *The Critic and Good Literature* 1 (29 March 1884): 145–46; idem, "The Humor of Women," *The Critic and Good Literature* 1 (28 June 1884): 301–2; [Anon.], *Wit and Humor of Women* (Philadelphia: George W. Jacobs, 1907); Edith Slater and Frances H. Freshfield, "The Sense of Humour in Men," *Cornhill Magazine* 6 (March 1899): 347–52; R. Y. Tyrrell, "Sense of Humour in Women," *Cornhill Magazine* 6 (May 1899): 627–35; [Anon.], "A Bit of the Gospel according to Stevenson," *The Atlantic* 86 (December 1900): 858–60; [Anon.], "Wit, Humor, and Women," *Century* 59 (April 1900): 958–59; Edith Baker Brown, "Woman's Humor," *The Bookman* 19 (August 1904): 611–13; Constant Coquelin, "Have Women a Sense of Humor?" *Harper's Bazaar* 34 (12 January 1901): 67–69; [Anon.], "Woman among Humorists," *New York Times Saturday Review* (20 January 1900): 40, and the responses by letter writers in the issues of 27 January, 10 February, and 17 February 1900; Arthur B. Maurice, "Feminine Humorists," *Good Housekeeping* 50 (January 1910): 34–39.

58. Coquelin, "Have Women a Sense of Humor?" 67; [Anon.], "Woman among Humorists," 40.

59. Nancy F. Cott, *The Grounding of Modern Feminism* (New Haven: Yale University Press, 1987).

60. See, for instance, Catherine Clinton, "Me and My Feminist Humor: All Alone and Feeling Blue," *Popular Culture in America*, ed. Paul Buhle (Minneapolis: University Of Minnesota Press, 1987): 251–56.

61. Brander Matthews, "The Penalty of Humor," *Harper's* 92 (May 1896): 898. See also Harold Nicholson, *"The English Sense of Humour" and Other Essays* (London: Constable, 1956), 4.

62. Matthews, "Penalty of Humor," 898.

63. William James, *Psychology* (New York: Henry Holt, 1892), 179–81; Charles Horton Cooley, *Human Nature and the Social Order*, (1902; reprint New York: Schocken Books, 1964), esp. 168–263; Franklin Henry Giddings, *The Principles of Sociology: An Analysis of the Phenomena of Association and of Social Organization* (New York: Macmillan, 1896), 17ff, 100–152. For a reading of Cooley, see David W. Noble, *The Paradox of Progressive Thought* (Minneapolis: University of Minnesota Press, 1958), 103–24.

64. George Herbert Mead, *Mind, Self and Society* (1934; reprint Chicago: University of Chicago Press, 1959); Erving Goffman, *The Presentation of Self in Everyday Life* (New York: Doubleday, 1959). On the relationship between this tradition of social psychology and the notion of the self in American culture, see John P. Hewitt, *Dilemmas of the American Self* (Philadelphia: Temple University Press, 1989).

65. Burges Johnson, "The New Humor," *Critic* 40 (April 1902): 331.

66. Mary Whiton Calkins, *An Introduction to Psychology* (New York: Macmillan, 1902), 284.

67. Crothers, "The Mission of Humor," 373–74.

68. "Wit and Humor," *Atlantic Monthly* 100 (September 1907): 427.

69. William Burnham, *The Wholesome Personality: A Contribution to Mental Hygiene* (New York: D. Appleton, 1932), 595.

70. Wallin, *Personality Maladjustments and Mental Hygiene*, 312.

71. Harry Emerson Fosdick, *On Being a Real Person* (New York: Harper and Bros., 1943), 104–5.

72. Gordon W. Allport, *Personality: A Psychological Interpretation* (New York: Henry Holt, 1937), 222–25. For examples of the kind of analytical-empirical psychology of personality traits that Allport rejected, especially in regard to the idea of the sense of humor, see Polyxenie Kambouropoulou, "Individual Differences in the Sense of Humor and Their Relation to Temperamental Differences," *Archives of Psychology* 121 (October 1930): 1–83; M. Hesty, "Variations in the Sense of Humor According to Age and Mental Condition" (M.A. thesis, Columbia University, 1924); Carney Landis and John W. H. Ross, "Humor and Its Relation to Other Personality Traits," *Journal of Social Psychology* 4 (1933): 156–75; Louise Omwake, "A Study of Sense of Humor: Its Relation to Sex, Age, and Personal Characteristics," *Journal of Applied Psychology* 21 (1937): 688–704; N. Franklin Stump, "Sense of Humor and Its Relationship to Personality, Scholastic Aptitude, Emotional Maturity, Height, and Weight," *Journal of General Psychology* 20 (1939): 25–32.

73. Gordon Allport, *The Nature of Prejudice* (Cambridge, Mass.: Addison-Wesley, 1954), 437, 509.

74. Mahadev L. Apte, "Ethnic Humor versus 'Sense of Humor': An American Sociocultural Dilemma," *American Behavioral Scientist* 30 (January-February 1987): 28–30. On the post-World War II liberal ethic of tolerance and cultural pluralism, see Philip Gleason, *Speaking of Diversity*. For a critique of the notion of humor as an aspect of a "tolerant society," see Charles Husband, "Racist Humour," in *Humour in Society: Resistance and Control*, ed. Chris Powell and George E. C. Paton (New York: St. Martin's Press, 1988), 149–50.

75. Roving Eye [pseud.], "Humor, Brickbats, Cheers and Susie Belle," *Wilson Bulletin for Librarians* (January 1938): 322–23, quoted in Florence N. Brumbaugh, "Stimuli Which Cause Laughter in Children" (Ph.D. diss., New York University, 1939), 8.

76. Margery Wilson, *The Woman You Want to Be* (Philadelphia: J. B. Lippincott, 1942), 396–97.

77. Laird, *The Technique of Personal Analysis*, 404.

78. Donald McLean, *Knowing Yourself and Others: Mental Hygiene for Young People* (n.p.: Henry Holt, 1938), 42.

79. Betty Allen and Mitchell Pirie Briggs, *If You Please! A Book of Manners for Young Moderns* (Chicago: J. B. Lippincott, 1942), 15.

80. Knight Dunlap, *Old and New Viewpoints in Psychology* (St. Louis: C. V. Mosby Co., 1925), 125. This essay was originally delivered as a lecture to the Johns Hopkins Women's Club, May 31, 1921.

81. Edwin P. Whipple, "Cheerfulness," in *Success and Its Conditions* (Boston: James R. Osgood and Co., 1871), 195, 194. For a particularly didactic version of the ethic of cheerfulness in the form of children's literature, see Peter Parley, *Make the Best of It; or, Cheerful Cherry, and Other Tales* (New York: Sheldon, 1843).

82. Edward O. Sisson, *The Essentials of Character: A Practical Study of the Aim of Moral Education* (New York: Macmillan, 1910), 44ff.

83. Whipple, "Cheerfulness," 196.

84. Ibid., 203–4; C. Wright Mills, *White Collar: The American Middle Classes* (New York: Oxford University Press, 1951), 233–35; idem, *The Sociological Imagination* (New York: Oxford University Press, 1959), 169–76.

85. *OED*, 2d ed., s.v. "tact."

86. See, for instance, Katherine M. H. Blackford and Arthur Newcomb, *Analyzing Character* (New York: Henry Alden, 1917), 458–59; John Robert Powers and Mary Sue Miller, *Secrets of Charm* (Philadelphia: John C. Winston Co., 1954), 359; Donald A. Laird, *How to Use Psychology in Business* (New York: McGraw-Hill, 1936), 116–18.

87. Emory S. Bogardus and Robert H. Lewis, *Social Life and Personality* (New York: Silver Burdett, 1942), 40–41.

88. Emory S. Bogardus, *Leaders and Leadership* (New York: D. Appleton, 1934), 172–82.

89. S. H. Kraines and E. S. Thetford, *Live and Help Live* (New York: Macmillan, 1951), 75–76.

90. Harold Höffding, *Outlines of Psychology*, trans. Mary E. Lowndes (New York: Macmillan, 1896), 298; Overstreet, *About Ourselves*, 264.

91. William Moulton Marston, *Try Living* (New York: Thomas Y. Crowell, 1937), 135–38.

92. Ibid., 139.

93. Ibid., 142.

94. William Moulton Marston, *March On! Facing Life with Courage* (New York: Doubleday, Doran, 1941), 177–78.

95. Donald S. Napoli, *Architects of Adjustment: The History of the Psychological Profession in the United States* (Port Washington, N.Y.: Kennikat Press, 1981), 30ff. See also Loren Baritz, *The Servants of Power: A History of the Use of Social Science in American Industry* (Westport, Conn.: Greenwood Press, 1960).

96. For a typical high-school text of the period, see Herbert Sorenson and Marguerite Malm, *Psychology for Living* (New York: McGraw-Hill, 1948). For examples of college texts, see Richard Wellington Husband, *General Psychology* (New York: Rinehart and Co., 1940); J. P. Guilford, *Personality* (New York: McGraw-Hill, 1959). For an interesting use of social science textbooks as source materials, see C. Wright Mills, "The Professional Ideology of Social Pathologists," *American Journal of Sociology* 49 (September 1943): 165–80.

97. For an example of the opposition to conflict in corporate management, see Zunz, *Making America Corporate 1880–1920*, 192. On the need for adjustment and control to avoid conflict in the workplace, and more generally in the broader sphere of social life, see Carol Zisowitz Stearns and Peter N. Stearns, *Anger: The Struggle for Emotional Control in America's History* (Chicago: University of Chicago Press, 1986), 110–56ff; Peter N. Stearns, "Suppressing Unpleasant Emotions: The Development of a Twentieth-Century American Style," in *Social History and Issues in Human Consciousness: Some Interdisciplinary Connections*, ed. Andrew E. Barnes and Peter N. Stearns (New York: New York University Press, 1989), 230–61; idem, *Jealousy: The Evolution of an Emotion in American History* (New York: New York University Press, 1989); idem, *American Cool: Constructing a Twentieth-Century Emotional Style* (New York: New York University Press, 1994).

98. William Mathews, *Wit and Humor: Their Use and Abuse* (Chicago: S. C. Griggs, 1888), 75–77.

99. Ralph A. Habas, *The Art of Self-Control: How to Make Your Habits Work for You* (New York: Royal and Hitchcock, 1941), 234.

100. Henry A. Bowman, *Marriage for Moderns* (New York: McGraw-Hill, 1942), 312.

101. Frank E. Howard and Frederick L. Patry, *Mental Health: Its Principles and Practice* (New York: Harper Bros., 1935), 188–89.

102. Charles E. Foster, *Psychology for Life Adjustment* (Chicago: American Technical Society, 1951), 417–18; see also 190–93.

103. Floyd L. Ruch, *Psychology and Life: A Study of the Thinking, Feeling, and Doing of People* (Chicago: Scott, Foresman, 1937), 164.

104. Markun, *How to Develop Your Sense of Humor*, 17; John Erskine, "Humor, a Sense of It, Is a Thing to Cultivate and Achieve," *Century* 115 (February 1928): 421.

105. Henry S. Pritchett, "Politicians and the Sense of Humor," *Scribner's* 55 (January 1914): 79; William Burnham, *The Normal Mind: An Introduction to Mental Hygiene and the Hygiene of School Instruction* (New York: D. Appleton, 1924), 399–401.

106. Erskine, "Humor, a Sense of It," 421. For an interesting discussion of Erskine as a characteristically "middlebrow" figure, see Joan Shelley Rubin, *The Making of Middlebrow Culture* (Chapel Hill: University of North Carolina Press, 1992), 148–86.

107. Mathews, *Wit and Humor*, 57.

108. Pritchett, "Politicians and the Sense of Humor," 79.

109. "Extols Sense of Humor," *New York Times*, 16 April 1923, p. 17.

110. Arthur Gilbert Bills, *The Psychology of Efficiency: A Discussion of the Hygiene of Mental Work* (New York: Harper and Bros., 1943), 186–98.

111. Lawrence B. Goodrich, *Living with Others: A Book on Social Conduct* (New York: American Book Co., 1939), 53.

112. [Mrs. Nella Braddy Henny], *The Book of Business Etiquette* (Garden City, N.Y.: Doubleday, Page, 1922), 34–35.

113. Mary Brockman, *What Is She Like? A Personality Book for Girls* (New York: Charles Scribner's Sons, 1936), 159.

114. Laird, *The Technique of Personal Analysis*, 402.

115. On the foregrounding of "everyday life" as a level of cultural reality in modern bureaucratic societies, see Henri Lefebvre, *Critique de la vie quotidienne*, 3 vols. (Paris: L'Arche, 1958–81). The current interest by historians in everyday life as an object of study can be seen as part of this process of foregrounding. For an interesting use of Lefebvre's conception of everyday life as a level of reality, see Thomas C. Holt, "Marking: Race, Race-making, and the Writing of History," *American Historical Review*, 100 (February 1995): 1–20.

116. Norbert Elias, *The History of Manners*, trans. Edmund Jephcott (New York: Pantheon, 1978); John F. Kasson, *Rudeness and Civility: Manners in Nineteenth-Century Urban America* (New York: Hill and Wang, 1990).

4. The Commodity Form of the Joke

1. Brander Matthews, *"The American of the Future" and Other Essays* (New York: Charles Scribner's Sons, 1910), 162.

2. Jonathan Swift quoted in Norman Knox, *The Word Irony and Its Context, 1500–1755* (Durham: Duke University Press, 1961), 203.

3. William Shakespeare, *Love's Labour's Lost*, 5.2.863–65.

4. *OED*, 2d ed., s.v. "jest" and "joke"; Albert F. McLean, Jr., *American Vaudeville as Ritual* (Lexington: University of Kentucky Press, 1965), 113. I am indebted to McLean's notion of the relative novelty of the things designated as jokes in the late nineteenth century and of the way in which the term "joke" narrowed its meaning from the seventeenth through the nineteenth centuries. However, I find his interpretation of the joke as an urban ethnic form, rooted in the language and experience of the city, unpersuasive.

5. On the formal distinction between tale and joke as literary forms, see the insightful essay by Elliott Oring, "Between Jokes and Tales," in *Jokes and Their Relations* (Lexington: University Press of Kentucky, 1992), 81–93. Oring's stress on the punch line as the fundamental distinguishing feature of the joke is very much in line with the interpretation of the formal elements of the joke offered in the present book.

6. See, for instance, the success of Garrison Keillor's *A Prairie Home Companion* radio program on National Public Radio in the 1980s.

7. This idea continues to the present day in the scholarship on American humor. See, for instance, the standard overview of the field, Walter Blair and Hamlin Hill, *America's Humor: From Poor Richard to Doonesbury* (New York: Oxford University Press, 1978), 17–25.

8. Constance Rourke, *American Humor: A Study of the National Character* (New York: Harcourt, Brace, and Co., 1931); Walter Blair, *Native American Humor* (New York: Ameri-

can Book Co., 1930); idem, *Horse Sense in American Humor* (Chicago: University of Chicago Press, 1942); Franklin J. Meine, ed., *Tall Tales of the Southwest: An Anthology of Southern and Southwestern Humor, 1830–1860* (New York: Knopf, 1931). This scholarly "discovery" of American humor had precedents in the 1920s. See, for instance, Jennette Tandy, *Crackerbox Philosophers in American Humor and Satire* (New York: Columbia University Press, 1925). The concern with laughter and humor in the 1930s extended beyond those who were intent on recovering an American "folk" culture, although such a recovery was an important part of that concern. It also embraced critics such as Max Eastman, novelists like Nathanael West, and filmmakers such as Preston Sturges, all of whom gave a prominent place to the analysis and meaning of laughter and humor within their work. As much as some have seen the emergence of a new humor "movement" in the 1980s, guided by a concern with the psychological, therapeutic, medical, and corporate "uses" of laughter, an earlier version of that movement appears to have taken place in the 1930s, although its interests were much more frankly cultural.

9. The issue of genre and school—"southwestern," "Down East," "local color," etc.— plays a dominant organizational role in Blair and Hill, *America's Humor;* the status of humor itself is pushed into the background. See also Louis D. Rubin, Jr., ed., *The Comic Imagination in American Literature* (New Brunswick: Rutgers University Press, 1973); Kenneth S. Lynn, *Mark Twain and Southwestern Humor* (Boston: Little, Brown, 1960); Jesse Bier, *The Rise and Fall of American Humor* (New York: Holt, Rinehart, and Winston, 1968).

10. See, for instance, [H. W], "Slick, Crockett, Downing, etc.," *Westminster Review* 32 (December 1838): 136–45; "American Humor," *Eclectic Magazine* 33 (September 1854): 137–44, and 35 (June 1855): 267–72; "Traits of American Humor," *Irish Quarterly Review* 2 (1852): 171–96.

11. Norris W. Yates, *William T. Porter and the Spirit of the Times* (Baton Rouge: Louisiana State University Press, 1957); Lynn, *Mark Twain and Southwestern Humor.*

12. One recent reinvention of the early minstrel show as a comic form from its inception is in Alexander Saxton, *The Rise and Fall of the White Republic: Class Politics and Mass Culture in Nineteenth-Century America* (New York: Verso, 1990), 165–82.

13. Robert C. Toll, *Blacking Up: The Minstrel Show in Nineteenth Century America* (New York: Oxford University Press, 1979), 51–57. Also, on the sentimental content of the minstrel show, see Eric Lott, *Love and Theft: Blackface Minstrelsy and the American Working Class* (New York: Oxford University Press, 1993).

14. The standard text on *Punch* is Richard Geoffrey George Price, *A History of Punch* (London: Collins, 1957). For a brief overview, see Alvin Sullivan, ed., *British Literary Magazines: The Victorian and Edwardian Age, 1837–1913* (Westport, Conn.: Greenwood Press, 1984), 325–29.

15. Edwin Lawrence Godkin, "The 'Comic Paper' Question," in *Reflections and Comments 1865–1895* (New York: Charles Scribner's Sons, 1895), 29–39.

16. On mid-nineteenth-century British humor and its turn-of-the-century heirs, see Roger B. Henkle, *Comedy and Culture: England 1820–1900* (Princeton: Princeton University Press, 1980); Richard S. Carlson, *The Benign Humorists* (n.p.: Archon Books, 1975).

17. Ralph Waldo Emerson, *Emerson in His Journals*, ed. Joel Porte (Cambridge: Harvard University Press, Belknap, 1982), 387.

18. Karen Halttunen, *Confidence Men and Painted Women: A Study of Middle-Class Culture in America, 1830–1870* (New Haven: Yale University Press, 1982), 185–90.

19. Frank Bellew, *The Art of Amusing* (New York: Carleton, 1866; reprint New York: Arno Press, 1974), 7.

20. Godkin, "The 'Comic Paper' Question," 29–30.

21. James C. Austin, *Artemus Ward* (New York: Twayne, 1964); idem, *Petroleum Vesuvius Nasby (David Ross Locke)* (New York: Twayne, 1965); John M. Harrison, *The Man Who*

Made Nasby (Chapel Hill: University of North Carolina Press, 1969); David B. Kesterson, *Josh Billings (Henry Wheeler Shaw)* (New York: Twayne, 1973).

22. William Mathews, *"The Great Conversers," and Other Essays* (Chicago: S. C. Griggs, 1874), 161.

23. Godkin, "The 'Comic Paper' Question," 30–31.

24. H. H. Boyesen, "The Plague of Jocularity," *North American Review* 161 (November 1895): 328–55; reprinted in Per Seyersted, *From Norwegian Romantic to American Realist: Studies in the Life and Writings of Hjalmar Hjorth Boyesen* (Atlantic Highlands, N.J.: Humanities Press, 1984), 167–73.

25. See, for instance, Eleanor Kirk, ed., *Beecher as a Humorist: Selections from the Published Works* (New York: Fords, Howard, and Hulbert, 1894).

26. On the history of American humor periodicals from the 1870s to the 1930s, see David E. E. Sloane, ed., *American Humor Magazines and Comic Periodicals* (Westport, Conn.: Greenwood Press, 1987), 111–20, 141–52, 219–26; Frank L. Mott, *A History of American Magazines* (Cambridge: Harvard University Press, 1938), 3: 263–71, 520–32, 552–68.

27. Frank L. Mott, *A History of American Magazines* (Cambridge: Harvard University Press, 1957), 4: 383.

28. On the transformation of the university and its purposes in the later nineteenth century, see Burton Bledstein, *The Culture of Professionalism: The Middle Class and the Development of Higher Education in America* (New York: Norton, 1976). On the dominance of the peer group in twentieth-century higher education, see Paula S. Fass, *The Damned and the Beautiful: American Youth in the 1920s* (New York: Oxford University Press, 1977).

29. Sloane, ed., *American Humor Magazines and Comic Periodicals*, 532–34.

30. The literature on vaudeville is voluminous. The most recent historical study is Robert W. Snyder, *The Voice of the City: Vaudeville and Popular Culture in New York* (New York: Oxford University Press, 1989). The best interpretive work remains McLean, *American Vaudeville as Ritual.* I have also drawn on Douglas Gilbert, *American Vaudeville: Its Life and Times* (New York: McGraw-Hill, 1940); Joe Laurie, Jr., *Vaudeville: From the Honky-tonks to the Palace* (New York: Henry Holt, 1953).

31. Elliott Gorn, *The Manly Art: Bare-Knuckle Prize Fighting in America* (Ithaca: Cornell University Press, 1986), 129–47, esp. 141–42.

32. Gilbert, *American Vaudeville*, 10.

33. On the history of burlesque and its relationship to class and cultural transformations in the post-Civil War era, see Robert C. Allen, *Horrible Prettiness: Burlesque and American Culture* (Chapel Hill: University of North Carolina Press, 1991).

34. Snyder, *The Voice of the City*, 82–103, discusses the big-time/small-time distinction.

35. Edwin Milton Royce, "The Vaudeville Theatre," in *American Vaudeville as Seen by Its Contemporaries*, ed. Charles W. Stein (New York: Knopf, 1984), 26. Royce's essay was first published in 1899.

36. The debate on twentieth-century mass culture and its relationship to nineteenth-century predecessors, and particularly its class basis, is a wide-ranging one. Without revisiting the history of this debate and its many offshoots, it is fair to say that the general view developed since World War II by Marxist and liberal critics alike has held that mass culture differed from nineteenth-century forms by creating a homogeneous national audience for its commercial products, bringing the working class and the middle class together in a shared ethic of consumption and "entertainment." A fair sampling of the postwar debate can be found in Bernard Rosenberg and David Manning White, eds., *Mass Culture: The Popular Arts in America* (Glencoe, Ill.: Free Press, 1957). Recently this view has been challenged by Lawrence Levine, *Highbrow/Lowbrow: The Emergence of Cultural Hierarchy in America* (Cambridge: Harvard University Press, 1988), who argues that a common culture in nineteenth-century America was bifurcated by the elite sacralization of "culture": where

once there had been unity, now there was "high culture" and "mass culture." There is obviously some truth to this argument. The critique of mass culture has come from a position associated with the values of high culture and has tended to judge "mass" by its failure to meet the standards of "high." The very existence of the critique of mass culture reaffirms an alternative "higher" culture. Another rejection of the idea that mass culture has had a homogenizing effect, and has co-opted workers through an accommodation to bourgeois consumerism, has stressed the resilient particularism of worker communities in the face of the universalizing tendencies of commercial forms. See, for instance, Lizabeth Cohen, *Making a New Deal: Industrial Workers in Chicago, 1919–1939* (Cambridge: Cambridge University Press, 1990). The entire field of "cultural studies," which has its foundations in the Marxist critique of mass culture, has in recent years turned toward a notion of worker "resistance" to capitalist social relations *within* the sphere of mass culture. See, for instance, George Lipsitz, *Time Passages: Collective Memory and American Popular Culture* (Minneapolis: University of Minnesota Press, 1990). While all of these perspectives modify the previously dominant view of mass culture as a "totalitarian," stultifying, and aesthetically degraded phenomenon, none challenge the essential truth in the notion of a *tendency* toward universalization of consumer values across social class. For a recent discussion of where historians stand on issues of popular culture—although the ground is always shifting—see Lawrence W. Levine, Robin D. G. Kelley, Natalie Zemon Davis, and T. J. Jackson Lears, "AHR Forum," *American Historical Review* 97 (December 1992): 1369–1430.

37. Marshall P. Wilder, *The Sunny Side of the Street* (New York: Funk and Wagnalls, 1905), 116–17.

38. George Rowland Collins, *Platform Speaking: A Practical Study for Business and Professional Men* (New York: Harper and Bros., 1923), 194. See also William Norwood Brigance, *The Spoken Word: A Text-book of Speech Composition* (New York: F. S. Crofts, 1927), 297.

39. Richard C. Borden, *Public Speaking—As Listeners Like It!* (New York: Harper and Bros., 1935), 41.

40. Sinclair Lewis, *Babbitt* (New York: Harcourt, Brace, 1922), 180. For a general understanding of the role after-dinner speaking had come to play in American life by the 1920s, I have consulted many texts on popular speech. See, for instance, Wilbur D. Nesbit, *After-Dinner Speeches and How to Make Them* (Chicago: Reilly and Lee, 1927).

41. William Mathews, *Wit and Humor: Their Use and Abuse* (Chicago: S.C. Griggs, 1888), 97.

42. Jerome K. Jerome, "You Can't Be Funny All the Time," *Cosmopolitan* 41 (1906): 110.

43. Stephen Butler Leacock, *Humor and Humanity: An Introduction to the Study of Humor* (New York: Henry Holt, 1938), 194–95.

44. Evan Esar, *The Humor of Humor* (New York: Horizon Press, 1952).

45. Mark Twain, "How to Tell a Story," in *The Complete Essays of Mark Twain*, ed. Charles Neider (Garden City, N.Y.: Doubleday, 1963), 155.

46. Ibid., 156.

47. Ibid., 155, 158. The notion of the joke as a mechanically produced entity requiring no human inventiveness is echoed in the work of Nathanael West in the 1930s. See, for instance, the following passage from *Miss Lonelyhearts* (1933): "Miss Lonelyhearts had again begun to smile. Like Shrike, the man they imitated, they were machines for making jokes. A button machine makes buttons, no matter what the power used, foot, steam or electricity. They, no matter what the motivating force, death, love or God, made jokes." Nathanael West, *Miss Lonelyhearts & The Day of the Locust* (New York: New Directions, 1969), 15.

48. Twain, "How to Tell a Story," 157, 158.

49. Ibid., 156.

50. On Dunne, see Grace Eckley, *Finley Peter Dunne* (Boston: G. K. Hall, 1981); Charles

Fanning, *Finley Peter Dunne and Mr. Dooley: The Chicago Years* (Lexington: University Press of Kentucky, 1978). On Ade, see Lee Coyle, *George Ade* (New York: Twayne, 1964).

51. Blair and Hill, *America's Humor*, 372–74.

52. Arthur Sullivan Hoffmann, "Who Writes the Jokes?" *The Bookman* 26 (October 1907): 171–81.

53. *New York Times*, 19 June 1934, p. 19. Masson's publications include a book of essays, *Well, Why Not?* (Garden City, N.Y.: Doubleday, Page, 1921); an edited collection, *American Wit and Humor*, 6 vols. (Garden City, N.Y.: Doubleday, Page, 1924); as well as numerous articles on humor, such as "Humor and Comic Journals," *Yale Review*, n.s., 15 (October 1925): 113–23, and "Has America a Sense of Humor?" *North American Review* 228 (August 1929): 178–84.

54. Thomas L. Masson, "How I Wrote 50,000 Jokes in 20 Years," *American Magazine* 89 (June 1920): 234.

55. John Albert Macy, "The Career of the Joke," *Atlantic Monthly* 96 (1905): 449.

56. Masson, "How I Wrote 50,000 Jokes," 233.

57. Ibid., 26.

58. Ibid.

59. Ibid., 234.

60. Ibid., 26, 234.

61. Of course, stock characters had been elements of jesting for hundreds of years; a quick glance at the famous *Joe Miller's Jests* of 1739, for instance, would reveal such well-known character types as the vain and aging woman (no. 99), the country clergyman (nos. 30–32), the cuckold (no. 216), and the cowardly servant (no. 237). See *Joe Miller's Jests; or, The Wits Vade-mecum* (1739; reprint New York: Dover, 1963).

62. Ibid., 27.

63. Norris Yates, *The American Humorist: Conscience of the Twentieth Century* (Ames: Iowa State University Press, 1964).

64. Masson, "How I Wrote 50,000 Jokes," 233.

65. Hoffmann, "Who Writes the Jokes?" 171.

66. For an example of Rogers's "style" and his fixation on the abbreviated joke form, see Will Rogers, "How to Be Funny," in *"How to Be Funny" and Other Writings of Will Rogers*, ed. Steven K. Gracent (Stillwater: Oklahoma State University Press, 1983), 112–15.

67. Dr. Doran, "Old-New Jokes," *Argosy* 5 (1 January 1868): 141–42. See also Brander Matthews, "On the Antiquity of Jests," in *The World's Best Essays: From Confucius to Mencken*, ed. F. H. Pritchard (New York: Harper and Bros., 1929), 913–22.

68. Mathews, *Wit and Humor*, 328–29.

69. L. H. Robbins, "The Adam of Gag Men," *New York Times Magazine* (26 November 1939): 6, 24.

70. Milton Wright, *What's Funny — and Why: An Outline of Humor* (New York: McGraw-Hill, 1939), 219–20.

71. Frank J. Wilstach, "Nothing New under the Sun—Except Jokes," *New York Times Magazine* (4 June 1922): 2.

72. Edward (Senator) Ford, "Jokes: New Variations on Old Themes," *New York Times Magazine* (20 February 1944): 8.

73. Ibid.

74. John Wardroper, ed. *Jest upon Jest: A Selection from the Jestbooks and Collections of Merry Tales Published from the Reign of Richard III to George III* (London: Routledge and Kegan Paul, 1970), 28. Similarly, Pearl Buck found that there was nothing akin to the mother-in-law joke in twentieth-century Chinese humor. See *New York Times*, 21 April 1933, p. 19.

75. Wright, *What's Funny — and Why*, 262.

76. Carolyn V. Wells, "You Can't Kill These Fifteen Immortal Jokes," *American Magazine* 95 (April 1923): 25, 111–21.

77. *New York Times*, 30 April 1908, p. 16.

78. "New Jokes? There Are No New Jokes. There Is Only One Joke," *New York Times*, 2 May 1909, sec. 5, p. 6.

79. Wright, *What's Funny—and Why*, 30–53.

80. "New Jokes? There Are No New Jokes," 6.

81. Wright, *What's Funny—and Why*, 30–53.

82. See, for instance, Larry Wilde, *How the Great Comedy Writers Create Laughter* (Chicago: Nelson-Hall, 1976), 25, 120. The source of the idea of the seven original jokes is obscure. The number seven was clearly appealing, perhaps on the analogy of the seven deadly sins, especially when one considers comedians' desire to "kill" or "slay" their audiences with jokes. For some, just as all jokes were universal and of ancient pedigree, so the idea that there were only seven jokes had a similar derivation. M. B. Levich, for instance, writing in 1926, made such a claim: "As all drama has been tabulated into thirty-six dramatic situations, so all comedy has been compressed into the seven deadly jokes. The analysis has been attributed to Mark Twain; it has also been traced back to Tzetzes, a Byzantine scholar, and through him to the ancients" See Levich, *New York Times Magazine* (24 January 1926): 2. The offhand attribution to a tradition leading to Twain is not supported by any specific citation, but rather by a will to believe in the "antiquity" of the idea as a sign of its authority. Twain was known for belittling the staleness of jokes he deemed thousands of years old, but there is no specific analysis of the seven jokes in his writings. Its attribution to him was based more on his authority as the nineteenth century's greatest humorist than on whether he did or did not make such a claim. John Tzetzes did assert (c. 1110–80) that "the laughter of comedy arises from diction . . . in seven ways," but his list of verbal devices hardly constitutes what comedians meant when they referred to "jokes." See Tzetzes, excerpt from *First Proem to Aristophanes*, trans. Lane Cooper, in *Theories of Comedy*, ed. Paul Lauter (Garden City, N.Y.: Doubleday, Anchor Books, 1964), 33–34.
In fact, the most likely source for the idea of the seven original jokes is the work of a rather obscure eighteenth-century philosopher and aesthetician, George Friedrich Meier. Meier's second edition of *Thoughts on Jesting* (1754), the first modern work specifically dedicated to the aesthetics of jesting rather than to laughter, ridicule, or humor, analyzed seven rules for making jests. Through the English translation of 1764, the ideas contained in this work filtered into the Anglo-American world of comic practice, where its rules of jesting were transformed into a typology of jokes. Meier's intellectual context and the publication history of his text are briefly examined by Joseph Jones in his introduction to the reprint edition. See George Friedrich Meier, *Thoughts on Jesting*, ed. Joseph Jones (Austin: University of Texas Press, 1947). For a detailed analysis of Meier's text and its relationship to twentieth-century ideas of the seven universal jokes, see Daniel Wickberg, "The Sense of Humor in American Culture, 1850–1960" (Ph.D. diss., Yale University, 1993), 272–79.

83. Laurie, *Vaudeville: From the Honky-tonks to the Palace*, 170–95.

84. Allen, *Horrible Prettiness*, 238.

85. David Marc, *Demographic Vistas: Television in American Culture* (Philadelphia: University of Pennsylvania Press, 1984), 21–29.

86. Brett Page, *Writing for Vaudeville* (Springfield, Mass.: Home Correspondence School, 1915), 64–70.

87. *OED*, 2d ed., s.v. "material."

88. Gilbert, *American Vaudeville*, 135; Fred Allen, *Much Ado about Me* (New York: Little, Brown, 1956), 247–78; Robert C. Toll, *The Entertainment Machine: Show Business in the Twentieth Century* (New York: Oxford University Press, 1982), 226.

89. Page, *Writing for Vaudeville*, 91; Gilbert, *American Vaudeville*, 274–75; Arthur Frank Wertheim, *Radio Comedy* (New York: Oxford University Press, 1979), 6.

90. Wright, *What's Funny—and Why*, 255–59. For a latter-day example of a joke file, see Milton Berle, *Milton Berle's Private Joke File: Over 10,000 of His Best Gags, Anecdotes, and One-liners* (New York: Crown, 1989).

91. Fred Allen, *Treadmill to Oblivion* (New York: Little, Brown, 1954), 70.

92. Walter Blair and Hamlin Hill remark of the motif indexes: "Thanks to these compilers, anyone who has encountered any joke anywhere probably can track down in these indexes a summary of that same joke from which practically every smidgeon of humor has disappeared, get a list of versions, and then read every version. The conclusion, based upon excruciating research, will be that essentially the same joke—in fact, every conceivable joke—has been told everywhere again and again." Thus, the idea of the universal joke is reproduced in contemporary scholarship. See Blair and Hill, *America's Humor*, 18–19.

The indexes include Antti Aarne and Stith Thompson, *The Types of the Folk-tale: A Classification and Bibliography*, 2d ed. (Helsinki: Suomalainen Tredeakatemia, 1961); Stith Thompson, *Motif-Index of Folk Literature: A Classification of Narrative Elements in Folktales, Ballads, Myths, Fables, Medieval Romances, Exempla, Fabliaux, Jest-Books, and Local Legends*, 6 vols. (Bloomington: Indiana University Press, 1955–58); Ernest W. Baugham, *Type and Motif-Index of the Folktales of England and North America* (The Hague: Mouton, 1966); Gershon Legman, *Rationale of the Dirty Joke: An Analysis of Sexual Humor* (New York: Grove Press, 1968).

93. "The Commercial Humorist at Work in His Sanctum," *New York Times*, 26 January 1908, sec. 4, p. 6.

94. *New York Times*, 10 December 1936, p. 26.

95. *New York Times*, 28 July 1938, p. 18.

96. *New York Times*, 28 August 1908, p. 6.

97. Clifton Fadiman, *Party of One: The Selected Writings* (Cleveland: World, 1955), 272.

98. The debt to Taylorism and scientific management is evident in the doctrine of "the one best way." See Daniel T. Rodgers, *The Work Ethic in Industrial America, 1850–1920* (Chicago: University of Chicago Press, 1978), 53–57.

99. Sherwood Schwartz quoted in Lloyd Shearer, "It's the Gag That Gets the 'Boff,'" *New York Times Magazine* (21 October 1945): 18–19.

100. Frank Fogarty quoted in Page, *Writing for Vaudeville*, 74–76.

101. Walter Winchell, "The Wisecrack and the Gag," *The Bookman* 66 (October 1927): 152–57.

102. Esar, *The Humor of Humor*, 25–27.

103. Page, *Writing for Vaudeville*, 86–87.

104. Ibid., 87.

105. Wilde, *How the Great Comedy Writers Create Laughter*, 150–51.

106. Wertheim, *Radio Comedy*, 97.

107. On Hope's consumption of massive quantities of "material" in the process of routining a monologue, see Wilde, *How the Great Comedy Writers Create Laughter*, 149; Toll, *The Entertainment Machine*, 232.

108. Allen, *Treadmill to Oblivion*, 155.

109. Ibid., 240.

110. Wright, *What's Funny—and Why*, 251. On what Wright refers to as "the gag industry," see pp. 246–73.

111. Sidney Reznick, "Want to Be Funny?" *New York Times*, 9 November 1941, sec. 9, p. 10.

112. Laurie quoted in Robert Schiffer, "The Jokes Are Old," *New York Times*, 29 July 1945, sec. 2, p. 5.

113. Art Henley, *Radio Comedy: How to Write It, including The Mathematics of Humor* (n.p.: Art Henley, 1948), 1: 6.

114. Ibid., 1: 35.

115. Ibid., 1: 6–16, 31–35.

116. On applied psychology in the 1920s and 1930s, see Loren Baritz, *The Servants of Power: A History of the Use of Social Science in American Industry* (Westport, Conn.: Greenwood Press, 1960); Donald S. Napoli, *Architects of Adjustment: The History of the Psychological Profession in the United States* (Port Washington, N.Y.: Kennikat Press, 1981). The primary figure in developing and promoting intelligence testing was Lewis Terman, a Stanford colleague and coauthor with John C. Almack, who developed the first sense-of-humor test in the 1920s. On Terman, see Paul David Chapman, *Schools as Sorters: Lewis M. Terman, Applied Psychology, and the Intelligence Testing Movement, 1890–1930* (New York: New York University Press, 1988). The text coauthored by Terman and Almack was *The Hygiene of the School Child*, 2d ed. (Boston: Houghton Mifflin, 1929).

117. For a bibliography of empirical research from 1897 to 1966, see Yvonne Treadwell, "Bibliography of Empirical Studies of Wit and Humor," *Psychological Reports* 20 (June 1967): 1079–83.

118. N. Franklin Stump, "Sense of Humor and Its Relationship to Personality, Scholastic Aptitude, Emotional Maturity, Height and Weight," *Journal of General Psychology* 20 (1939): 31.

119. John C. Almack, "The Nature of Humor," *Century Magazine* 116 (September 1928): 567–73. For a more recent sense-of-humor test, the Antioch Sense of Humor Inventory (ASHI), see Harvey Mindess et al., *The Antioch Humor Test: Making Sense of Humor* (New York: Avon, 1985).

120. Ford, "Jokes: New Variations on Old Themes," 8, 45.

121. Henley, *Radio Comedy*, 1: 6.

5. The Humorous and the Serious

1. Michael Mulkay, *On Humor: Its Nature and Place in Modern Society* (New York: Basil Blackwell, 1988).

2. Ibid., 156.

3. See, for instance, John Morreall, ed. *The Philosophy of Laughter and Humor* (Albany: State University of New York Press, 1987).

4. Immanuel Kant, *Critique of Judgment*, trans. J. H. Bernard (London: Macmillan, 1892), pt. 1, div. 1, 54, quoted ibid., 47–49.

5. Herbert Spencer, "The Physiology of Laughter," *Essays on Education* (London: Dent, 1911), quoted in Morreall, ed. *The Philosophy of Laughter and Humor*, 108.

6. Laurent Joubert, *Treatise on Laughter*, trans. Gregory David de Rocher (University: University of Alabama Press, 1980); René Descartes, *The Passions of the Soul*, trans. Elizabeth Haldane and G. Ross (Cambridge: Cambridge University Press, 1911), pt. 2, arts. 124–27, and pt. 3, arts. 178–81.

7. Carl Georg Lange and William James, *The Emotions* (Baltimore: Williams and Wilkins, 1922); H. M. Gardiner, Ruth Clark Metcalf, and John G. Beebe-Center, *Feeling and Emotion: A History of Theories* (New York: American Book Co., 1937), 295–99.

8. Spencer, "The Physiology of Laughter," 104.

9. Ibid., 105.

10. John Dewey, "The Theory of Emotion" (1895), in *The Early Works, 1882–1898* (Carbondale: Southern Illinois University Press, 1971), 4: 158.

11. Ibid.

12. Boris Sidis, *The Psychology of Laughter* (New York: D. Appleton, 1919), 68.

13. J. C. Gregory, *The Nature of Laughter* (New York: Harcourt, Brace, 1924), 27–29.

14. Sylvia Bliss, "The Origin of Laughter," *American Journal of Psychology* 26 (1915): 236–46.

15. G. Stanley Hall and Arthur Allin, "The Psychology of Tickling, Laughing, and the Comic," *American Journal of Psychology* 9 (October 1897): 1–41.

16. Henri Bergson, *Laughter: An Essay on the Meaning of the Comic* (New York: Macmillan, 1911).

17. H. T. Tuckerman, "Humor," *Godey's Lady's Book* 39 (July-December 1849): 7.

18. William Mathews, *Wit and Humor: Their Uses and Abuses* (Chicago: S. C. Griggs and Co., 1888), 62; Milton Harrington, *A Biological Approach to Abnormal Behavior* (Lancaster, Pa.: Science Press Printing Co., 1938), 267; C. H. Scherf, *Do Your Own Thinking* (New York: McGraw-Hill, 1948), 320–21.

19. The notion of humor as a safety valve appeared in American culture at the same moment that workers were increasingly being associated with machines; the hydraulic model of the person and his "energies" seems to represent a literal understanding of the person as a machine. On the new, and troubling, conception of workers as machines, see Daniel T. Rodgers, *The Work Ethic in Industrial America, 1850–1920* (Chicago: University of Chicago Press, 1978), 65–93.

20. E. P. Thompson, "Time, Work-Discipline, and Industrial Capitalism," *Past and Present* 38 (December 1967): 56–97; Roy Rosenzweig, *Eight Hours for What We Will: Workers and Leisure in an Industrial City, 1870–1920* (Cambridge: Cambridge University Press, 1983); Hugh Cunningham, *Leisure in the Industrial Revolution, c. 1780–1880* (London: Croom Helms, 1980); Kathy Peiss, *Cheap Amusements: Working Women and Leisure in Turn-of-the-Century New York* (Philadelphia: Temple University Press, 1986); Benjamin Kline Hunnicutt, *Work without End: Abandoning Shorter Hours for the Right to Work* (Philadelphia: Temple University Press, 1988); Richard Butsch, ed., *For Fun and Profit: The Transformation of Leisure into Consumption* (Philadelphia: Temple University Press, 1990).

21. For general discussions of the transformation of leisure through the social order, see Witold Rybczynski, *Waiting for the Weekend* (New York: Viking, 1991); Sebastian de Grazia, *Of Time, Work, and Leisure* (New York: Random House, Vintage Books, 1994).

22. This point has been made by Joseph Boskin, who sees a twentieth-century disregard for the importance of humor as a consequence of the division between work and play, seriousness and humor. See Boskin, *Humor and Social Change in Twentieth-Century America* (Boston: Trustees of the Public Library of the City of Boston, 1979).

23. Mathews, *Wit and Humor,* 60–62.

24. B[enjamin] F[ranklin] Clark, *Mirthfulness and Its Exciters; or, Rational Laughter and Its Promoters* (Boston: Lee and Shepard, 1870), 21–22.

25. Gregory, *The Nature of Laughter,* 94–96.

26. Sidis, *The Psychology of Laughter,* 74–81. The quotation is from p. 75.

27. George Thomas White Patrick, *The Psychology of Relaxation* (Boston: Houghton Mifflin, 1916), 102, 107–8.

28. H. A. Overstreet, *Influencing Human Behavior* (New York: W. W. Norton and Co., 1925), 256ff.

29. Max Eastman, *Enjoyment of Laughter* (New York: Halcyon House, 1936), 15. See Johan Huizinga, *Homo Ludens: A Study of the Play Element in Culture* (Boston: Beacon Press, 1955); the original edition was completed in 1938. See also Dudley Zuver, *Salvation by Laughter* (New York: Harper and Bros., 1933), 1–35; Samuel S. Seward, Jr., *The Paradox of the Ludicrous* (Stanford: Stanford University Press, 1930), 16.

30. J. Y. T. Grieg, *The Psychology of Laughter and Comedy* (London: George Allen and Unwin, 1923), 67.

31. L. W. Kline, "The Psychology of Humor," *American Journal of Psychology* 18 (1907): 421–41. The quotation is from pp. 436–37. See also Horace M. Kallen, *Liberty, Laughter and Tears: Reflections on the Relations of Comedy and Tragedy to Human Freedom* (De Kalb: Northern Illinois University Press, 1968).

32. Donald E. Gibson, "Humor Consulting: Laughs for Power and Profit in Organizations," *Humor* 7 (1994): 403–28. See also Glenn Collins, "How Punch Lines Bolster the Bottom Line," *New York Times,* 30 April 1988, pp. 37, 39. One of the most prominent of the new breed of humor consultants in the 1980s was Joel Goodman, director of the HUMOR Project at Sagamore Institute in Saratoga Springs, New York, and editor of the quarterly journal *Laughing Matters.* Others include C. W. Metcalf, Malcolm L. Kushner, Barbara Mackoff, and Michael Iapoce. For examples of the prescriptions of these humor consultants, see Iapoce, *"A Funny Thing Happened on the Way to the Boardroom": Using Humor in Business Speaking* (New York: John Wiley and Sons, 1988); Mackoff, *What Mona Lisa Knew: A Women's Guide to Getting Ahead in Business by Lightening Up* (Los Angeles: Lowell House, 1990); Kushner, *The Light Touch: How to Use Humor for Business Success* (New York: Simon and Schuster, 1990).

33. John F. Kasson, *Rudeness and Civility: Manners in Nineteenth-Century Urban America* (New York: Hill and Wang, 1990), 162–65.

34. Michel Foucault, *The History of Sexuality,* vol. 1: *An Introduction,* trans. Robert Hurley (New York: Pantheon, 1978).

35. This is in contrast to those who believe that the entire tradition of Western thought is antipathetic to humor and laughter. See John Morreall, "The Rejection of Humor in Western Thought," *Philosophy East and West* 39 (July 1989): 243–65. Morreall contrasts Western rationalism, and its rejection of the incongruity and hostility of humor, with the embrace of humor in Zen Buddhism. Interestingly, Morreall's arguments for the benefits of humor sound very much like those made in American culture since the nineteenth century—relief, perspective, self-awareness. In other words, Morreall fails to distinguish between the antipathetic view of laughter characteristic of the period before the eighteenth century and the modern Western view of humor as beneficial, even as he reproduces that modern view in his own writing.

36. Mrs. [Caroline] Kirkland, *The Evening Book; or, Fireside Talks on Morals and Manners, with Sketches of Western Life* (New York: Charles Scribner's, 1953), 86–87. For a further discussion of Kasson's argument, particularly his reliance on Lord Chesterfield as a representative figure, see Daniel Wickberg, "The Sense of Humor in American Culture, 1850–1960" (Ph.D. diss., Yale University, 1993), 335–36.

37. James D. McCabe, *The National Encyclopaedia of Business and Social Forms* (Philadelphia: National Publishing Co., 1879), 44. The rejection of boisterous laughter in public was a common theme in etiquette manuals as late as the 1920s. See, for instance, *Vogue's Book of Etiquette* (Garden City, N.Y.: Doubleday, Doran, and Co., 1929), 21.

38. Mrs. M. L. Rayne, *Gems of Deportment and Hints of Etiquette* (Detroit: Tyler, 1882), 397–98.

39. McCabe, *National Encyclopaedia of Business and Social Forms,* 81.

40. Margaret E. Sangster, *Good Manners for All Occasions* (New York: Christian Herald, 1904), 222.

41. "About Humor and Its Sphere," *Hours at Home* 5 (June 1867): 150.

42. Stephen Leacock, *Humor and Humanity: An Introduction to the Study of Humor* (New York: Henry Holt, 1938), 177–78.

43. Horace M. Kallen, "The Aesthetic Principle in Comedy," *American Journal of Psy-*

chology 22 (April 1911): 138; Elizabeth Woodbridge, "The Humor-Fetish," *"Days Out" and Other Papers* (Boston: Houghton Mifflin, 1917), 85–92.

44. "A Plea for Seriousness," *The Atlantic* 69 (May 1892): 630.

45. Katharine Roof, "The American Sense of Humor," *Outlook* 96 (8 October 1910): 311.

46. Woodbridge, "The Humor-Fetish," 86–87.

47. Eunice Tietjens, "Our Over-developed Sense of Humor," *Arena* 41 (March 1909): 320.

48. Ibid.

49. Roof, "The American Sense of Humor," 311.

50. "A Plea for Seriousness," 629.

51. Mathews, *Wit and Humor*, 225.

52. On "cultural custodians" see Henry May, *The End of American Innocence: A Study of the First Years of Our Own Time, 1912–1917* (New York: Oxford University Press, 1979), 30–51.

53. Matthew Arnold quoted in Lawrence Levine, *Highbrow/Lowbrow: The Emergence of Cultural Hierarchy in America* (Cambridge: Harvard University Press, 1988), 212.

54. "A Plea for Seriousness," 629.

55. Roof, "The American Sense of Humor," 312.

56. Tietjens, "Our Over-developed Sense of Humor," 320–21.

57. Roof, "The American Sense of Humor," 312.

58. "The Dominant Joke," *The Atlantic* 91 (1903): 432.

59. Agnes Repplier, "A Plea for Humor," *The Atlantic* 63 (1889): 179.

60. Agnes Repplier, "The Mission of Humor," *Americans and Others* (Boston: Houghton Mifflin, 1912), 51–52.

61. Agnes Repplier, *In Pursuit of Laughter* (Boston: Houghton Mifflin, 1936), 3, 222, 182.

62. Agnes Repplier, "Cruelty and Humor," *Points of Friction* (Boston: Houghton Mifflin, 1920), 275–76.

63. Agnes Repplier, "The American Laughs," *Under Dispute* (Boston: Houghton Mifflin, 1924), 286–311.

64. J. E. Wallace Wallin, *Personality Maladjustments and Mental Hygiene*, 2d ed. (New York: McGraw-Hill, 1949), 313–15.

65. William Lyon Phelps, *As I Like It* (New York: Charles Scribner's Sons, 1923), 50.

66. Katharine M. Wilson, "The Sense of Humour," *Contemporary Review* 131 (1927): 632.

67. Overstreet, *Influencing Human Behavior*, 259.

68. Leo Markun, *How to Develop Your Sense of Humor* (Girard, Kans.: Haldeman-Julius, [1928]), 35.

69. See, for instance, Hall and Allin, "The Psychology of Tickling, Laughing, and the Comic."

70. Repplier, "The American Laughs," 301.

71. Gage William Chapel, "Humor in the White House: And [*sic*] Interview with Presidential Speechwriter Robert Orben," *Communication Quarterly* 26 (Winter 1978): 44–49; "Talking to Don Penny," *Vogue* 178 (September 1988): 584, 594, 602, 608.

72. There are numerous examples of the genre. They include Maxwell Meyersohn, ed., *The Wit and Wisdom of Franklin D. Roosevelt* (Boston: Beacon Press, 1950); George S. Caldwell, ed., *Good Old Harry: The Wit and Wisdom of Harry S. Truman* (New York: Hawthorn Books, 1966); Bill Adler, ed., *The Kennedy Wit* (New York: Citadel Press, [1964]); Bill Adler, ed. *The Johnson Humor* (New York: Simon and Schuster, [1965]); Bill Adler, ed.

The Wit and Humor of Richard Nixon (New York: Popular Library, 1969); Gerald R. Ford, *Humor and the Presidency* (New York: Arbor House, 1987); Bill Adler, ed., *The Wit and Wisdom of Jimmy Carter* (Secaucus, N.J.: Citadel Press, 1977); James S. Denton and Peter Schweizer, eds., *Grinning with the Gipper: A Celebration of the Wit, Wisdom, and Wisecracks of Ronald Reagan* (New York: Atlantic Monthly Press, 1988); Ken Brady and Jeremy Solemon, eds., *The Wit and Wisdom of George Bush: With Some Reflections from Dan Quayle* (New York: St. Martin's Press, 1989); *Willy Nilly: Bill Clinton Speaks Out* (Nashville: Caliban Books, 1994).

73. On Earl Butz's racist gaffe, see Peter Carroll, *It Seemed Like Nothing Happened: America in the 1970s* (New Brunswick: Rutgers University Press, 1990), 203.

74. See, for instance, S. S. Cox, "Legislative Humor," *Harper's* 52 (December 1875): 119–29, and (January 1876): 271–81.

75. "Humor in High Places," *The Nation* 83 (12 July 1906): 28.

76. Hubert Bruce Fuller, "How Humor Enlivens the Solemn Work of Congress," *New York Times*, 28 April 1912, sec. 6, p. 9.

77. "Humorists as Campaigners," *New York Times*, 28 October 1922, p. 12.

78. Albert J. Beveridge, *The Art of Public Speaking* (Boston: Houghton Mifflin, 1924), 41. See also Charles Willis Thompson, "Humor and Presidential Candidates," *New York Times Magazine* (21 September 1924): 9.

79. W. H. Sheldon with S. S. Stevens, *The Varieties of Temperament: A Psychology of Constitutional Differences* (New York: Harper and Bros., 1942), 53.

80. "Wit and Public Men," *New York Times*, 24 February 1925, p. 18.

81. Porter McKeever, *Adlai Stevenson: His Life and Legacy* (New York: William Morrow, 1989), 250–51; T. V. Smith, "The Serious Problem of Campaign Humor," *New York Times Magazine* (28 September 1952): 11, 51, 53; TRB, *New Republic* (15 September 1952): 3; TRB, *New Republic* (23 September 1952): 3.

82. Eisenhower quoted in Hollington K. Tong, *American Sense of Humor* (n.p.: [1958]), 8–9. The speech was given before the U.S. Naval Academy graduating class, June 4, 1958.

83. My understanding of the changes in the structure, content, and "style" of political life in the twentieth century is drawn from a wide variety of sources. See, in particular, Michael E. McGerr, *The Decline of Popular Politics: The American North, 1865–1928* (New York: Oxford University Press, 1986); Robert Westbrook, "Politics as Consumption: Managing the Modern American Election," in *The Culture of Consumption: Critical Essays in American History*, ed. Richard Wightman Fox and T. J. Jackson Lears (New York: Pantheon, 1983), 143–73; Kenneth Cmiel, *Democratic Eloquence: The Fight over Popular Speech in Nineteenth-Century America* (Berkeley: University of California Press, 1990).

84. Henry S. Pritchett, "Politicians and the Sense of Humor," *Scribner's Magazine* 55 (January 1914): 77–78.

85. Ibid., 79.

86. Interview with Stephen Leacock, *New York Times Magazine* (8 April 1917): 7.

87. Christine Ladd Franklin, "Humor and Journalism," *New York Times*, 22 May 1917, p. 12.

88. Letter to editor, *New York Times*, 5 November 1936, p. 26.

89. Letter to editor, *New York Times*, 13 November 1940, p. 16.

90. *New York Times*, 22 September 1938, p. 21.

91. See, for instance, Emory S. Bogardus, *Leaders and Leadership* (New York: D. Appleton-Century, 1934), 178.

92. Franklin Delano Roosevelt, "Address Delivered at Savannah, Georgia: 'The American March of Progress,' November 18, 1933," in *The Public Papers and Addresses of Franklin D. Roosevelt*, comp. Samuel I. Rosenman (New York: Random House, 1938), vol. 2: *The Year of Crisis: 1933*, 491.

93. Brooks Atkinson, "Sense of Humor," *New York Times*, 15 June 1941, sec. 9, p. 1; *New York Times*, 22 September 1938, p. 21; Frederick Elmore Lumley, *Means of Social Control* (New York: Century, 1925), 276; Stewart W. McClelland, "Dictators Don't Laugh," *Vital Speeches of the Day* 8 (1 March 1942): 300–303. McClelland's address was delivered before the Lincoln Club of Los Angeles, 12 February 1942. For remarks on a similar theme, see also Nat Schmulowitz, "Liberty, Laughter and the Law," *Vital Speeches of the Day* 13 (15 August 1947): 660, delivered at the Judicial Conference of the U.S. Circuit and District Judges for the Ninth Judicial Circuit, San Francisco, 23 July 1947; George E. Vincent's speech of 31 March 1936 to the Chicago Rotary Club, as reported in "Humor Held Barrier to Dictatorship Here," *New York Times*, 1 April 1936, p. 13; a speech by William M. Lewis, president of Lafayette College, reported in the *New York Times*, 2 November 1935, p. 15, in which he claimed that Mussolini "does not possess a sense of humor, or he would not have developed that omnipotent complex which is threatening the peace of the world"; Robert Withington, "Laughter in Our Time," *School and Society* 59 (3 June 1944): 393–95.

94. *New York Times*, 7 November 1939, p. 24.

95. McClelland, "Dictators Don't Laugh," 300. See also [Anon.], "Warriors with Humor," *New York Times*, 30 August 1945, p. 20.

96. Bob Hope, "Sure-fire Gags for the Foxhole," *New York Times Magazine* (28 May 1944): 8.

97. John Biesanz and Mavis Biesanz, *Modern Society: An Introduction to Social Science* (New York: Prentice-Hall, 1954), 620.

98. Joost A. M. Meerloo, *Mental Seduction and Menticide: The Psychology of Thought Control and Brainwashing* (London: Jonathan Cape, 1956), 147.

99. On the "end of ideology" see, for instance, Stephen J. Whitfield, *The Culture of the Cold War* (Baltimore: Johns Hopkins University Press, 1991), 54; Richard H. Pells, *The Liberal Mind in a Conservative Age: American Intellectuals in the 1940s and 1950s* (Hanover, NH: Wesleyan University Press, 1989), 117–82.

100. Anton Zijderveld, "The Sociology of Humor and Laughter," *Current Sociology* 31 (Winter 1983): 58.

101. Leon Ormond, *Laugh and Learn: The Art of Teaching with Humor* (New York: Greenberg, 1941), 56, 74.

102. This credo is taken from a statement of editorial purpose that appeared on the masthead of *The Masses*. I am grateful to Christopher Shannon for the reference.

103. Abbie Hoffman, *Revolution for the Hell of It* (New York: Dial Press, 1968), 153.

104. William Burnham, *The Normal Mind: An Introduction to Mental Hygiene and the Hygiene of School Instruction* (New York: D. Appleton, 1924), 399.

105. Florence Brumbaugh, "We Study Wit and Humor," *Childhood Education* 16 (May 1940): 403–4. See also idem, "Laughter and Teachers," *Educational Method* 20 (November 1940): 69–70; idem, "The Place of Humor in the Curriculum," *Journal of Experimental Education* 8 (June 1940): 403–10; idem, "Stimuli Which Cause Laughter in Children" (Ph.D. diss., New York University, 1939); Lucien Aigner, "Why Children Laugh," *New York Times Magazine* (17 May 1942): 10–11.

106. James E. Warren, Jr., "The English Teacher as Humorist," *Clearing House* 24 (October 1949): 83.

107. Ormond, *Laugh and Learn*, 15.

108. Brumbaugh, "We Study Wit and Humor," 401.

109. Ormond, *Laugh and Learn*, 267.

110. Ibid., 42.

111. Winifred H. Nash, "Let Laughter In!" *Journal of Education* 121 (April 1938): 116.

112. Ormond, *Laugh and Learn*, 30.

113. "College Humor," *New York Times*, 26 December 1923, p. 14.

114. "Courses in Humor at Colleges Urged," *New York Times*, 5 February 1934, p. 17.

115. "Coals to Newcastle," *New York Times*, 6 February 1934, p. 20; "Learning to Laugh," *The Nation* (14 March 1934): 292.

116. Ida Benfey Judd, letter, *New York Times*, 23 February 1934, p. 18.

117. *New York Times*, 11 February 1934, sec. 4, p. 20; ibid., 27 September 1936, sec. 2, p. 10.

118. T. J. Jackson Lears, "From Salvation to Self-Realization: Advertising and the Therapeutic Roots of the Consumer Culture, 1880–1930," in *The Culture of Consumption*, ed. Fox and Lears, 1–38.

119. Dudley Zuver, *Salvation by Laughter* (New York: Harper and Bros., 1933), 25. See also Leslie B. Flynn, *Serve Him with Mirth: The Place of Humor in the Christian Life* (Grand Rapids, Mich.: Zondervan, 1960); Elton Trueblood, *The Humor of Christ* (New York: Harper and Row, 1964).

120. Bruce Barton, *The Man Nobody Knows: A Discovery of Jesus* (Indianapolis: Bobbs-Merrill, 1925), 57–88; idem, *The Book Nobody Knows* (Indianapolis: Bobbs-Merrill, 1926), 27. On Barton, see T. J. Jackson Lears, "From Salvation to Self-Realization," 30–38; Leo Ribuffo, "Jesus Christ as Business Statesman: Bruce Barton and the Selling of Corporate Capitalism," *American Quarterly* 33 (Summer 1981): 206–31.

121. Donald Meyer, *The Positive Thinkers: A Study of the American Quest for Health, Wealth and Personal Power from Mary Baker Eddy to Norman Vincent Peale* (Garden City, N.Y.: Doubleday, Anchor Books, 1966).

122. Orison Swett Marden, *Peace, Power, and Plenty* (New York: Thomas Y. Crowell, 1909), 298–300.

123. On neo-orthodoxy, see Sydney Ahlstrom, *A Religious History of the American People* (New Haven: Yale University Press, 1972), 932–48.

124. Reinhold Niebuhr, "Humour and Faith," in *Discerning the Signs of the Times: Sermons for Today and Tomorrow* (New York: Charles Scribner's Sons, 1946), 112. See Richard Wightman Fox, *Reinhold Niebuhr: A Biography* (New York: Pantheon, 1985), 225, 245–56.

125. Niebuhr, "Humour and Faith," 119–20.

126. Joshua Loth Liebman, *Peace of Mind* (New York: Simon and Schuster, 1946), 190.

127. Reinhold Niebuhr, *The Irony of American History* (New York: Charles Scribner's Sons, 1952), 169–70.

128. Niebuhr, "Humour and Faith," 120–21, 131.

129. M. Conrad Hyers, *The Comic Vision and the Christian Faith: A Celebration of Life and Laughter* (New York: Pilgrim Press, 1981), 24.

Conclusion

1. An enormous literature on the various aspects of the benefits of humor and laughter has been produced over the past two decades. To get a sense of the role of humor in medical treatment, see Vera M. Robinson, *Humor and the Health Professions* (Thorofare, N.J.: C. B. Slack, 1977); Raymond A. Moody, *Laugh after Laugh: The Healing Power of Humor* (Jacksonville, Fla.: Headwaters Press, 1978); Norman Cousins, *Anatomy of an Illness* (New York: Penguin, 1979). Specifically in the field of gerontology, see, for instance, Kathleen C. Buckwalter et al., "Shining Through: The Humor and Individuality of Persons with Alzheimer's Disease," *Journal of Gerontological Nursing* 21 (March 1995): 11–16. For a recent brief on the professional use of humor, see R. Wayne King, "If You're Raising Money Today, You Need a Sense of Humor," *Fund Raising Management* 26 (May 1995):

26–27. On corporate humor consultants, see Donald E. Gibson, "Humor Consulting: Laughs for Power and Profit in Organizations," *Humor* 7 (1994): 403–28. For examples of writings by humor consultants, see Michael Iapoce, *"A Funny Thing Happened on the Way to the Boardroom": Using Humor in Business Speaking* (New York: John Wiley and Sons, 1988); Barbara Mackoff, *What Mona Lisa Knew: A Woman's Guide to Getting Ahead in Business by Lightening Up* (Los Angeles: Lowell House, 1990). On academic literature, consult the journal *Humor* (Berlin and New York: Mouton de Gruyter, 1988-). An excellent synthesis of anthropological concern with humor is Mahadev L. Apte, *Humor and Laughter: An Anthropological Approach* (Ithaca: Cornell University Press, 1985).

2. Claude C. Hopkins, *My Life in Advertising/Scientific Advertising* (Chicago: Advertising Publications, 1966), 183–84.

3. Gerald B. Wadsworth, "Principles and Practice of Advertising," *Advertising and Selling* 22 (September 1912): 70.

4. Don Herold, *Humor in Advertising . . . And How to Make It Pay* (New York: McGraw-Hill, 1963), 9, 195. On Freberg and Graham, see "Funny," *Newsweek* 55 (14 March 1960): 76–79.

5. Marc G. Weinberger and Charles S. Gulas, "The Impact of Humor in Advertising: A Review," *Journal of Advertising* 21 (December 1992): 35–59.

Index

Bergson, Henri, 178
Bernard, John, 33
Beveridge, Albert J., 198
Billings, Josh (Henry Wheeler Shaw), 126–127
Bills, Arthur, 117
Blackface minstrelsy, 33, 124–126, 153
Blair, Hugh, 38, 42–43
Blair, Walter, 123, 211–212
Bliss, Sylvia, 178
"Blue" humor, 130
Bogardus, Emory, 110
Bourgeois consciousness, 6, 59–64, 91, 96, 133
Bowman, Henry A., 115
Boyesen, H. H., 127–128, 133
Brevity, in jokes, 159
Browne, Charles Farrar. *See* Ward, Artemus
Bruce, Lenny, 222
Brumbaugh, Florence, 207–208
Burdette, Robert, 92–93
Bureaucratic individualism, 8–9, 74–119, 210, 235n1
Burlesque, 130, 153
Burnet, James. *See* Monboddo, Lord
Burnham, William, 102, 207
Butcher, S. H., 91
Butz, Earl, 197

Calhoun, John C., 128
Calkins, Mary Whiton, 100
Cambridge platonists, 71
"Camp" sensibility, 11
Campbell, George, 38, 52–54
Capitalism, 76, 77–78, 79–80, 87, 221–222; work/leisure distinction and, 179–180
Carlyle, Thomas, 21, 65, 93, 100, 227n44
Cazamian, Louis, 23, 28–29
Chaplin, Charlie, 66, 212
Characterology, 78, 97, 103, 144. *See also* Personhood
Cheerfulness, 108–110
Choate, Joseph, 151

Christ, image of, 212–213
Cicero, 48; concept of common sense, 70
Clark, Benjamin Franklin, 180
Clay, Henry, 128
College humor magazines, 129
Collingwood, R. G., 2
Comedy of humors, 21–25, 58. *See also* Jonson, Ben; Shadwell, Thomas
Comic monologue, 124, 130, 153–154, 158, 160.
Comic periodicals, 125, 128–129, 139–140, 142
Comic relief, 178. *See also* Relief
Comic story, opposed to humor, 136–137
Comic timing, 138, 160
Commodification, 15; jokes and, 134–146
Common sense: concept of, 16, 69–70, 74, 83; Scottish philosophy of, 37
Communism, 199, 204–205
Community/society distinction, 75–76
Conflict, sense of humor and, 114–115, 118
Congreve, William, 41–42
Conrad, Eugene, 156
Conversation, laughter in, 52–53
Cooley, Charles Horton, 99
Coquelin, Constant, 96
Corwin, Tom, 197
Cott, Nancy, 96
Cousins, Norman, 219, 222
Cox, Samuel S. (U.S. Senator), 29, 43–44, 61, 198
Crothers, Samuel, 88–89, 102
Cult of the sense of humor, 133, 186–196
Cultural custodians, 188–190
Cultural history: base and superstructure in, 152–153; debate within, 239n48; genre conventions of, 222; as mode of analysis, 2–4, 11–12
Culture of sensibility, 8, 16, 45, 64, 69–73, 74, 83, 99, 125, 126, 173, 233n46

Deformity, and meaning of laughter, 47–49, 63, 64; and jokes, 151
Democracy, humor and, 196–206
Depersonalization, idea of humor and, 35–41
Descartes, René, 175
Descending incongruity, 174–177. *See also* Incongruity
Dewey, John, 3, 174, 177–178
Dickens, Charles, 73, 125
Dictatorship, humor opposed to, 201–205, 216–217
Discourse, humor as a form of, 35–41
Disney, Walt, 3, 65–66, 156
Domesticity. *See* Gender ideology
Donald Duck, 66
Douglas, Mary, 171
Downing, Major Jack, 127, 196
Dryden, John, 58–59
Dumont, Louis, 14–15
Dunlap, Knight, 106–107
Dunne, Finley Peter (Mr. Dooley), 139, 196

Eastman, Max, 66, 134, 181, 205–206, 244n8
Eccentricity, humor and, 20, 23, 24, 27–28, 32, 35, 36, 43–44, 68, 97, 101, 107, 137
Education, humor and, 206–212
Eisenhower, Dwight, 199–200, 204
Elias, Norbert, 119
Elitism, and wit/humor distinction, 61–62. *See also* Aristocracy
Emerson, Ralph Waldo, 125, 277n44
"End of ideology," 205
Energy, idea of, 176–177
English liberty, 41–45, 182. *See also* Freedom
Erskine, John, 116–117
Esar, Evan, 134, 159
Etiquette. *See* Manners

Fadiman, Clifton, 158
Farquhar, George, 43

Fellow-feeling. *See* Sympathy
Feminists, lack of sense of humor and, 96–97
Folktale: form of, 121–122; index, 121, 157, 249n92; "native humor" and, 125
Ford, Edward "Senator," 149, 168
Ford, Gerald, 197
Fosdick, Harry Emerson, 103
Foster, Charles E., 115
Foucault, Michel, 5, 183
Fowler, O. S., 82
Franklin, Christine Ladd, 201–202
Freberg, Stan, 221
Frederic, Harold, 81
Freedman, Dave, 156
Freedom, idea of humor and, 10, 41–45, 75, 181–182, 194–195, 199, 201–206, 214, 217, 222
Freud, Sigmund, 174, 178
Fuller, H. B., 198

Gag, 159. *See also* Joke
Gag thieves, 155
Gagmen. *See* Joke writers
Galen. *See* Humoral medicine
Geertz, Clifford, 2, 83
Gemeinschaft/gesellschaft distinction. *See* Community/society distinction
Gender ideology, 91–97
Geniality, 78
Gerard, Alexander, 72
Giddings, Franklin, 99
Godkin, E. L., 125, 127
Goffman, Erving, 99
Gorn, Elliott, 129
Gospel of amusement, 193, 220
Graham, Ed, 221
Gregory, J. C., 66, 178, 180
Grieg, J. Y. T., 66, 181
Grimes, James S., 82

Habas, Ralph A., 115
Haliburton, Thomas Chandler, 125
Hall, G. Stanley, 178
Halttunen, Karen, 126

Hardin, Ben, 197
Harrington, Milton, 178
Harris, George Washington, 124
Harvard Lampoon, 129
Hawthorne, Nathaniel, 81
Haywarde, Richard, 65
Hazlitt, William, 56, 61, 80–81
Health, humor and, 219
Henley, Art, 3, 163–164, 169
Herold, Don, 221
Hitler, Adolph, image of, 203
Hobbes, Thomas, 47–49, 50, 51, 54–57, 64, 183, 230n10
Höffding, Harold, 111
Hoffman, Abbie, 206
Holism, opposed to individualism, 14–15
Hollingworth, H. L., 90
Holmes, John Haynes, 117
Holmes, Oliver Wendell, 72–73
Home, Henry. *See* Kames
Hooker, Edward, 16
Hope, Bob, 3, 160–161, 203–204
Hopkins, Claude, 220–221
Horne, Hal, 156
Huizinga, Johan, 181
Humanitarian sensibility. *See* Culture of sensibility
Humor: as bourgeois concept, 59–64; as business matter, 140–146; as character, 22–24; cultural status of, 123–134; idea of, 7, 13–45; joke as unit of, 134–145; as literary genre, 124–125, 134–135; as mode of being, 27; as mode of seeing, 27, 167–168, 196; as safety valve, 178–179, 185–186, 202, 251n19; vs. sense of humor, 120; sociology of, 170–171
Humoral medicine, 6, 8, 16–21, 26, 39, 45, 103, 116, 214; Ben Jonson's use of, 22–23, 25
Humor consultants, 182, 219, 221
Humorist, concept of, 25, 29–34, 62, 137, 227n44. *See also* Professional humorists
Hunt, Leigh, 40–41, 80–81

Hutcheson, Francis, 3, 51, 56, 71–72, 228n51, 230n10
Hyers, Conrad, 217

Incongruity: faith and, 214–217; humor and idea of, 8, 39–41, 107, 118, 137, 170–171, 198; joke form and, 123, 134, 136, 159; meaning of laughter and, 56–57, 59, 60, 63–64, 66, 98, 101, 173–175, 185; self and, 111–113; Sydney Smith on, 39–40; theories of laughter, 47, 173–174. *See also* Descending incongruity
Individualism, 7, 20–21, 24, 28, 29, 32, 35, 41–45, 62, 68, 74, 81, 97, 119, 147; bourgeois characterology and, 144; definition of, 13–16; personality psychology and, 103; in twentieth-century social thought, 75–78. *See also* Bureaucratic individualism; Personhood; Self
Insight, and sense of humor, 104, 115
intelligence testing, 167
Internalization. *See* Subjectification
Irony, 11, 63, 214–217

James, William, 99
James-Lange theory of emotions, 176
Jerome, Jerome K., 133
Jester, 52
Jests, 52, 120–121, 122
Joe Miller's Jests, 147, 148, 150
Johnson, Burges, 89, 92
Joke, 120–169, 177, 190, 197, 243n4
Joke books, 62–63, 122, 131
Joke characters, 143–145, 247n61
Joke files, 156–157, 158, 161–164, 166–167
Joke submission, 145, 155
Joke technologies, 152–164
Joke writers, 122–123, 139–146, 148–152, 155–164, 168–169
Joke writing, 141–146, 152–164
Jones, William A., 3, 32, 43
Jonson, Ben, 3, 21–25, 27, 30, 31, 34, 36, 64

McConaughy, James L., 202–203
McDougall, William, 67–68, 90
McKnight, George, 25
McLean, Donald, 106
Mead, George Herbert, 99
Meerloo, Joost, 204–205
Meier, George Friedrich, 248n82
Meine, Franklin J., 123
Melville, Herman, 32–33, 227n44
Mental hygiene, 102–103, 113
Merrill, Dana K., 211
Meyer, Donald, 213–214
Mickey Mouse, 66
Millar, John, 44–45
Miller, Joe. *See Joe Miller's Jests*
Mills, C. Wright, 109
Mindcure. *See* Psychology: popular
Mirth, faculty of, 82
Monboddo, Lord (James Burnet), 31, 38
Moore, W. E., 211
Moral sense, concept of, 16, 71, 74, 83, 225n10
Moran, Appleton, 95
Morris, Corbyn, 29–32, 33, 42–43, 59–60
Mother-in-law joke, 150
Mulkay, Michael, 170–171
Multiculturalism, 15, 105
Mussolini, Benito, image of, 203

Nasby, Petroleum V. (David Ross Locke), 126–127
Nash, Winifred, 209–210
Nast, Thomas, 196
Nationalism, humor and, 42
National Lampoon, 129
Natural/artificial distinction. *See* Artificial/natural distinction
Neo-orthodoxy, 212, 214–217
Nicholson, Meredith, 211
Niebuhr, Reinhold, 3, 214–217
Nixon, Richard, 197
Novel: and characterology, 80–82; as modern literary form, 9, 20, 122, 147, 154

Object-subject relations, 4–6, 15, 25, 34, 35–36, 40, 58, 64, 68, 101, 113, 168–169, 210, 222
Objectivity. *See* Object-subject relations
Oratory, 128, 131–132, 200. *See also* Rhetoric
Orben, Robert, 197
Ormond, Leon, 88, 205, 208–210
Overstreet, H. A., 86, 111, 181, 194–195

Page, Brett, 153–154, 160
Paine, Thomas, 70
Pastor, Tony, 129
Patrick, G. T. W., 181
Penny, Don, 197
Perception, humor as a mode of, 35–36, 98, 113, 167–169, 196
Perkins, Eli. *See* Landon, Melville D.
Personhood, 5–9, 14–19, 20–21, 23–25, 26, 32, 29, 41, 45, 59, 62, 73, 89, 147, 167–168, 178–179, 210
Phelps, William Lyon, 194
Phrenology, 81–82, 237–238n18
Play: humor and, 10, 55, 66, 115, 208; "the ludicrous" and, 51; as relief, 180–182
Political campaigning, 197
"Politically correct," 96
Politics, humor and, 196–206
Popular culture, 6, 172, 188–190
Porter, William T., 125
Postmodernism, 11
Presidential elections, 199
Price, Orlo J., 202
Pritchett, Henry, 117, 200–201
Professional humorists, 126–128, 135–146, 191. *See also* Joke writers
Progressive education, 206–210
Psychology: academic, 165–168; in American culture, 90; Hobbes and, 48; and humoral medicine, 18; industrial, 114; personality (Allport), 103–105; popular, 106, 107, 111–113, 213–214; Shadwell and, 27; social, 99, 104; of tension and release, 172

Public laughter, 55–56
Puck, 128
Punch, 125
Punch line, 136, 142–143, 163, 243n5
Puritans, 54

Radio comedy, 124, 156–164
Raillery, 51–53, 54, 58, 68
Reagan, Ronald, 197
"Real life," as a forum for humor, 27, 30–33, 60, 97, 169
Realism, 24, 28, 60
Refining, joke technology of, 158–160
Relief: and humor, 10, 170–171, 191, 202, 212; release and, 177; theory of laughter, 47, 66, 173–178, 195
Religion, 50, 54, 184–185, 212–217
Repartee, 52
Repplier, Agnes, 3, 89, 151, 190–194, 195, 216, 220
Representation, humor as a mode of, 35, 38, 40
Republicanism, 61
Restoration drama, 26–28, 58
Reznick, Sidney, 162
Rhetoric, 38, 52–53, 54
Rickles, Don, 132
Ridicule, 49–54, 55–57, 58, 63–64, 68, 72, 92, 231n12; as the test of truth, 50–51, 53, 77, 183–184, 230n9
Riesman, David, 76–77, 86–87, 110
Riley, James Whitcomb, 137
Risibility, 47, 53, 57
Robbins, L. H., 148
Robbins, Tom, 81
Rogers, Will, 146, 202
Roof, Katharine, 187–190
Roosevelt, Franklin D., 197, 202–203
Ross, Edward, 76
Routining, joke technology of, 138, 160–162
Rourke, Constance, 123, 211–212
Rubin, Jerry, 206
Ruch, Floyd L., 116

Sam Slick, 127
Sambo characterization, 33, 125, 228n47
Sangster, Margaret, 184
Satire, 51, 63
Scherf, C. H., 178
Schizophrenia, 90
"Science of humor," 134
Scorn, laughter and, 51, 54–57, 63. *See also* Antipathy
Scottish Enlightenment, 31, 37, 56, 70, 228n51
Self: concept of, 14–15, 23, 28, 108, 119; culture of sensibility and, 69; laughter at, 67–68; modes of, 9, 76–78, 87; as source of authority, 79; in 1890s, 99. *See also* Personhood
Self-adjustment, 113–119
Self-objectification, 8–9, 24, 98–107, 165, 215, 222
Sense, idea of, 69–72, 83
Sense of beauty, 71, 84
Sense of honor, 84
Sense of humor: joke and, 164–169; lack of, 84–97, 194–195, 197–198, 202–206, 217; as means of social exclusion, 92
Sense-of-humor tests, 166–168, 211
Sense of perspective, 106, 212
Sense of proportion, 95, 108–113, 175, 191, 203, 212
Sense of ridicule, 72
Sense of the ludicrous, 80
Sense of the ridiculous, 72–73, 80
Sensibility. *See* Culture of sensibility
Sentimentalism. *See* Culture of sensibility
Separate spheres. *See* Gender ideology
Seriousness, 10, 68, 79, 93, 113; opposed to humor, 170–218
"Seven deadly jokes," 151–152, 248n82
Shadwell, Thomas, 26–29, 30, 31, 58
Shaftesbury, Third Earl of (Anthony Ashley Cooper), 50–51, 54, 71–72
Shakespeare, William, 19, 120

Wit, 36–37, 68, 231n12. *See also* Wit/humor distinction

Wit/humor distinction, 36–37, 40, 57–64, 65, 72, 80, 92, 201

Witherspoon, John, 37

Wits, company of, 52, 57

Wolfe, W. Béran, 90

Women: sense of humor and, 82, 91–97; vaudeville and, 130

Woodbridge, Elizabeth, 186–187

Work/leisure distinction, 172, 179–182

Working class, 179

World humor movement, 219–220, 243–244n8

Wright, Milton, 134, 148, 150, 151, 162

Yale Record, 129

Yippies, 206

Zuver, Dudley, 212–213